Selected Cultural Relics from

Haidian District

Edited by Haidian Museum

Cultural Relics Press

海淀博物馆 编

海淀文物
精选集

文物出版社

目录
Catelogo

红叶黄花自一川 [1]
——海淀古代文物概说

秦大树

一、海淀的地理环境与历史沿革

海淀区位于北京市区的西部和西北部，地处华北平原北部边缘与太行山余脉——西山山脉交汇地带，兼有山地平原，地形西高东低。西部山峦起伏，有大小山峰 60 多座。东部的海淀区平原属华北平原北部边缘，位于西山东部，向东微倾斜，可分两部分：百望山以南称山前平原区，以北称山后平原区。山前平原为永定河洪积扇，山后平原为南沙河、南口冲积扇，平原海拔为 35~50 米。

海淀区历史上河、湖、泉众多，水流交错，不仅是北京早期农业发展重要的灌溉之源，也是后来金、元、明、清乃至如今都城供水的重要地表水源地。主要河流有南长河、清河、万泉河、小月河、南沙河、北沙河等 [2]。

可以说，海淀区是倚山拥水，群山雄峙，众水交流，古往今来，就是人类的宜居之地，有着丰富的古代遗存；又景色雄奇，寺庙园林星罗棋布，历史上兴修了众多的水利工程，成为古代农业生产高度发达之地。历史时期以来，这里人文荟萃，被视为风水宝地，使海淀区成为依附重要城市和都城的文物汇聚之地。

历史上海淀区现辖地区没有设置过单独的行政建制，而分属不同的行政区域。区境南半部自秦汉以来主要是隶属于历代北京城的附郭县，金、元两代还曾有少部分地区分别是金中都、元大都的城区，明清时期，绝大部分划入京师直辖区域。而北半部历来都是以北京为中心的大行政区属县（州）的辖区 [3]。

至迟在商代后期，今北京地区已有燕、蓟等方国，是商的属国。周武王灭商后，分封燕、蓟两个诸侯国于今北京地区。燕国于北部"置设上谷、渔阳、右北平、辽西、辽东郡以拒胡" [4]，今海淀区辖域西北部的部分地区可能属于燕国上谷郡管辖。秦统一后，在原燕国北部保留上谷、渔阳等五郡，又设广阳郡，其中海淀部分地区可能属广阳郡（或上谷郡）蓟县、上谷郡军都县所辖。西汉一朝，海淀地区可能属于广阳国蓟县、上谷郡军都县。到东汉末年，则分属蓟、军都和昌平县（均为广阳郡辖县）。三国、魏晋、南北朝时期，绝大部分时间内今海淀区辖区南部始终为燕郡蓟县辖地。其北部在三国至北魏前期分属于燕郡军都、昌平两县，至北魏末年则属军都县，东魏至北齐可能分属于军都县及昌平、万年（又称"万言"）、广武、沃野等 4 个侨置县 [5]。

隋大业三年（607 年）废幽州，置涿郡，今北京地区大部分属涿郡所辖。唐建国后复置幽州，今海淀区辖域在唐天宝元年（742 年）前后可能分属幽州（范阳郡）的蓟、广平、广宁、昌平县和带州孤竹县（寄治），其后一直到五代后唐，可能分属于蓟、幽都、玉河、燕平等县。值得一提的是，705 年后，羁縻州带州及其属县孤竹县寄治于昌平县境，"孤竹，旧治营州界。州陷契丹后，寄治于昌平县之清水店，为州治" [6]，即今海淀区太舟坞村，这是海淀地区范围内历史上最早见于史料的县级治所。可见，海淀区自先秦迄隋唐，一直是方国或地方重镇的附郭之地。

自契丹天显十一年（936 年）起，今北京地区先后由契丹、女真、蒙古等少数民族政权统治达 400 多年。辽在此置南京，金中都则为实际使用的正式都城，后又成为元、明、清三个大一统王朝的首都。契丹会同元年（938 年），"升幽州为南京"，又称燕京，为陪都，设南京道。开泰元年（1012 年）十一月"改

1 "红叶黄花自一川"句出自（金）周昂诗：《香山》："山林朝市两茫然，红叶黄花自一川。野水趁人如有约，长松阅世不知年。千篇未暇偿诗债，一饭聊从结净缘。欲问安心已了了，手书谁识是生前。"这里用此句意在表达海淀文物的多样和独特。载（金）元好问：《中州集》卷四，第 167 页，中华书局，1959 年。

2 北京市海淀区地方志编纂委员会：《北京市海淀区志》第二编，第一章，北京出版社，2004 年。

3 北京市海淀区地方志编纂委员会：《北京市海淀区志》第一编，第一章，北京出版社，2004 年。

4 （汉）司马迁：《史记》卷一百十《匈奴列传》，第 2886 页，中华书局，1959 年。

5 （北齐）魏收：《魏书》卷一〇六上《地形志二上第五》，第 2493-2494 页，中华书局，1974 年。

6 （后晋）刘昫等：《旧唐书》卷三十九《地理二》，第 1524 页，中华书局，1975 年。

幽都府为析津府，蓟北县为析津县，幽都县为宛平县"[7]，海淀地区分属于辽南京道析津府的析津、宛平、玉河、昌平等县。尽管辽南京还是一个陪都，但作为中原和北方地区、农耕区与游牧区或山林部族的交界之处，其扮演的连接与交汇的角色日益彰显，作为民族涵化、文明冲突和交融最激烈的区域，在古代历史和文物制度方面都留下了深刻的印记。

金天德三年（1151年）四月，弑兄即位的海陵王下诏迁都燕京，贞元元年（1153年）改为"中都"[8]。金贞元二年，析津县改称大兴县，大兴、宛平两县分治中都城。金中都由辽南京扩建而成，西北方向将今海淀区羊坊店路以东、黄亭子至会城门一线以南地区括入，其他区域的归属大体仍辽之旧。至金代末年，分属于中都路大兴府的大兴、宛平、昌平等县。据已发现的辽代石刻记载，今魏公村、西二里沟、公主坟一带属宛平县，今北安河、大觉寺一带属玉河县[9]。

金贞祐三年（1215年），蒙古军攻占金中都，"克燕，初为燕京路，总管大兴府"[10]，至元四年（1267年）开始在金中都旧城东北兴建新都[11]，至元八年（1271年）蒙古改国号为"大元"，次年二月"改中都为大都"[12]，今海淀区东部偏南一部分地区划入新都城垣内（即今元代土城以内地区）。至元十一年（1274年）重置大兴、宛平两县衙署。至元二十四年，筑城工程全部告成，有元一代，海淀地区南半部大体宛平县，北半部大体属昌平县。一些重要的寺庙也分布于海淀地区，是元大都最重要的附属地区。

明洪武元年（1368年）八月明军攻占大都城，随即将大都路改为北平府。永乐元年（1403年）正月，"建北京于顺天府，称为行在"[13]，辖今北京市大部分地区。永乐十九年（1421年）正月，称北京为"京师"，正式定都于此。明代海淀地区仍分属宛平、昌平两县（州）。明初，据《永乐大典》辑本《顺天府志》记载，海淀地区内宛平、昌平两县分界，与元代大体相同。清朝沿明旧制，于京师仍置顺天府。清代顺天府所领州县多有变化，大兴、宛平始终为京县，直辖于府，昌平等州县在康熙十五年

（1676年），"始以昌平等十九州县来隶"[14]。康熙二十六年（1687年），顺天府辖区内设东、西、南、北四路厅，大兴、宛平等县属西路厅，昌平州等地属北路厅。清代，今海淀区南半部和温泉、冷泉、北安河一带隶属于宛平县，北半部大部隶属于昌平州。康熙三十一年（1692年）以后，随着玉泉山静明园和此后圆明园的兴建，宛、昌分界才发生较大变动。

可见，自金代以后，海淀随着北京整体地位的变化，从一个地方重镇和陪都的属县辖区，变为都城的一部分和周边地域，特别是清代，在海淀建设了圆明园及附属的苑囿以后，这里实际扮演了一个陪都或夏都的角色。这些构成了海淀文物在帝国时期前、后阶段出土文物的不同特色。

二、文明的曙光——史前时期海淀的文化遗存

1. 古生物化石发现地点

北京这片山前平原地区，河流纵横，是生物和人类的宜居地区，在海淀区的土地上，多年来发现了大量远古时期的古生物化石。1956年，于海淀区黑山扈安河桥挖井过程中，在山前清河上游冲积层地下10米砾石层发现象臼齿，周明镇检测属于更新世晚期[15]。1956年秋，海淀区羊坊店北柳林馆永定河引水工程中，在永定河洪积扇地下6.5米砂砾石中发现有原始牛头骨，中国科学院古脊椎动物与古人类研究所的胡长康对其进行检测，确认其属于更新世晚期[16]。1957年，北京自然博物馆李凤林在海淀区白家疃做调查时，在山前丘陵石灰岩裂隙中发现獾化石，证明其属于更新世晚期[17]。1976年7月，海淀区羊坊店北蜂窝修筑人防工程时，在永定河洪积扇地下6.8米的砂砾石中发现有原始牛头骨，由中国科学院古脊椎动物与古人类研究所的阎德发采集了标本，并进行检测，确认其属于更新世晚期[18]。1999年，海淀区四季青乡玉泉砂石厂在采石过程中，在永定河沉积带发现了古菱齿象牙，属更新世晚期[19]。2005年，在海淀区上地地下

7　（元）脱脱等：《辽史》卷十五《圣宗本纪六》，第171页，中华书局，1974年。

8　（元）脱脱等：《金史》卷二四《地理上》，第572页，中华书局，1975年。

9　北京市海淀区地方志编纂委员会：《北京市海淀区志》，第50页，北京出版社，2004年。

10　（明）宋濂等：《元史》卷五八《地理一》，第1347页，中华书局，1976年。

11　（清）于敏中引《元史·地理志》："（至元）四年，始于中都之东北置今城而迁都焉。"（清）于敏中：《日下旧闻考》卷四，第61页，北京古籍出版社，2000年。

12　（明）宋濂等：《元史》卷七《世祖本纪四》，第140页，中华书局，1976年。

13　（清）张廷玉等：《明史》卷四十《地理一》，第883页，中华书局，1974年。

14　《清史稿》卷一百一十六《职官三》，第3335页，中华书局，1976年。

15　周明镇：《北京西郊的Palaeoloxodon化石及中国Namadicus类象化石的初步讨论》《古生物学报》1957年第2期，第283-294页。

16　胡长康《北京西郊一原始牛（Bos primigenius）头骨化石》，《古脊椎动物与古人类》，1959年第1期，41-42页。

17　郭京宁著，宋大川主编：《北京考古史·史前卷》，第109页，上海古籍出版社，2012年。

18　郭京宁著，宋大川主编：《北京考古史·史前卷》，第109页，上海古籍出版社，2012年。

19　焦晋林：《丹棱撷贝——京西出土文物品鉴》，第224页，学苑出版社，2010年。

9 米深沙层中发现了古菱齿象牙，证明属于晚更新世晚期[20]。2007年，在海淀区知春里，也发现古菱齿象牙化石[21]。海淀博物馆收藏有出土于玉泉山南部地区的菱齿象牙化石和原始牛角化石[22]。菱齿象是生存于晚更新世时期（距今约 10 万 ~1 万年）的大型哺乳动物，海淀区众多的菱齿象化石的出土，表明在远古时期，今天的海淀大地上水草丰美，林木茂密。

距今六七十万年前，人类的远古祖先——北京猿人即在北京这片土地上繁衍生息，北京猿人的行迹一定也到达过海淀的地面，充分表明这里在远古时期是一片生机勃勃的动物和人类的家园。

2. 新石器时代晚期

新石器时代晚期，人类的文明已遍及海淀。从海淀镇向东北延伸的清河台地，被称为海淀台地，是人类文明密集分布的地带。海淀博物馆收藏的出土于北京大学校园内的石斧，就是海淀台地出土的新时期时代晚期的遗物。1982 年，在位于苏家坨镇苏二村苏家坨砖厂东侧，发现了一处古代遗址，时代从新石器时代晚期至汉代，在属于新石器时代晚期的地层中出土了红陶片[23]。1956 年，北京大学佟府甲三号院发现有做工精致的石斧[24]，同年，校园内十楼前发现细石器，采集有石器 100 多件，废片等 200 多块[25]。1997 年北大理科楼群建筑工地发现一批陶器、石器、兽骨及植物标本。陶器以屑云母的红陶为主，次为夹砂陶、泥质陶，器形以罐为主。基本为手制，素面，部分磨光，据碳十四测年，这处被称为燕园遗址的时代为 4400±100 年[26]。此处属于斜穿海淀台地的古水沟，时代约与北京的史前文化雪山一期略同[27]。此外，海淀区还有中关村、清河、白家疃、田村等处发现过细石器和磨制石器[28]，可见海淀区的新石器时代文化大体属

于雪山文化的范畴。

三、燕蓟霞光——夏商周时期海淀的文化遗存

进入原史时期以后，北京地区在夏商两代均属边地，位于文明与蛮荒的交界地域。至西周时，分封了燕、蓟两个方国于今北京地区，燕并蓟后，都蓟城，后成为战国七雄之一。今海淀一带地处古蓟城的西北郊，是北方草原民族同中原农耕民族经济、文化交往的重要通道。战国时期，这里的手工业、商业较为发达，有成熟的制陶业和多种金属货币的铸造业。海淀区朱房村古城城墙夯土中发现的典型战国陶片，表明在战国时期这里已开始建城，可能属于蓟城的外围城镇。

海淀区目前发现的此期的古代遗迹主要是战国时期的墓葬和一些钱币窖藏，其分布的区域大体与新石器时代相同而略有扩展，主要分布在海淀台地和周边地区。1949 年在八里庄街道玲珑路发现瓮棺墓 2 座，南北向，均由相对接的陶瓮组成，瓮内有不足 3 岁的幼儿遗体一具，头北足南[29]。1955 年在海淀区中关村中关园内修建北京大学教工宿舍基建工程中发现了几座战国时期的瓮棺墓，墓呈正南北向，长 0.5 米、宽 0.3 米。瓮棺由两件"鱼骨盆"类陶瓮相对接而成，瓮棺北端用几片素面泥质灰陶片覆盖其上，棺内尸体腐朽，无任何随葬品[30]。1991~2001 年，为配合上地开发区的建设，北京市文物研究所在海淀上地信息产业基地发现较大规模的墓群，其中有 8 座为战国墓葬，均为竖穴土坑墓，出土了一些陶器、铜镜、铜印和带勾等金属器[31]。2007 年，在海淀区青龙桥新村房地产开发工地发现战国瓮棺墓 5 座，每件瓮棺均由两件直腹深底、口沿外侈的陶釜相对接而成，大型陶釜长 50 厘米，小型釜长 30 厘米左右，瓮棺内均盛敛小孩骸骨[32]。

海淀区还多次发现了战国时期的钱币窖藏。1982 年，在苏家坨镇苏二村苏家坨砖厂东侧的遗址发现战国刀币，该遗址的时代从新石器时代晚期至汉代[33]。1953 年 6 月，在海淀区紫竹桥

20　董育纲：《北京山地出土古菱齿象牙与现场收取保护》，《北京文博》2006年 2 期，第 93-95 页。

21　焦晋林：《丹稜撷贝——京西出土文物品鉴》，第 224 页，学苑出版社，2010 年。

22　李昂主编：《沉香越千年——海淀历史文物展》，2-3 页，海淀博物馆，2012 年。

23　国家文物局主编：《中国文物地图集》北京分册（下），科学出版社 2008 年，第 209 页。

24　岳升阳：《北大燕园的文化埋藏》，《北京大学学报（哲学社会科学版）》1998 年第 35 卷 31 期，第 55-61 页。

25　魏效祖：《北京海淀区发现细石器》，《文物参考资料》，1956 年 7 期，第 73 页。

26　岳升阳等：《燕园遗址调查简报》，《考古与文物》2002 年增刊（先秦考古），第 9-12 页。

27　郭京宁著，宋大川主编：《北京考古史·史前卷》，上海古籍出版社，2012 年，第 173 页。

28　关成和译：《北京北部清河镇发现新石器时代磨光石斧》，《文物参考资料》1953 年 12 期，第 109 页，原文发表在自苏联《图书馆员》1953 年 7 期。魏效祖：《北京海淀区发现细石器》，《文物参考资料》1956 年 7 期。

29　国家文物局主编：《中国文物地图集》北京分册（下），科学出版社 2008 年，第 212 页。

30　王克林：《北京西郊中关园内发现瓮棺葬》，《文物参考资料》1955 年 11 期，第 121 页。

31　国家文物局主编：《中国文物地图集》北京分册（下），第 212 页，科学出版社，2008 年；宋大川：《近年来北京考古新成果》，《北京文物与考古》第 5 辑，第 6 页，北京燕山出版社，2002 年。

32　北京市文物研究所编：《北京考古四十年》，62-63 页，北京燕山出版社，1990 年。

33　国家文物局主编：《中国文物地图集》北京分册（下），第 209 页，科学出版社，2008 年。

发现方折式"匽"字刀币，总量约4公斤[34]。1976年，在海淀区温泉公社东埠头村地下2米深处发现方折式"匽"字刀币，共数百枚[35]。1978年，在海淀区梁家园西山农场果树三队，生产中发现了方折式"匽"字刀币约2公斤[36]。1989年海淀区谷香园食品厂也出土了明刀窖藏，出土的刀币现藏海淀博物馆[37]。

此外，海淀区还发现了一些战国时期的其他遗物。1957年5月，在海淀区东北旺村北农场，发现战国时期铜簋一件，器底有铭文[38]。零星发现的战国陶器就更多了，主要是灰陶质的陶罐和壶等。1971年8月，海淀区八里庄出土战国陶壶一件[39]。在北京大学燕南园的管线施工中，也曾出土过战国灰陶罐。

可以看到，战国以来，海淀区出土的文物迅速增加，表明燕、蓟对北京地区开发的效果。特别是密集的铜币窖藏的发现，表明海淀地区在战国时已成为一个得到高度开发，农业、商业、手工业都迅速发展的地区。

四、边陲巨邑——汉唐时期海淀的文化遗存

1. 两汉时期，海淀地区可能属于广阳国蓟县、上谷郡军都县，社会经济较前更加繁荣，表明这时期农耕文明已延伸到了这里，北京一带成为北部边陲的重镇和经济中心。海淀区范围内的两汉文化遗存十分丰富，以小型的墓葬为主，此外还有少量城址和建筑遗迹。

1951年，在海淀区清河镇至朱房村的区域内，曾先后发现许多西汉和东汉土坑墓，出土有灰陶绳纹大瓮、壶、鼎等陶器，还有砖瓦、半两钱、五铢钱等[40]。1962年冬，在海淀区永定路清理了一座汉代墓葬，墓葬为长方形小型土坑墓，骨架保存完好，出土陶器、西汉五铢钱及铜镜一面[41]。1982年，在位于苏家坨镇苏二村苏家坨砖厂东侧的一处时代从新石器时代晚期至汉代的遗址，清理了汉代墓葬6座，墓葬多为单室砖墓，大部分遭破坏。出土器物有铜镜、铜车马饰、灰陶壶、罐、盆及汉代陶片[42]。1982年，在海淀区万寿路五棵松附近的炮兵司令部大院内发现3座汉代墓葬，出土有陶器和丝织品[43]。2004~2005年，海淀区复兴路五棵松篮球馆工程占地范围内发掘了7座汉墓，均为长方形竖穴土坑式墓葬，其中M3及M5为西汉时期的墓葬，出土有红陶壶、红陶钵、灰陶壶、灰陶罐。其他主要随葬灰陶罐，为东汉时期墓葬[44]。棒球馆内发掘1座汉代砖室墓，为前单室，后双室墓，出土铜钱及一面铜镜，发掘者将年代定在东汉中晚期[45]。1984年，在海淀区海淀街道万泉庄南发现2座西汉陶井，3座西汉土坑墓，墓葬出土陶壶、仓等陶器，还发现有汉代五铢钱[46]。1985年，在西玉河一带发现多座砖室汉墓，破坏严重，形制模糊，其中一座单室墓出土陶罐等陶器和数件银器[47]。海淀区最大规模的汉墓群发现于海淀区上地街道上地信息产业基地，1991~2001年，北京市文物研究所在这里先后发掘了300多座汉代墓葬[48]。此外，近年配合上地佳园的兴建，在原上地村的菜地、果园中进行了一系列的勘探工作，发现一批墓葬，该墓葬区属战国、秦汉时期，应该是一条高于地面约3米的台地。其中98座墓葬属于汉代墓葬，形制多为长方形、多边形，极少量耳室墓，均为竖穴，部分青砖铺设墓地，也有砌筑墓圹、券拱的[49]。2007年，在海淀区青龙桥新村开发区内发现墓葬遗存，属于汉代墓葬的有M2及M4，均为长方形竖穴土坑墓，随葬品有陶罐、钵、鼎、仓等[50]。

34　周耿：《介绍北京市的出土文物展览》，《文物参考资料》，1954年第8期，第70页。

35　北京市文物研究所编：《北京考古四十年》，第64页，北京燕山出版社，1990年。

36　北京市文物研究所编：《北京考古四十年》，第64页，北京燕山出版社，1990年。

37　李昂主编：《沉香越千年—海淀历史文物展》，6-7页，海淀博物馆，2012年。

38　北京市文物组：《海淀区发现春秋时代铜器》，《文物参考资料》1958年第5期，第72页。

39　北京市文物研究所编：《北京考古四十年》，第59页，北京燕山出版社，1990年。

40　周耿：《介绍北京市的出土文物展览》，《文物参考资料》，1954年第8期，第70页。

41　喻震：《北京永定路东汉墓》，《考古》1963年3期，第170-171页。

42　国家文物局主编：《中国文物地图集》北京分册（下），第209页，科学出版社，2008年。

43　国家文物局主编：《中国文物地图集》北京分册（下），第212页，科学出版社，2008年。

44　北京市文物研究所：《五棵松篮球馆工程考古发掘报告》，《北京奥运场馆考古发掘报告》，第1-71页，科学出版社，2007年。

45　北京市文物研究所：《五棵松棒球场工程考古发掘报告》，《北京奥运场馆考古发掘报告》，第381-382页，科学出版社，2007年。

46　国家文物局主编：《中国文物地图集》北京分册（下），第209页，科学出版社，2008年。

47　国家文物局主编：《中国文物地图集》北京分册（下），第212页，科学出版社，2008年。

48　李达：《海淀上地村东汉墓》，《中国考古学年鉴（1992）》，第146页，文物出版社，1994年。其中公布发现的5座东汉墓。宋大川：《近年来北京考古新成果》，《北京文物与考古》第5辑，第6页，北京燕山出版社，2002年；国家文物局主编：《中国文物地图集》北京分册（下），第212页，科学出版社，2008年。

49　郭立展执笔，宋大川主编：《实创房地产开发公司上地佳园考古勘探报告》，《北京考古工作报告（2000-2009）》海淀卷，第348-349页，上海古籍出版社，2011年。

50　郭立展执笔，宋大川主编：《青龙桥新村考古发掘报告》，《北京考古工作报告（2000-2009）》海淀卷、第348-349页，上海古籍出版社，2011年。

位于海淀区清河街道朱房村的是一座汉代古城遗址，1955年对其进行了局部发掘。城址平面呈正方形，发现陶井十几处，出土夹砂红陶、泥质灰陶及板瓦、瓦当、筒瓦等，另发现一批铁器，包括铁剑、铁刀、铁锄、铁镜等，还发现了铜印[51]。海淀区还发现了大批的汉井遗迹，主要分布在今颐和园到玉泉山一带，都用巨大的灰陶井圈建造，尽管这些遗迹的资料并未得到报告，但可以看到，这时期在海淀区的西部地区农业已得到了高度的发展。此外，在清河镇朱房村发现了汉代窑址，清理了汉代的窑基[52]。这些发现都很好地诠释了两汉时期海淀一带生产发达，人口滋殖的繁庶景象。

2. 三国两晋南北朝时期，北方地方行政区划基本上是州、郡、县三级制度。位于北京市的蓟城为幽州治所，也始终为燕郡（燕国）治所，经济文化都比较发达，是北方边陲的巨邑。

此期最重要的考古发现之一是海淀区玉潭乡八里庄魏墓。此墓1987年发掘，位于八里庄东北，墓为双室砖室墓，南北向，由墓道、墓门、前室、甬道、后室组成，出土了成套的黄釉俑和模型明器，包括两件生动的舞俑、仓、灶、井、磨、臼、猪圈等模型明器，用作酒具的樽和勺、奁、榼、扁壶和虎子等用具。自汉代以来，北方地区就流行成套的釉陶明器，但在今黄河沿线的地区流行绿釉明器，河北省邯郸以北的地区则流行一整套的黄釉明器，这座魏墓出土的黄釉明器，为接近北方边地的区域提供了一套较为完整的黄釉陶明器组合。此外，八里庄魏墓还发现了五铢钱，特别是这座墓葬中出土了一件铜质弩机，上有规整的阴刻铭文："正始五年三月卅日左尚方造步弩耳监作吏王昭匠马广师张雄"[53]，证明这座墓的时代为曹魏正始五年（244年）以后不久。与八里庄魏墓颇为相似的还有草场西晋墓，1962年发现于苏家坨镇草场村，共2座。两墓均为砖室墓，斜坡墓道，拱券顶，也出土了成组的黄釉陶明器，如车夫俑、牛车、牛、鸡、灶等，另有铜钱、铜镜、铜铃[54]。

海淀区还清理出另外的一些南北朝时期的墓葬。1953年在清河镇发掘了一座魏晋大型砖室墓，该墓葬为悬棺下葬，出土了铜镜、铜刀、陶盏、五铢钱等。离该墓不远还发现了砖坑，出土铁犁铧2件[55]。1953年，在海淀镇八一小学发现有魏晋北朝土坑墓1座。1962年，在海淀区景王坟西北还发现2座西晋砖室墓[56]。

两晋南北朝时期考古的一项重要工作是古代水利工程的考察。在今紫竹桥西南至石景山的永定河畔有一条古渠，据岳升阳研究，这就是始建于曹魏的车厢渠。根据零星的考古发现相连后可以得到古渠的走向，南端相当于在紫竹院旁边的高梁河畔，北端在成府村至清华大学一带汇入万泉河。其南段与白石桥路大致重叠，北段与海淀路大致平行，但在当代商城以北似乎又分支[57]。车厢渠走向的明了，对于了解两晋时期渠流经地区的农业和民居都有重要作用。

3. 隋唐时期，是北京地区得到进一步开发的时期。幽州是唐代的大州，占地超过16坊，是北方重镇。"安史之乱"中，史思明以幽州城为"燕京"（759年），这是历史上首次称北京为"燕京"。晚唐藩镇割据时又是三大藩镇之一的幽州节度使（兼卢龙节度使）辖地，为后来北京成为帝国的都城奠定了基础。

这一时期北京发现过一些重要的唐墓，海淀是较大型唐墓的集中发现区域。1980年在海淀区钓鱼台国宾馆东门外发现了一座唐代早中期的砖室墓，墓南北向，门朝南，券顶，出土有白彩陶片，大致包括罐、碗、盆等，另有墓志一方[58]。1973年，在清河镇朱房村发现一座唐代天宝年间的墓葬，墓葬为长方形砖室墓，由墓道、墓门、墓室组成，随葬器物仅剩黑陶碗、彩陶四系盖罐、陶盘和墓志一合。据墓志可知，该墓主人王徽，是开元观道士[59]。

1985年，在海淀区翠微路14号院内发现唐墓一座。该墓为圆形穹隆顶单室砖墓，墓内绘有壁画，还有砖雕的门窗、灯檠和仿木构建筑等，皆涂油朱彩。棺床在墓室北部，其中出土墓志一件。据墓志可知，该墓为唐大中元年（847年）游击将军纪制夫妇墓[60]。这座墓是晚唐时期北方地区最早的仿木构砖室

51 北京大葆台西汉墓博物馆编：《北京地区汉代城址调查与研究》，第124-127页，北京燕山出版社，2009年；胡传耸著，宋大川主编：《北京考古史·汉代卷》第38-41页，上海古籍出版社，2012年。

52 周耿：《介绍北京市的出土文物展览》，《文物参考资料》，1954年第8期，第71页。

53 董坤玉著，宋大川主编：《北京考古史·魏晋南北朝隋唐卷》，第16页，上海古籍出版社，2012年。

54 国家文物局主编：《中国文物地图集》北京分册（下），第213页，科学出版社，2008年。

55 周耿：《介绍北京市的出土文物展览》，《文物参考资料》，1954年第8期，第71页。

56 董坤玉著，宋大川主编：《北京考古史·魏晋南北朝隋唐卷》，第2页，上海古籍出版社，2012年。

57 岳升阳：《双榆树古渠遗址与车箱渠》，载北京市文物研究所编：《北京文物与考古》第4辑，第126-127页，1994年。

58 洪欣：《北京近年来发现的几座唐墓》，《文物》1990年第12期，第16页。

59 北京市文物工作队：《北京市发现的几座唐墓》，《考古》1980年第6期，总498-500页。

60 洪欣：《北京近年来发现的几座唐墓》，《文物》1990年第12期，第20页。

墓之一。

1992年，海淀区文管所在八里庄某单位施工现场清理一座唐墓。墓为弧方形单室砖墓，由墓道、墓门、墓室三部分组成，墓门朝南，墓道为斜坡式，墓内有砖砌棂窗、壁龛，墓内顶部及四壁均有壁画装饰。重要的是在墓室后壁较完好的保存了一幅长2.9米，高1.56米的通景画式的屏风画，内容是牡丹芦雁图，为晚唐五代时期北方地区墓葬的装饰特点和唐代绘画史研究，特别是花鸟画发展历史的研究提供了不可多得的重要资料。因墓内早年被盗，仅有少量器物碎片和墓志一合，根据墓志记载，此墓为唐大中六年（852年）幽州节度判官王公淑墓[61]。

1984年，在海淀区二里沟发现唐墓1座。墓葬为圆形单室砖墓，南北向，由墓道、墓门、墓室组成，墓门开在南边，北部为棺床，北壁上抹白灰并绘朱红色花纹。随葬品仅见陶器碎片和墓志一合，从墓志可知为唐广明元年（880年）兵马使充使宅将副将茹洪庆墓[62]。1966年在修建京密引水工程中发现一座唐墓，墓早年已毁，仅存墓志一合，根据墓志可知为唐乾元二年（759年）青山州（羁縻州）刺史李永定墓[63]。此外，发现的较重要的纪年唐墓还有海淀区万寿路唐懿宗咸通十五年（874年）温令绥墓[64]、海淀区二里沟进出口大楼院内发现的唐广明元年（880年）墓[65]、海淀区温泉白家疃文德元年（888年）要氏夫人墓等[66]。

此外，在偏北部的地区，即距离幽州城更远一些的地方，还发现了一些唐代的不带壁面装饰的简单砖室墓和小型土坑墓。1988年，在清华大学院内偏东南部的一处建筑工地上，发现了一批小型竖穴土坑墓，海淀区文管所进行了清理，墓葬的等级并不高，但出土了一些精美的遗物，如唐代邢窑的碗、巩义窑的高足杯和精美的花鸟纹菱花镜等，这些遗物现存海淀博物馆[67]。1991-2001年，北京市文物研究所在海淀上地街道上地信息产业基地发掘的墓群，其中有2座为唐代墓葬[68]。2003年，在物

资储备学校发现唐墓1座。墓葬为长方形斜坡式砖室墓，方向185°，由墓道、墓门和墓室组成，墓道在墓室南侧。出土人骨2具，头朝南，随葬品包括陶缸2个，棺环3个[69]。2006年，在北京市香山植物园卧佛寺公交车站改造工地中发现唐墓一座。该墓葬为半椭圆形砖室墓，券顶，出土了陶罐、陶器座及盖、还有开元通宝2枚[70]。

五、交融与涵化——宋辽金元时期海淀的文化遗存

辽金元时期（包括宋代短暂的占领时间），长城南北一线经历了复杂的政治演变，契丹、女真、蒙古等骑马民族交替南下。以北京为中心，包括周边冀晋北部、内蒙古东南部和辽宁西隅地区在这种动荡的时局之下，表现出人群族属与文化传统的多样性与交融性，而这种擅代文化之变和族属涵化现象使北京地区的古代文化面貌出现了多样性和丰富性。也恰恰是在这时，作为沟通中原农耕民族和北方草原民族重镇的燕京，以其独有的地理位置和经济基础，成为了中国巨大帝国的都邑。展现了都城文化的特有面貌。

1. 辽统治时期。公元936年，辽统治者获得燕云十六州后，升幽州为辽五京之一，称南京。开泰元年改称析津府。北京地区从中原王朝的北部边陲，变成了边境王朝的南界，成为汉文化与契丹文化交流、交融的中心地区。经过考古勘察，结合文献记载，证明辽南京的西北角约在今海淀区东南角位置，有小部分区域重合。

在海淀区发现有一些辽代墓葬，并出土有不少精美文物。1953年，在西翠路修下水道过程中发现辽墓，北京市文物局随即对该墓进行了清理。此墓为仿木构圆形单室砖墓，墓内保存有较丰富的壁画，题材包括假门、花卉、水鸟等，漫漶严重，未见棺椁。出土有开元通宝、乾元通宝等钱币，及大小玉带扣、薄银片，精美的定窑白釉素面葵花口大碗、武士陶俑等[71]。

1985年，在海淀区苏家坨镇聂各庄西北发现四座圆形单室砖室墓，海淀区文管所进行了清理。4座墓葬均被盗，多有壁画的痕迹，但破坏严重，其中一座墓还保存有一幅较完整的壁画，为备茶图中的风炉和汤瓶部分。4座墓的葬式都采用了火葬，

61　北京市海淀区文物管理所：《北京市海淀区八里庄唐墓》，《文物》1995年第11期，45-53页。

62　洪欣：《北京近年来发现的几座唐墓》，《文物》1990年第12期，第17页。

63　国家文物局主编：《中国文物地图集》北京分册（下），第213页，科学出版社，2008年。

64　董坤玉著，宋大川主编：《北京考古史·魏晋南北朝隋唐卷》，第52页，上海古籍出版社，2012年。

65　董坤玉著，宋大川主编：《北京考古史·魏晋南北朝隋唐卷》，第52页，上海古籍出版社，2012年。

66　董坤玉著，宋大川主编：《北京考古史·魏晋南北朝隋唐卷》，第53页，上海古籍出版社，2012年。

67　北京市海淀区博物馆编：《海淀博物馆》，12-15、154页，文物出版社，2005年。

68　北京市文物研究所编：《北京考古四十年》，62-63页，北京燕山出版社，1990年。

69　郭立展执笔，宋大川主编：《物资储备学校住宅区考古发掘报告》，《北京考古工作报告（2000-2009）》海淀卷，第126页，上海古籍出版社，2011年。

70　郭立展执笔，宋大川主编：《香山北京植物园卧佛寺公交车站改造工地考古发掘报告》，《北京考古工作报告（2000-2009）》海淀卷，第280-281页，上海古籍出版社，2011年。

71　苏天钧：《北京郊区辽墓发掘简报》，《考古》，1959年第2期，第89-93页。

墓中出土了一些残陶器和宋辽铜钱[72]。

1991年，北京市文物研究所抢救性发掘了海淀区羊坊店邮电局宿舍以北基建施工中发现的1座长方形券顶单室砖室墓。该墓保存较好，南北向，墓顶上铺有平砖一层，墓北端0.4米处有祭台一个。头顶部随葬有鸡冠壶、小黑陶罐、灰陶罐、骨质粉盒、贝壳、刷子柄、骨簪、铁剪刀等器物，此外还有一些漆器遗痕。在墓主胸部正中有铜镜一面，祭品台上有大型牲畜头骨一颗。这座墓形制较特别，出土物也十分丰富[73]。

1991~2001年在上地信息产业基地建设工程中发掘的从战国到明清的墓葬群中，发现辽金时代墓葬30座，分为砖室墓和石椁墓两种，出土有铜镜、陶器、瓷器、玉器、铁器等[74]。

2002年，海淀区增光路中国工运学院住宿楼北部施工发现1座辽墓，北京市文物研究所进行了抢救性发掘。该墓为仿木结构圆形单室砖墓，墓南向，由墓道、影风墙、甬道、墓室四部分组成；墓中出土了灰陶盆、灰陶碟、灰陶罐3件陶器，另有墓志一方。墓志记载墓主人逝于咸雍七年（1071年），墓志内容丰富了史料，有助于我们了解家族墓的分围列葬情况[75]。奥运前夕，在营建五棵松奥运场馆过程中，发现辽金墓3座，其中2座可确定为辽墓。两座辽墓皆为椭圆形砖室墓，出土器物多为陶器，包括陶盆、陶盘、陶盏等，亦出土有零星瓷器，如瓷碗、瓷盘之类，还发现有鸡腿瓶，质地较粗。

总体而言，海淀区发现的辽墓基本包括了北京所发现辽墓的各种类型，并有一些规格较高、出土物较丰富的辽墓发现。目前对于辽墓的研究主要集中在分区分期、形制研究、壁画研究、随葬品研究等多个方面。不过，与北京其他区县比，海淀区发现的辽墓并未显示出特殊的区域特征，因此在研究中，多将海淀区辽墓作为北京辽墓的一个部分进行阐释。

2. 金代的繁盛。1125年，金军伐宋获幽燕地区，改燕山府为南京。1153年，海陵王完颜亮迁都南京，升为中都。在北京城市发展史上，金中都的建立，开辟了北京作为首都的新纪元，此后，元明清一直沿袭至今。因此，金代是北京地区发展的重要时代。目前认为金中都的北垣与辽南京基本重合，与海淀区有小区域重合。

海淀区发现的金代墓葬颇多。1956年，在甘家口街道二里沟发现张汝猷墓。此墓早年被毁，出土墓志一合，志文载，张汝猷殁于金泰和七年（1207年）[76]。1978年在青龙桥街道娘娘府村发现蒲察胡沙墓。蒲察胡沙为金代贵族，娶世宗公主，姐姐为世宗妃子。其墓早年被盗，为土坑石椁墓，用六块石板砌建，棺底有一长方形石棺床，有火烧痕迹，出土有墓志一合[77]。1979年，在甘家口街道半截塔村南发现金墓，为长方形单室砖墓，墓室东西长1.75米，南北宽1.15米，高0.6米。在墓室北壁近中部有小墓道，墓顶向上逐渐收缩，盖青石板，为火葬墓。出土有围棋子、绿松石饰品和铜钱等[78]。

1985年，在四季青镇南辛庄西发现金墓，海淀区文管所进行了清理。M1、M2均为土坑石椁墓。M1早年遭日军盗掘，出土有定窑白瓷碗、瓜棱注子、盘、盒等，还出土有墓志一合，题墓主为宣武将军骑都尉张□震，考证其时代为金海陵王贞元至正隆年间（1153~1160年）。M2为夫妻合葬墓，此墓没有被盗，墓内有木棺痕迹。出土有定窑绿釉划花瓷枕、定窑白瓷盒、碗、盘、水注、罐、碟、粉盒、定窑黑釉托盏和陶砚，一个纸盒内放置的一整套化妆用具等遗物，体现了一套完整的金代前期墓葬随葬品的组合[79]。此墓出土的一组早期定窑瓷器，表现出了制作工艺精粗的不同，但整体上体现出定窑精细白瓷的主要特征，包括黑定托盏，定窑受磁州窑影响生产的绿釉划花瓷枕，在报告发表时对于了解定窑金代前期的烧造情况起到十分重要的作用。

1987年，在四季青镇金山山麓发现金代前期的土坑石椁墓，海淀区文管所进行了清理。此墓早年被盗，石椁为六块青石凿榫卯相接，椁长2.5米，宽1.41米，高1.2米，是一座金代前期的墓葬。清理出钧窑玉壶春瓶、盘、碗各一件，红黑两色缠枝花卉漆盒盖二件。另外，在盗洞口处发现有钧窑菱口钵及龙泉

72 国家文物局编：《中国文物考古地图集·北京分册（下）》，第213页，科学出版社，2008年。

73 刘连成、李达：《海淀区羊坊店辽墓》，引自《中国考古学年鉴-1992》，第149页，文物出版社，1994年。

74 王有泉：《一九九八年北京地区地下文物保护工作主要成就》，《北京文博》，1999年第1期，第10-12页。

75 朱志刚：《海淀中国工运学院辽墓及其墓志》，《北京文物与考古》第六辑，第27-34页，民族出版社，2004年。

76 侯珺：《金〈张汝猷墓志〉考释》，《北京文物与考古》第2辑，152-157页，北京燕山出版社，1991年；北京市文物局：《北京辽金史迹图志》（上），第217页，北京燕山出版社，2003年。

77 齐心：《金代蒲察墓志考》，《北京史论文集》，第一辑，101-105页，北京史研究会编印，1980年。另见北京市文物研究所：《北京考古四十年》，第166页，北京燕山出版社，1990年。

78 国家文物局编：《中国文物地图集·北京卷（下）》，第214页，科学出版社，2008年。

79 北京市海淀区文化文物局：《北京市海淀区南辛庄金墓清理简报》，《文物》1988年7期，56-66页。

窑梅瓶残片[80]。此墓的时代为金代前期，土坑石椁墓证明主要是女真贵族及家属使用，因此这座墓葬出土的几件钧窑瓷器，成为确定钧窑创烧时间的最重要的考古证据之一。

1998年，海淀区文管所在在北京植物园内清理了一座金代长方形券顶砖室墓，出土了一件磁州窑椭圆形白地黑花婴戏纹瓷枕和金"大定通宝"铜钱，证明此墓的年代为金世宗"大定十八年"（1178年）始铸此钱之后[81]。此墓出土的瓷枕以往一向被认为是北宋的产品，此墓证明这类瓷枕的实际生产年代是金代后期。

此外，在北京大学院内[82]、海淀区北安河等地也曾发现金墓[83]，但并无详细报道。海淀区发现的金代墓葬大部分是在金代流行并十分有特点的土坑石椁墓，这类墓葬从金代开始在北京和周边的河北地区出现，主要是女真贵族和降金的契丹贵族使用、等级均比较高，往往出土一些高等级的文物。这类墓葬目前以北京地区发现的最多，集中分布在房山县金陵区域附近和海淀区，这似乎表明海淀区当时曾是女真贵族聚居的地区。

金代北京地区有一段十分特别的历史，即在宋金战争初期，金二帅完颜宗翰（粘翰）和完颜宗望（斡离不）分别驻扎在云州和燕，是攻击宋朝的前进基地。靖康之变以后，二帝挟宋二帝北上金源的五国头城，是从燕经行的，此外，二帅也曾继续驻扎两地，手下的一些官兵曾从北宋两京核心地区掠来大批北宋时期，特别是北宋后期的精美器物，部分就散落在了北京周边地区，这些文物对了解北宋后期的一些文物制度和手工业生产情况具有重要意义。前述四季青镇金山金墓出土的一组钧窑瓷器，可能就是北宋后期在河南地区生产的，宋金战争时被金兵掠来，回到驻地燕以后随葬在金初期墓葬中，这是钧窑始烧于北宋末期的重要证据。此外，1986年在四季青乡的河道挖沙时，出土了一枚"大晟"编钟，现藏海淀区博物馆[84]。大晟编钟是北宋徽宗时恢复礼制，大批制作"新成礼器"的重要代表，靖康之变时大部分被掠往金源之地的上京，金代中期逐渐用于金王

朝的礼制性活动，目前保存下来的"大晟"编钟主要藏于北京、台北两故宫。这件编钟是唯一后期出土的个案，很有可能是当时掳掠此器的金兵所遗弃的。这是女真人从宋宫廷掠来的大批文物的少数出土的器物，具有十分重要的学术意义。

3. 蒙元时期。金贞祐三年（1215年），蒙古军攻占金中都，此后对金中都的经营是从蒙古人改变"得地不守"政策开始的，因此是金宋统治区内最早进入稳定发展的地区。中统二年（1261年）世祖忽必烈曾修过一次燕京城墙，但旋即放弃了重修金中都的打算。至元四年（1267年）开始在金中都东北修建新都，到至元二十四年主城工程基本完成，前后筑城达二十年，使北京由一个地方性中心而成为了整个蒙元帝国的政治、经济、文化中心。关于元大都的考古工作是最早引起学界关注的，民国时期营造学社就开展了一些工作。1964~1974年中国科学院考古研究所与北京市文物工作队共同组成了元大都考古队，勘查了元大都的城垣、街道、河湖水系等遗迹，这是宋元明时期考古最早的专门的城市考古队。因此北京元代考古最重要也最富有成果的工作，毫无疑问是元大都相关的考古工作。

元大都位于金中都东北方向。元大都遗址西北部分分布在今海淀区范围内（北土城的西半部），北城墙西门健德门，西城墙北门肃清门，均在海淀区。目前在海淀区北太平庄街道学院南路明光村向北至知春路口向东，保存有部分元大都北城墙西段和西城墙北端遗迹，全长4公里。元大都考古队曾在北部城墙清理了三处水涵洞遗址，其中花园路和学院路的两处都在海淀区范围内[85]。残存最高处约8米，基宽22~24米，夯土版筑，夯窝明显[86]。1992年，北京市文物研究所对太平庄以北的元大都城墙进行了解剖发掘，证明城墙由四种土质分层夯筑，表明大都的城墙曾多次补筑[87]。同时，海淀区文管所也曾配合整修乾隆时修建的燕京八景中"蓟门烟树"景点部分清理了大都西墙北段的部分城墙，出土了两门明末的大铜炮。

另外，在西土城路西侧有水涵洞遗址。位于北城西段墙下，肃清门北部的水涵洞，涵洞的金门底与两壁均用石板铺砌，顶部用砖起券，可见三券三袱，为都城之制。涵洞内外侧各用石块砌出6.5米长的摆手，整个涵洞的石底略向外倾斜。这处水涵

80　秦大树、王晓军：《记北京市海淀区出土的一组早期钧窑瓷器及相关问题探讨》，《文物》2002年第11期，80-92页。另见国家文物局编：《中国文物地图集·北京卷（下）》，第214页，科学出版社，2008年。

81　高二岳：《海淀出土一件磁州窑瓷枕》，《北京文博》2000年1期，第76页。

82　苏天钧：《十年来北京市所发现的重要古代墓葬和遗址》，《考古》，1959年第3期，第160页。

83　北京市文物研究所：《北京考古四十年》，第167页，北京燕山出版社，1990年。

84　北京市海淀区博物馆编：《海淀博物馆》，156-159页，文物出版社，2005年。

85　元大都考古队：《元大都的勘查与发掘》，《考古》1972年1期，19-28页；徐苹芳：《元大都的勘察与发掘》，载徐苹芳：《中国历史考古学论丛》，159-172页，台北：允晨文化，1995年。

86　国家文物局编：《中国文物考古地图集·北京分册（下）》，209页，科学出版社，2008年。

87　国家文物局编：《中国文物考古地图集·北京分册（下）》，209页，科学出版社，2008年。

洞本经过元大都考古队的清理，后由于保护不利有所破坏，2002年北京市文物研究所对这处水涵洞遗址再次进行了发掘，进一步了解其结构，并进行了保护。通过发掘可知，水涵洞的建造是筑夯土城墙之前预先构筑的，水关涵洞南北走向，长9.5米，高3.45米，底部和两侧都是用石板砌成，顶部为砖券，在涵洞中心部位装有一排断面呈菱形的铁栅棍，间距10-15厘米，底石和两壁皆以铁锭（细腰）加固。它对我们了解和研究元大都排水系统工程具有重要意义[88]。

海淀区发现的元墓不多，1998年北京市文物研究所在颐和园内发掘了至元二十二年（1285年）耶律铸夫妇合葬墓，是这一时期较重要的墓葬[89]。耶律铸为耶律楚材次子，官居中书左丞相，在元代有较高的政治地位。此墓为多室仿木构砖墓，由墓道、墓门、前室、前室东西侧室、后室及后室东西侧室组成。墓道位于前室南侧正中，距墓门不远墓道上方并列立有圆额墓志两块。墓室内壁均绘制有壁画，不过大多漫漶，仅可见云朵、花草、鸟兽等图案。此墓早年被盗，出土随葬品仍十分丰富，包括瓷器、陶器、银器、石器等装饰品计180余件。其中瓷器有青白釉高足碗、双鱼盘、玉壶春瓶等。青白釉高足碗口径12.5厘米，足径4.5厘米，通高9.5厘米。侈口，尖唇，曲腹下收，圈足较高，足端外撇。腹部饰有云雷纹，并有"白"、"王"二字。陶俑共有48件，俑的质量都很差，多数为神煞类俑，有手执书牌的十二时俑，捧持各类生活用器的男女仆役俑等，及龙、凤、马、骆驼等动物。石器有汉白玉石马、石狗等，一组8件玉石质明器有盘、碗、钵、盏托等。汉白玉天马长64厘米，宽30厘米，通高50厘米，座长55厘米，马身修长，四足较短，置于卷云纹中，下面有一长方形基座，雕刻精细。耶律铸墓独特的形制和丰富的随葬品，为元代前期葬制研究和文物研究提供了不可多得的重要资料。

此外，1971年在大有庄村、1986年在永定路也分别发现了元代单室砖墓，出土有一些陶瓷器和铜钱[90]。1985年海淀区文管所在航天部二院清理元代小型砖室墓一座，其中出土了一件元代景德镇窑青白瓷梅瓶和一组黑陶明器，包括罐、盆、碗、釜、尊等[91]。

作为重要墓葬遗迹的还有耶律楚材的墓和祠，其位于颐和园昆明湖东岸，文昌阁以北，为墓、祠合一的两进双层套院。第一进院落正房为祠堂，面阔三间，内供奉耶律楚材泥塑像。院内有高达3米的石碑一座，碑阳为乾隆十五年（1750年）御制《耶律楚材墓碑记》，碑阴为大学士汪由敦撰《元臣耶律楚材墓碑记》，旁立石翁仲一。第二进院落北房三间，内有耶律楚材及续弦夫人苏氏合葬的丘冢。耶律楚材墓始建于元代，按生前要求葬于瓮山泊（昆明湖）畔，时建庙立像，极为隆重，并成为大都西郊名迹，供人凭吊题咏。明初墓地遭到彻底破坏，清乾隆年间修造清漪园时，于原地恢复了祠墓，并立碑记其始末，昭其功德。1860年，祠、墓均为英法联军焚毁。现存地面建筑系光绪时（1875-1908年）重修，祠堂、墓丘一如旧制[92]。

此外，1983年在羊坊店街道公主坟南发现三座元代窑址，窑壁高约1米，壁厚0.3米。出土物除少量黑釉瓷片外，主要是各色琉璃建筑构件和窑具，其中有白琉璃砖、绿琉璃砖、素面砖、沟纹砖、筒瓦、板瓦、绿琉璃宝顶等物，此外还出土了一些窑具。根据窑址的地理位置、出土器物及文献记载等情况，推测是元代至元四年所建的西窑厂[93]。

从总体来看，北京地区元代的考古工作实际以元大都的勘察与发掘为核心，在海淀区范围内也发现有不少非常重要的城市考古遗迹。另外，在元大都的考古过程中，还发现了不少重要的遗物和文字材料，进一步推动了元大都的研究。在北京地区发现的元代墓葬至2009年约有50座左右，相对于辽金墓葬来说，数量较少，不过分布范围较广。海淀区内的元代墓葬数量很少，不过出土了耶律铸夫妇墓这种等级较高的墓葬，并发现了墓志，这为我们了解元代的政治、宗教、思想、民族融合等信息提供了宝贵的材料。另外在羊坊店街道发现的琉璃窑址，为此前所少见，为我们研究元代宫廷的琉璃烧造提供了重要实物证据。

88 李华：《元大都北土城花园路段城墙勘探及水关遗址清理简报》，《北京考古》第一辑，北京燕山出版社，2008年。

89 程利：《耶律铸夫妇合葬墓简况》，《北京文博》，1998年第4期，彩三-彩四；北京市文物研究所：《北京元耶律铸夫妇合葬墓》，《1998中国重要考古发现》，第111-115页，文物出版社，2000年。

90 国家文物局编：《中国文物地图集·北京分册（下）》，第215页，科学出版社，2008年。

91 李昂主编：《沉香越千年——海淀历史文物展》，45-47页，海淀博物馆，2012年。

92 北京辽金城垣博物馆：《北京元代史迹图志》，283页，北京燕山出版社，2009年。

93 赵光林：《近年北京地区发现的几处古代琉璃窑址》，《考古》，1986年第7期，第628-631页。

六、郊居选胜——明清时期海淀的文化遗存 [94]

1. 明代的海淀。明军攻占元大都城，旋即将城市向南收缩了 5 里，构成了以后的明清北京城的内城，今海淀区原纳入元大都城的部分也基本被废弃了，海淀区辖地成为了名副其实的郊区。永乐十九年（1421 年）明成祖迁都北京，城市格局一仍其旧，海淀地区辖地分属宛平、昌平两县（州）。明代海淀区辖地成为重要的墓葬区，不仅有位于董四墓山脚下的妃嫔墓群，还有紧傍卧佛寺的四王子村一带的王子公主墓区，特别是在青龙桥镇金山口，安葬了葬于明十三陵以外的三个帝王之一的景泰帝，这座由原郕王墓扩修而成的皇陵，埋葬着在宫廷斗争中落败而死的景泰帝，不论当时英宗使用了多少伎俩，景泰帝最终下葬于此，还是由于这里已经有了相应的机构，被认为是风水合宜，景色佳好之地。仔细查看，这里的风水、景色与十三陵有异曲同工之妙。正因为如此，王公贵胄均趋之若鹜，选择这里作为茔地，明朝曾有"一溜边山府，七十二座坟"的佳话。特别值得一提的是，在明代的政治配置中占有举足轻重地位的太监群体，看中了这里风水和景色的佳绝，以及寺庙林立、佛境幽深的特点，也大批埋葬于这里 [95]。

海淀区明代墓葬发掘较多，高等级墓葬主要有妃嫔墓、皇子墓、公主墓、外戚墓及太监墓，另有较多的平民墓葬。其中的高等级墓的一般特征是：三合土技术广泛使用，还有少量石室（石椁）墓，并有精美的石刻装饰 [96]；墓葬封护严密；墓志均是带字面扣合，外加铁箍两道；墓中随葬前朝旧钱或形态丰富的厌胜钱等。

就墓葬形制而言，有竖穴土坑墓、砖室墓、罐装骨灰的火葬、三合土浇筑墓、八角（或六角）砖穴墓和石室墓等多种形制，其中以竖穴土坑墓为主。竖穴土坑墓中一般都有木质葬具，有棺无椁。根据埋葬人数，又有单棺葬、双棺葬、和多棺葬，前两种较多，多棺葬少见 [97]。砖室墓虽然大小不一，形制也有一定的差异，但大多是用砖砌出墓框，用石条或石板盖顶，墓内有石棺床，上置葬具。这类墓大多等级较高，出土物丰富，首都博物馆和海淀区博物馆所藏的大批明代精美文物都是从这类墓葬中出土的。

明陵不似宋陵，陵区里不设皇室宗亲的陪陵墓，明朝皇帝之子多被封为藩王，藩王分据各地，各自在当地安葬。皇后又与皇帝同陵合葬，所以在陵区或在北京，独立存在的只有妃嫔墓葬，明代妃嫔葬制分从葬和不从葬两种。据顾炎武《昌平山水记》载："自英宗既止宫人从葬，于是妃墓始名，或在陵山之内，或在他山。[98]"妃嫔葬所在北京有两处，一处在十三陵内的东西二井，另一处在海淀区金山，即今海淀区青龙桥西北，明朝时称为金山。葬在金山的还有诸王、公主。《长安客话》载："凡诸王、公主夭殇者，并葬金山口，其地与景皇陵相属，又诸妃亦多葬此。[99]"是北京地区十三陵以外另一处嫔妃墓的主要分布区，且数量多于十三陵区的妃嫔墓 [100]，据文献记载到清顺治十一年有 53 处。后以墓名村，有东四墓、西四墓等村。

海淀区发掘过的妃嫔墓较为重要的有董四墓村天启、万历帝嫔妃墓。1951 年 8 月至 11 月，在金山董四墓村清理了两座明代妃嫔墓，共葬十个妃嫔。一号墓埋葬天启帝的三个妃子，墓有宝顶、墓门、前室、主室组成。宝顶呈截尖圆锥形，平顶，高约 4 米。用土掺石灰夯成，位于主室之后，并不直接压于地下墓室建筑之上。地下墓室是一座平面呈"工"字形的宫殿式建筑，分为前室和主室两部分，"工"字形殿是明代的制度，在墓室中也反映出来。各室用石门相连，且都有实际用作墓顶的仿木结构建筑。主室为四阿式顶，正脊长 13.8 米，高 7.2 米，并使用实际的琉璃构件。主室靠后墓壁用石条筑成石棺床，放置 3 口棺椁。在每个椁底靠后墙处棺尾附近，各置 1 合墓志，铭文合在中间，外面绕有两条铁箍，再外覆木匣。从墓志位置，可知左侧是天启帝的张裕妃、中间是段纯妃、右侧是李成妃。墓室被盗，出土遗物不多，有"大明万历年制"款青花、青白瓷梅瓶 3 件，有凤冠上的装饰品及金簪等。玉器可分为两类，一类是镶嵌在凤冠上的饰物，另外一类是玉扣，浮雕植物花纹。出土珍珠大小不等，可能是凤冠上的装饰品，也有的是镶嵌在金饰上面的，共千余粒。另外还有钱币、梳和篦等 [101]。

二号墓埋葬万历帝的七个内嫔，位于一号墓东北约 300 米处。形制由宝顶、墓门、前室、后室组成。平面呈"工"字形。

---

94 此句出自（明）王嘉谟：《丹棱沜记》，内录元上都路制使荣里真文，云："负山丛丛，盖神皋之佳丽，郊居之选胜也。"载（清）孙承泽：《春明梦余录》卷六十五，第 1265-1266 页，北京古籍出版社，1992 年。

95 刘耀辉：《明代太监的丧葬》，《北京文博》2001 年第 3 期，第 25—39 页。

96 海淀区文管所曾清理 40 余座明太监或贵族墓，有不少是由石板制作的石椁，部分还有精美的石刻。这批石刻原藏于海淀区文管所，现下落不明。

97 宋大川主编：《北京考古发现与研究（1949-2009）》下，390 页，科学出版社，2009 年。

98 顾炎武：《昌平山水记》，卷上，18 页，北京古籍出版社，1982 年版。

99 （明）蒋一葵：《长安客话》，北京古籍出版社，1980 年版。

100 李永强著：《北京考古史（明代卷）》，34 页，上海古籍出版社，2012 年。

101 考古研究所通讯组：《北京西郊董四墓村明墓发掘记——第一号墓》，《文物参考资料》1952 年 2 期，78-87 页。

墓葬的结构与一号墓相似，墓室为使用石块和砖砌成的平房式建筑，屋脊用磨成半圆形的大砖接连而成。屋面上铺方砖一层，砖面以上为三合土台阶，南、北各三层，每层厚约 0.5 米。前室多陈列祭品，石门两侧各有石座一座，很像故宫三大殿的宝座，其靠背和两翼都刻有精细的花纹。石座前放置有香炉、烛台、插瓶及长明灯。东西两面各置有仪仗用的木架两副，西边有两对墓志，东边有三对墓志。后室有放置棺椁的棺床，棺床正中偏东有两对完整的墓志，7 具棺已七零八落，多半倒在棺床下面。其中 3 具没有被盗，随葬品主要有以下几类：第一类为各种实用器物，如金银质的盆、粉盒、胭脂盒、铜镜等，另外还有瓷器。第三棺出土"大明嘉靖年制"暗花白瓷梅瓶和"大明万历年制"青花缠枝番莲纹梅瓶，以及银元宝；第二棺出土 2 个各重五十两，上有款识，分别为万历十五年和十六年铸，都是福建省所缴纳的赋银；第二类是祭祀用法器，如第一棺出土的铜制钟形法器 2 件，上面刻有梵文、藏文的符号咒语；某些瓷器也可属于此类；第三类为钗冠等头面及饰品，如手镯、耳环、凤冠等，包括一些服装，第二棺出土 1 顶由 23 件钗簪等物组成的凤冠，镶以珠宝；第四类是自宋以来形成的所谓"刻木为车马、仆从、侍女，各执奉养之物，象平生而小。[102]"的明器。在二号墓前后两室共发现木俑百余件，以前室仪仗附近为最多，从装束看，有文臣、武将、宦官、皂隶、平民等类别，这种明器应该在高等级的明墓中是一类重要的随葬品，万历帝的定陵中也出土了锡质的这类明器（镴器），但制作十分粗糙，大体是意在示意，并不体现皇家气派。这两座墓葬中的出土器物大体概括了海淀区发现的高等级明墓出土的器物种类，海淀区博物馆展出的明代器物大体也都可以归类为这几种。根据出土圹志，二号墓内葬有万历七位内嫔，分别为张顺嫔、耿悼嫔、邵敬嫔、魏慎嫔、李荣嫔、李德嫔、梁和嫔[103]。

1963 年，在镶红旗营（现名厢红旗）发现明成化帝的妃子墓 7 座。南北向，在金山阴坡并列成一横排，宝顶已无存，从残存灰土渣判断系由三合土夯筑而成。墓室结构形制均为"工"字形的砖石结构的平房式建筑，由墓门、前室、后室等部分组成。前后室顶部两坡平铺方砖，脊饰已无存，后壁中央设宝座，其前置五供和万年灯等，后室中央设有大理石棺床，上置棺椁，棺床中央有方形金井。墓葬均被盗，其中有三座墓出土有墓志，

出土少量零散的金饰件、宝石、珍珠等，据出土圹志可知是成化帝庄静顺妃王氏、庄懿德妃张氏、和惠静妃岳氏[104]。另外还有 1996 年发掘的金山南麓武宗沈贤妃墓[105]和 1998 年发掘的香山街道正蓝旗西山国务院机关事务管理局西山管理处院内天顺六年（1462 年）荣淑贤妃墓[106]等，这两座墓可能因为时代较早，都是前后双室长方形券顶砖室墓，未使用"工"字型仿庑殿式的墓室。

在海淀区还发现数量较多的明代皇子、公主墓及几座外戚墓，多数被毁或被盗，墓葬形制多不清楚、出土物随葬品数量较少，但留下数量较多的出土墓志。经过考古发掘的皇子墓主要有成化八年（1473 年）明宪宗次子悼恭太子朱祐极墓[107]，其位于海淀区香山街道正蓝旗西山国务院机关事务管理局西山管理处院内。1998 年发现，为砖室墓，早年被盗，破坏严重。墓室南北长 11 米、东西宽 4 米，有墓道和前后室、券顶。出土绿釉陶鼎 2 件、绿釉陶壶 3 件、白釉陶缸 1 件，出土墓志一合，首题：悼恭太子圹志。另一座是位于北京海淀区香山路军事科学院内的成化二年（1547 年）宪宗长子朱见深墓，2001 年北京市文物研究所进行抢救性发掘。该墓为砖石结构，由墓道、墓门、前室、过道、后室组成。早年被盗，出土墓志一合，青花梅瓶 1 件，金饰 3 件及墓志。此墓墓道为长方形竖穴斜坡式，墓道尽头为城砖砌筑的金刚墙，金刚墙北部正中为两扇石门；前室长方形，四阿式屋顶，方砖铺地；北部中央设石质雕花宝座，前置五供和万年灯，灯顶端存一釉陶灯座；过道内有封门砖和石门；后室结构与前室相同而稍矮，正中置石棺床，中部有一长方形"金井"[108]。墓主人朱见深为成化宠妃万贵妃所生，所以墓葬的结构颇有一些独特之处。

经过发掘清理的公主墓主要有香山街道正蓝旗村东弘治十一年（1498 年）孝宗之女太康公主墓[109]，墓早年被毁，形制不详，仅存墓志一方。四季青镇鲍家窑村遂平长公主墓[110]。1999 年发现，为一座长方形券顶砖室墓，墓道内出土青铜器 2 件，圹志一合。

102　司马光：《书仪》卷七《丧仪三》"明器下帐苞筲祠版"条，文渊阁《四库全书》本，第 142 册，503 页，台北：商务印书馆影印本，1983 年。

103　中国科学院考古研究所京郊发掘团通讯组：《北京董四墓村明墓发掘续记——第二号墓》，《文物参考资料》1952 年第 2 期，第 88-100 页。

104　北京市文物研究所编：《北京考古四十年》，203 页，北京燕山出版社，1990 年。

105　李永强著：《北京考古史（明代卷）》，37 页，上海古籍出版社，2012 年。

106　李永强著：《北京考古史（明代卷）》，38 页，上海古籍出版社，2012 年。

107　国家文物局主编，北京市文物局编：《中国文物地图集·北京分册》，216 页，科学出版社，2008 年。

108　王燕玲：《海淀香山军科院明太子墓发掘简报》，《北京文物与考古》第五辑，2002 年。

109　国家文物局主编，北京市文物局编：《中国文物地图集·北京分册（下）》，215 页，科学出版社，2008 年。

110　国家文物局主编，北京市文物局编：《中国文物地图集·北京分册（下）》，216 页，科学出版社，2008 年。

此外还发掘了几座外戚墓，如宪宗之母孝肃皇太后之父周能墓[111]，位于苏家坨镇后柳林村北。当地人称之为周家坟。墓为长方形砖室墓，坐北朝南，建有围墙，墓园内原有石牌坊、石碑、石翁仲、石马和墓冢，"文革"中被毁，现存石马两件及明成化二十三年（1487 年）庆云侯周公神道碑及嘉靖朝太后祭告碑两通。万历帝生母之父武清侯赠太傅安国公李伟墓。位于八里庄街道慈寿寺塔西北 1 公里处。竖穴土坑墓，南北向，夫妻合葬，各一棺一椁；李伟棺椁被盗，仅出土银壶、小银元宝；其妻王氏墓出土有大银元宝、六角錾花错金执壶、银盆、银洗、金锭、金真武像、金簪、金镯等及玉带板，并出土墓志两合[112]。在各地发现的明墓中，北京地区发现的外戚墓无疑是十分重要的。除了海淀区清理的几座以外，还有东郊人民公园发现的世宗岳父安平候方锐墓、右安门外彭庄成化年间万贵妃之父万贵夫妇墓[113]，南苑苇子坑正德十年（1515 年）武宗毅皇后之父夏儒夫妇墓[114]，这几座墓的主人地位近似，墓葬规模略同。都采用三合土筑墓圹，然后用磨砖砌墓壁，内置木棺和椁，墓顶用青石条封盖，再以三合土夯筑封顶。由于墓室结构严密，墓内遗物保存完好。万贵墓出土了大量的金银、珠宝、玉器，金银器物的总重量达 500 余两。夏儒墓出土大批丝织品，图案复杂，样式齐全。这些器物多是宫廷制品，标有宫号、年号，十分珍贵。

明代是一个太监专权的王朝，北京作为都城，集中了大量的太监，他们死后大都葬在京城附近，自 1950 年以来，北京地区发现并清理了大量明代的太监墓，据不完全统计，总数不下百余座[115]。如广安门以北，西便门以南，可能是明太监的丛葬区。墓葬建筑规模大小不一，随葬品也多寡不等，但一般都有石或砖制的长方形墓室，内置木棺，也有许多采用塔墓的形式，随葬品有陶瓷器具和小件玉佩饰，而且都有墓志出土。海淀区发现数量也较多，时代主要集中在明代中晚期。一般太监的墓葬往往集中分布，采用小区域丛葬的方式。其中较为豪华并较重要的墓有位于香山饭店的嘉靖三十三年（1554 年）太监刘忠墓[116]。墓为砖石结构，墓室依山开凿，为前后双室墓，后室为长方形券顶砖室，并建有棺穴，棺穴在天然岩石上凿出，并以石板盖顶。墓门是用整块汉白玉制成的双扇石门，门额上刻有"栖霞岩"，前室有六块石雕，内容为各种鸟兽、花草树木，并有石碑、石香炉、石墩等；后室石门上刻有"清虚紫府刘仙翁之洞"，内出有小石阁、石供桌、石椅、石墩等精美的石雕 11 件。墓主人为"御马监太监署乙字库事"，曾担任三朝皇帝近侍太监的刘忠。由此墓可见明代太监权势之一斑。该墓非常独特，地势的选择、棺穴的安排、墓室彩绘、题刻及石制品的陈设都具有浓厚的道教色彩。

海淀区地质力学所内的万历四十七年（1619 年）尚衣监掌印太监杨太监墓，1999 年清理，在土坑中放置带有精美浅浮雕花纹的石椁木棺作为主要葬具，保存较好，椁为长方形、带盖，用石板以榫卯相接而成，椁底为须弥座式，椁壁饰有精美的浅浮雕结合线刻的图案，各壁四周为卷草纹，椁中部雕云鹤图、海水江崖、岁寒三友和阴阳八卦等图案，椁内有红漆描金的木棺，亦为云鹤图。出土物不多，有玉带、釉陶罐和买地券[117]。

北京西山太监王贵墓。此墓未经科学发掘，墓葬形制不明，但出土了"金银陶土玉石之器，凡百数十件。"是北京地区出土器物较多的太监墓[118]。2005 年，北京市文物研究所发掘了位于海淀区马神庙北京工商大学操场的 3 座明代墓葬，均为明代万历时期的太监墓[119]。1 号墓为长方形券顶砖室墓，由挡土墙、甬道、墓室组成。墓顶上方用青砖平铺后再封三合土，墓室长方形、券顶，石条铺地，两壁中部各有一长方形壁龛，南壁正中安两扇用整块石条做成的石门，雕成门楼形；墓室中部偏北砌棺床，长方形须弥座式，石条垒砌；随葬品有铜罍 1 件，酱黄色和茶叶末釉瓷瓶各 1 件，紫砂茶具 1 套（2 壶 4 杯），青玉带板 15 块。墓主为明代御用太监赵芬，葬于万历壬午年（1582 年）。2 号墓为长方形双室砖石混筑墓，由墓道、封门墙、甬道、前室、后室等部分组成。墓道为两侧砌砖的斜坡墓道，后接长方形甬道，东西两壁用青砖砌筑，顶部平铺 4 块石条；前室长方形，北侧有仿木构砖砌门楼，东西两壁各砌一长方形壁龛，壁龛上方有磨制青砖砌筑的门楼，室内中部靠壁站立两个石质童

111　国家文物局主编，北京市文物局编：《中国文物地图集·北京分册（下）》，科学出版社，2008 年，215 页。

112　国家文物局主编，北京市文物局编：《中国文物地图集·北京分册（下）》，科学出版社，2008 年，217 页。

113　北京市文物研究所：《北京考古四十年》，203-204 页，北京燕山出版社，1990 年。

114　北京市文物工作队：《北京南苑苇子坑明代墓葬清理简报》，《文物》1964 年 11 期，45-47 页。

115　宋大川主编：《北京考古发现与研究（1949-2009）》下 420 页，科学出版社，2009 年。

116　北京市文物工作队：《北京香山明太监刘忠墓》，《文物》1986 年 9 期，42-47 页。

117　程利：《地质力学所出土明太监墓》，《北京文博》2000 年期，封二，彩插一。

118　黄艺锡：《大招山发现古物记》，《地学杂志》第六卷，第 11 期，1915 年。

119　北京市文物研究所：《北京工商大学明代太监墓》，知识产权出版社，2005 年。

子，下连方形底座，通高 1.08 米。前室南部地面上置方形青砖 1 块，其上有朱砂字迹，应为买地券；前后室之间有石条铺地并盖顶的甬道，长方形后室，券顶；墓室中部偏北砌棺床，呈长方形须弥座式，四周用石条压栏，中间铺方砖，棺床中部有一亚腰形金井；随葬品有白玉带板 14 块，石俑 1 对，玉坠、金饰等；还出"万历通宝"铜钱；墓主姓董，为明代御用监太监。3 号墓形制与 2 号墓基本相同。随葬品有玉带板 13 块，石牌位 1 件，朱砂书买地券 1 件，另外还出土铜钱、玉石、陶罐、铜提梁等。根据买地券可知，墓主为明代御用监总理太监滑永形，葬于明万历乙未（1595 年）。

1991 年海淀区文管所在北下关街道北下关上园饭店西侧清理长方形券顶石室墓一座，墓室南北长 3.6 米、东西宽 2.86 米、高 2.95 米，券顶。南壁石门两扇，上有一对浮雕铺首，东、西、北壁设窗形小龛，皆有浮雕。石棺床的棺木乱置于石棺床上。随葬品有"大明嘉靖年制"款青花瓷罐和一块万历年款铜牌、大小玉带板和金银器，其中一块钟形镀金腰牌，正面书"御马监太监"，背面书"忠字叁拾捌号"；还出有压胜金币 2 枚，一枚正面书"天启通宝"，背面书"金五钱"，一枚为"吉祥图"，正背文均为旋读："南无消灾延寿药师佛"及猫眼石等宝石[120]。

1985 年海淀区文管所在八里庄百花印刷厂院内清理了明泰昌元年（1620 年）司礼监秉笔太监杜茂墓，此墓为长方形砖圹石顶墓，出土了不少精美的器物，包括一对灵芝双耳金杯，银錾花鸟人物纹盏托，银壶，铜爵杯等[121]。同年海淀区文管所还在国家气象局院内清理明太监墓一座，出土了一件明成化青花携琴访友纹大罐，十分精美。这件瓷器出土于墓室前部的墓道中，应该是用于祭祀的器具[122]。

明太监墓的等级也是十分明显的，北京海淀区历年清理的太监墓近 40 座，有些比刘忠墓的规模大，石刻更精美，但多数是地位较低的太监墓，使用单室的砖室石顶墓，出土物也数量不多，品质一般；较高等级的太监墓多为券顶砖室墓或石室墓，出土物比较高档，但基本不出成套的随葬品，以少数几件精美的瓷器，一些佛教法器、厌胜用品和小件的金银珠宝饰品为多，其中不乏十分精美的皇家御用器物，这与太监特殊的地位有关。另外，北京广安门老君地在明代时是太监从葬地之一，曾出土

有瓷制男性生殖器，可能是当时太监死后为了全尸入殓而使用的附葬品[123]。

北方以北京为中心，包括了今河北、河南、山东、山西等省市的地区的明墓发生了较大的变化。与元代流行正方形和多角形墓相比，明代的品官和富豪墓葬多使用长方形前后双室、单室或并列多室的砖室墓和石室墓，墓内有时饰以壁画，但仿木构的砖雕较少发现，常使用多重棺椁。总体上看，南北方的墓形和制作方法较多交错，趋于一致。

同样，北方地区的平民墓，一方面仍然保存了一些元墓的风格，如使用方形、圆形和多角形的砖室墓，有些还有仿木构雕砖或壁画装饰；同时，也开始在平民墓中使用长方形的砖室墓，有些不带装饰，但随葬较高级物品并有墓志的竖穴土坑石棺墓。如北京发现的许多八角形和六角形小墓，尽管墓的尺寸很小，随葬品很少，但在形制上仍保留了元代的风格[124]。

2. 清代的海淀。清代顺天府所领州县多有变化，康熙二十六年（1687 年），顺天府辖区内设东、西、南、北四路厅，大兴、宛平等县属西路厅，昌平州等地属北路厅。今海淀区南半部和温泉、冷泉、北安河一带隶属于宛平县；北半部大部隶属于昌平州。康熙三十一年（1692 年）以后，随着玉泉山静明园和此后圆明园的兴建，宛、昌分界才发生较大变动。圆明园的兴建又带动了周边地区的一系列园林的建设，海淀区实际扮演了一个清代陪都或夏都的角色。海淀区清代考古最重要的工作当属圆明园含经堂遗址的发掘。

含经堂遗址位于圆明园东部长春园的中央大岛上，四周为山水所绕，风景清丽优雅。遗址南北总长约 300 米、东西总宽约 200 米，总占地面积 6 万余平方米，建筑遗迹面积近 3 万平方米。含经堂遗址北邻西洋楼大水法遗址，东接玉玲珑馆遗址，南连长春桥和澹怀堂遗址，西与海岳开襟和思永斋遗址隔湖相望，该建筑建于乾隆十年至三十五年（1745-1770 年），是长春园中心区规模最大的一组寝宫型建筑群，内有各类建筑群组 30 余处，是圆明园内历史文化价值极高的宫殿群之一，代表了清代盛期皇家园林建筑设计和营建的最高水准，也是乾隆皇帝为自己预备的"归政娱老"、"退享林泉之乐"的颐养之地。含经堂建筑群在 1860 年的第二次鸦片战争和 1900 年的八国联军入侵中被焚毁，成为一片废墟。2001 年 4 月至 2002 年 12 月，北京市文

120 国家文物局主编，北京市文物局编：《中国文物地图集·北京分册（下）》，215 页，科学出版社，2008 年。另见李昂主编：《沉香越千年——海淀历史文物展》，71-73 页，海淀博物馆，2012 年。

121 北京市海淀区博物馆编：《海淀博物馆》，106-110 页，文物出版社，2005 年。

122 北京市海淀区博物馆编：《海淀博物馆》，36-39 页，文物出版社，2005 年。

123 杨宗安：《北京广安门老君地基建工地发现古物》，《文物参考资料》1955 年 4 期，103-104 页。

124 北京市文物研究所：《北京考古四十年》，206-207 页，北京燕山出版社，1990 年。

物研究所对长春园宫门区和含经堂遗址进行了有计划的科学发掘，总发掘面积为 32000 平方米[125]。

含经堂宫苑组群分为南、北两区：南区建筑沿革以中轴线为轴心，发掘了广场（牌楼、宫墙、甬道、铺地砖等）、宫门殿基、院落建筑（影壁、甬道、正殿、东西配殿、焚香楼、回廊、宫墙）等建筑遗迹；北区中路建筑群有淳化轩、蕴真斋、北院门等遗迹，东路则有渊映斋、扮戏房、戏台、看戏殿等遗迹，西路有涵光室、三友轩、待月楼、静莲斋和理心楼等遗迹。含经堂遗址还出土了清代铜、铁、玉、陶、瓷、螺钿、玻璃、石刻及各类建筑构件近千件，大多数为残件，具有一定的历史价值。

通过全面发掘，清楚了含经堂宫苑建筑景群的建筑格局、规模、结构特点及局部改建和添建的情况，确定主体建筑的年代是在乾隆十年至三十五年间，正值清朝兴盛时期，北区建筑的部分建筑为嘉庆十九年（1814 年）之后改建和添建。

此外，围绕着三山五园，驻扎着强悍的八旗兵，因此清代与明代多太监墓的情况略有不同，常常有重要的满族贵族墓葬发现。比较重要的如下。

索家坟清墓，1962 年，北京市文物工作队在西郊小西天的索家坟，配合基建发掘了 4 座墓葬[126]。皆为砖室墓，分为火葬和土葬两种；2 号墓为土葬墓，其余 3 座为火葬墓。1、2 号墓规格较高。1 号墓（黑舍里氏墓）室平面呈正方形，顶为三重券顶，正南北向。边长 1.82 米、高 2.95 米。东、西、北三壁分设壁龛，均做成悬山顶式仿木结构砖雕门楼，壁龛内分放瓷器、玉器等随葬品；南壁正中设甬道，券顶，南端有一青石质墓门；墓室北部棺床，约占全室 1/2，高出墓底地面 24 厘米。床面铺砖、中间放置长宽约 44 厘米、高 48 厘米木质骨灰盒 1 个。棺床正中设有汉白玉石供桌 1 个，上放置铜方炉、烛台等祭器。甬道中央有汉白玉碑一通，上刻"清故淑女黑舍里氏圹志铭"。墓葬出土大批具有皇家气派的精美随葬品，有瓷器、玉器、铜器等。瓷器以成化斗彩葡萄杯 2 件，成化五彩洗 1 件，成化、万历朝青花小杯 3 件三类最珍贵，另外还有白瓷暗花壶、黄釉盂各 1 件。玉器共 28 件，有玉瓶、杯、洗、砚和多种佩饰，多为明代制品，具有较高工艺水平。铜器 6 件，铜壶、方壶、炉、镜各 1 件，烛台 2 件，其中铜壶为宋仿战国铜壶。根据出土圹志可知，墓主黑舍里氏为清初辅政大臣一等公索尼的孙女，其父索额图，

官至保和殿大学士太子太傅，黑舍里氏 7 岁故去。2 号墓，长方形砖室石顶墓，长 5.4 米、宽 2.5 米、高 1.4 米，四壁青砖垒砌，地铺青砖，顶盖石板；东西两壁各有壁龛 1 个，内放青花小瓶和小罐各一。墓未设棺床，墓室中有长方形金丝楠木棺椁一具，尸体有单、夹、棉衣 7 层，外裹大衾，头部插满金饰件，左右手腕戴金镯。出土遗物大都为金器，有手镯、凤饰、钗、各种簪、耳挖、纽扣等，共 39 件。这些金饰品用累丝、盘丝、雕花、镂空及宝石镶嵌等工艺制作，技艺精湛。墓中出"康熙通宝"两枚。3、4 号墓比较简单，均为长方形砖室火葬墓，均出"康熙通宝"[127]。

清河永泰庄墓地。墓地位于海淀区清河镇永泰庄村。1993 年北京市文物研究所在该地清理出 1 处墓园基址及清代墓葬 8 座[128]。M10 为圆形单室砖墓，穹隆顶，有石门，由墓道、甬道和墓室组成；墓室直径 3.8 米、高 3.86 米，底铺青砖；墓壁上开 3 处壁龛，做成砖雕仿木构建筑门楼式样；墓室中发现一残墓志盖，未见尸骨、葬具和其他遗物。M11 为长方形券顶单室砖墓，由墓道和墓室组成，券门；墓室平面长 1.9 米、宽 1.6 米，底铺青砖；三合土夯筑宝顶，已坍塌。东西两壁各有一壁龛，砖雕仿木建筑结构门楼式。墓室内出土一残陶器。M12 为六角形单室砖室墓，推测为火葬墓，出土有铜镜 1 件、铁犁 2 件、石砚 1 方、瓷罐 1 件、瓷壶 1 件、鸡蛋壳 2 枚和 200 余枚"顺治通宝"钱。其他墓葬中，M3、M8 为火葬墓，葬具为瓷罐。M2、M4 为竖穴土坑墓，仰身直肢葬，葬具为木棺。M1 为 3 人合葬墓，其中一人为火葬。这些墓中出土常用的饰品和"乾隆通宝"钱。根据夯土墙、墓葬和房屋的布局看，该墓群应属于一个家族墓地，祖茔为 M10，另外几座有的可能属于同一家族并按照一定顺序安葬。根据墓志盖记载和文献记载，推测 M10 墓主人应为祖大寿之子祖松润。该墓地的布局应为固山一级官员的规制。

庄敬公主园寝，位于羊坊店街道公主坟，俗称"公主坟"，有两座园寝，坐北朝南，东、西排列。东部园寝为仁宗嘉庆帝之三女庄敬和硕公主夫妻合葬墓，西部为四女庄静固伦公主园寝。各有围墙、仪门、享殿等。1965 年修建地铁时，将地面建筑拆除，墓室发掘后拆毁，出土有蒙古刀、铜壶、玉如意、玉带板、扳指、烟壶、饰件及珐琅、金怀表等[129]。

125　北京市文物研究所圆明园考古队：《北京圆明园含经堂遗址 2001-2002 年度发掘简报》，《考古》2004 年第 2 期，第 41-65 页

126　苏天钧：《北京西郊小西天清代墓葬清理简报》，《文物》，1963 年 1 期。

127　北京市文物研究所编：《北京考古四十年》，209-211 页，北京燕山出版社，1990 年。

128　宋大川主编：《北京考古发现与研究（1949-2009）》483-484 页，科学出版社，2009 年。

129　国家文物局主编、北京市文物局编：《中国文物地图集·北京分册（下）》，219 页，科学出版社，2008 年。

清初洪承畴夫妻合葬墓，1952 年发掘，位于紫竹院街道车道沟村；墓南向，三合土筑墓冢高 2 米，直径 7 米，前有石翁仲、神道碑。墓室为方形券顶砖室墓，早年被盗，仅存杉木棺椁、衣物、残骨及墓志两合。墓旁还葬有其子洪士铭夫妻合葬墓，亦被盗，出土墓志两合。

除了这些规模较大的墓葬，还清理了一些小型清墓。

1977 年，西郊国家气象局院内发现 1 座清代火葬墓，墓室为方形单室砖室墓，用条石盖顶；墓门在北壁正中，东西两壁各置一龛；束腰须弥座式棺床，其中两块方砖上雕出四出钱纹，黑釉骨灰罐分别放在这两块方砖上[130]。清华南路墓群，位于燕园街道清华南路。2001 年发掘，共清理墓葬 36 座，多为长方形竖穴土坑墓。墓开口于现地表下 1 米左右，墓底距地表大约 3～4 米，出土陶器、青花瓷器、铜钱、玉器等[131]。2004 年，北京市文物研究所在海淀区复兴路五棵松篮球馆工地发掘清理了 25 座清代墓葬；全部为竖穴土坑墓，其中单人葬 9 座，2 人合葬 11 座，3 人合葬 4 座，无人骨 9 座；大部分尸骨保存完好，一般仰身直肢葬，少数二次葬；大部分都有葬具木棺，一座无葬具；出土器物有陶瓷、金银、铜和玉器等[132]。2007 年，在北京市物资储备职工中等专业学校南院清理出 8 座清代墓葬，其中 6 座为竖穴土坑墓，2 座为砖室墓；尸骨全部为仰身直肢葬，3 座墓葬中只葬骨灰；5 座墓葬的葬具为木棺，一人一棺，4 座中使用瓮棺；出土器物有瓷瓮、青花将军罐、金银饰品、铜饰品、玉器、珊瑚、铜钱等。这批墓葬规模相对较大，出土器物较精美，尤其是顶戴和朝珠，说明这些墓葬的主人生前有一定的官阶[133]。2007 年，北京市文物研究所在青龙桥新村开发区工程范围内进行了发掘，清理清代墓葬 28 座。全部为竖穴土坑墓，其中单人葬 9 座，双人合葬墓 15 座，三人合葬墓 4 座。大部分为仰身直肢葬，仅 1 例为仰身曲肢葬。葬具全部使用木棺。随葬品有陶器、瓷器、铜器、银器和铜钱等[134]。

上述我们梳理了北京市海淀区从上古时期到明清的古代遗存，从中可以看到以下几点：

第一，海淀区位于浅山和山前平原地区，适于人类生活，从很早以前，就有人类在此地生活，战国、秦汉时期已是农业高度开发的地区，留下了丰富的古代遗存。

第二，汉代以后，由于农业、手工业的发展，北京地区成为中原王朝下辖的边地重镇；成为中原农耕地区和草原地区交界的要塞和交往的重要通道，辽代在此建立陪都，也是为了联络中原汉地。文化面貌具有多样性和丰富性。是十分值得关注的地区。

第三，金元时期，北方的少数民族女真族和蒙古族先后南下，并将实际的都城安置在北京，其所包含的意思是立足于北方他们兴起的地区，将都城置于北京是为了更好地对中原汉地的控制，北京的文化表现出了交融与涵化的特质。海淀区作为都城的组成部分或郊区，出土了一些具有皇家气派的文物，十分有特色。

第四，明清两代北京一直持续作为都城使用，重要的变化是海淀区作为都城宫苑用水的水源地，山水秀美，被认为是风水宝地，因此，不仅皇家将这里作为茔地，还有大批权贵和明代具有重要地位的太监，将此处选为葬地，因此出土了数量众多的精美的皇家用器，在全国乃至北京周边地区都是独一无二的。清代在海淀区建造了许多苑宥，特别是规模宏大的圆明园，使海淀区实际扮演了夏都或离宫的角色，三山五园周边驻扎了大批的八旗军队，因此海淀区发现了许多满族贵族的墓葬，出土了高等级的文物。随着对清代考古的日益重视，还会有更多的文物出土。

130　北京市文物研究所编：《北京考古四十年》，213 页，北京燕山出版社，1990 年。

131　国家文物局主编，北京市文物局编：《中国文物地图集·北京分册（下）》，218 页，科学出版社，2008 年。

132　北京市文物研究所：《五棵松篮球馆工程考古发掘报告》，载北京市文物局、北京市文物研究所编：《北京奥运场馆考古发掘报告》，1-73 页，科学出版社，2007 年。

133　宋大川主编：《北京考古发现与研究（1949-2009）》，488 页，科学出版社，2009 年。

134　北京市文物研究所：《北京海淀区青龙桥新村工程发掘简报》，《北京文博》2010 年 2 期。

Red Leaves and Chrysanthemum Flowers were Cultivated at the Same Fertile Plains[1]:

Uniqueness of Cultural Diversity Discovered in Haidian District

Qin Dashu

I. Geographic environment and historical development

Haidian is a suburban district located in the north and northwest part of the municipality of Beijing, situated along the northern edge of the North China Plain partly surrounded by the West Mountain ranges-extensions of the Taihang Mountains. The vast plain is generally high in the west and low in the east, with more than 60 hills sitting in the west, but the marginal zone in the east within Haidian boundaries geographically belongs to the North China Plain to the north but slightly to the east. This zone can be divided into two parts: to the south side of the Baiwang Mountain is called Piedmont Plain Area shaped as the Fluvial Fan formed in the flows in the Yongding River, and to the north Mountain Back Plain Area shaped as Alluvial fan formed in the flows in the Nansha River. The plain is about 35 to 50 meters above the sea level.

There are numerous rivers, lakes and fountains flow through the Haidian area according to historical record. Not only are the important surface waters as natural resources responsible for the agricultural irrigations during early period in history, but also for the establishment of water supply systems in the city of Beijing throughout Jin, Yuan, Ming and Qing dynasties up to the very day. The main rivers in Haidian area are the Nanchang River, the Qing River, the Wanquan River, Xiaoyue River, Nansha River, and Beisha River, etc[2].

It can be said that lots of waters, lakes and grand mountains formed in ancient times in Haidian had made this area not only a livable place to have population growth, but also a wealthy cornucopia of ancient relics to discover in later times. Haidian also has magnificent sceneries, temples, gardens here and there, and many water projects completed in history that allow the geomantic treasure ground to become the highly developed land for agricultural products. Haidian positioned as subsidiary periphery to pivotal and metropolitan cities is the popular aggregation of human life and culture, the most crucial place where lots of cultural heritages and relics were found plentiful.

The directly governed area by Haidian local government had never been administratively independent in history but belonged to different divisions separately. The south part of Haidian had mainly become the subsidiary area to suburban counties of the

city of Beijing after Qin and Han dynasties, however, some regions were once comprised to the surrounding areas of the city of Zhongdu Capital of Jürchen Jin or Khanbaliq of Yuan dynasty. Majority of them were broke up and joined in the territory of Beijing directly under the central government during the Qing and Ming dynasties. The north part historically had always been divided into smaller administrative divisions as they were classified as the local level satellite districts around Beijing as the national core[3].

No later than the last years of the Shang dynasty, vassal states like Yan and Ji of the Shang had already existed in the lands of what is now Beijing area. The two vassal states turned out after the Shang dynasty was deposed by the King Wu of Zhou dynasty who conferred titles and Yan and Ji to the nobles within his domain. Some prefectures like Shanggu, Yuyang, Youbeiping, Liaoxi, Liaodong were set up to defend incursions from the Hu nomad faced by Yan[4]. The jurisdiction of some parts in the northwest of present Haidian presumably belonged to the Shanggu prefecture. The five prefectures mentioned above were kept there in the northern part of former Yan after the Qin unification and one more prefecture Guangyang was established thereafter. Some areas within the Haidian territory were possibly included in the spheres of Ji county of Guangyang (or Shanggu) and Jundu county of Shanggu prefecture. Haidian was probably under Ji county of the vassal state Guangyang and Jundu county of Shanggu prefecture throughout the years of Western Han dynasty. But by the end of Eastern Han dynasty, Haidian was under Ji, Jundu, and Changping the three counties of Guangyang prefecture. The southern part of Haidian for the most of the time was under Ji of Yan prefecture during the period of Three Kingdoms, Wei, Jin and Northern and Southern dynasties. From the period of Three Kingdoms to early Northern Wei dynasty the northern part of Haidian was separately under Jundu County and Changping county of Yan prefecture, but until the end of Northern Wei was exclusively under the Jundu county. From Eastern Wei to Northern Qi period, the northern Haidian possibly was partly under Jundu, partly under Changping, partly under Wannian (or Wanyan), partly Guangwu, and partly under Woye the four residing counties altogether[5].

In 607, the third year of Daye period of Sui dynasty, You prefecture as a level of administration was not used and renamed as Zhuo commandery by which most area of the present Beijing was under its control. Youzhou was revived after the establishment of Tang dynasty, the domain of Haidian district of nowadays was chronologically under the control of Ji, Guangping, Guangning, and Changping counties of the You commandery (or Fanyang prefecture), and of the administratively entrusted Guzhu county of the Dai commandery in the first year of Tianbao period of Tang dynasty that is to say the year of 742 thereafter, and until the Later Tang of the Five Dynasties period, Youzhou was presumably under the control of Ji, Youdu, Yuhe and Yanping the four counties. It is worth mentioning that Jimi commandery and Guzhu county of Dai commandery were administratively

---

1 This verse, "Red leaves and chrysanthemum are cultivated from the same plains", is from a poem, *The Fragrant Hill* composed by a poet named Zhou Ang (Jurchen Jin dynasty), in this poem he writes: "I got confused with the difference between the mountains, forests and the city in the morning, Red leaves and chrysanthemum are cultivated from the same plains. Flowing waters running through this area as promised to come that people are unware of what have happened. Pine trees who have lived for many years experienced what have happened before their eyes. I waste no time to have composed thousands of poems that I promised to compose but not yet finished, but I got a little bit peacefully relaxed after having a meal. Wished to ask myself whether I would feel relieved or not, but I never thought at this time my heart has already been disburdened. Nobody would know that what I have written is accomplished whether I live or die." I explain here about the diversity and uniqueness of cultural relics discovered in Haidian district by quoting this poem. Quoted from the *Collected Writings from ZhongZhou*, Vol. 4, Page 167, written by Yuan Haowen (Jurchen Jin dynasty), Published by Zhonghua Book Company, Beijing, 1959 edition.

2 *Haidian District Chronicles*, Composed by the Committee of Chronicles Compilation in Haidian District in Beijing, Part two, Chapter one, Beijing: Beijing press, 2004.

3 *Haidian District Chronicles*, Composed by the Committee of Chronicles Compilation in Haidian District in Beijing, Part one, Chapter one, Beijing: Beijing press, 2004.

4 Sima Qian of Han dynasty: *Records of the Grand Historian*, Vol. 110, *Hun Biography*, Page 2886, published by Zhonghua Book Company, 1959 edition.

5 *History of Wei Dynasty*, written by Wei Shou (from North Qi period), Vol. 106, *Topography II Part One Fifth Section*, pp. 2493-2494, Zhonghua Book Company, 1974 edition.

entrusted in the Changping county after 705. According to historical documents, Guzhu County was under the control of Ying commandery ever before its fall into the Khitans of Manchuria, and was administratively entrusted to Qingshuidian of Changping county which belonged to You commandery[6], in other words, to the Taizhouwu village of what is now Haidian. This is the first time seen in historical documents that the county-level governance was officially recorded. It can be said that Haidian district was taken as a crucial subsidiary area to vassal states or to local strongholds from pre-Qin period to Sui and Tang.

Minority groups like Khitan, Jurchen, and Mongol had ruled over the Beijing area for more than 400 years since the 11th year (936) of the Khitan Tianxian reign. Khitan Liao renamed the city to Nanjing (Southern Capital), but Jurchen Jin made Beijing their Central Capital as the political and cultural center of whole territories, later developed to an imperial metropolitan capital of, Yuan, Ming, and Qing, the three unified empires. At the first year (938) of Khitan Huitong reign, You prefecture was upgraded to Southern Capital or Yan Capital, the provisional capital to the central actual control, and the Nanjing Superior prefecture was established at the same time. In the first year of Kaitai reign November, under Liao Khitan's rule, Youdu prefecture was renamed to Xijin prefecture, Jibei county to Xijin county, and Youdu county to Wanping county[7]. The Haidian area at this time was administratively controlled under different counties like Xijin, Wanping, Yuhe, and Changping counties of Xijin prefecture of the Nanjing Superior prefecture. In spite of its secondary status concerned less by the Liao Khitan government, the Southern Capital had never lost its role played in political and cultural aggregations happened very often in the Central Plains and northern areas of China. As the most intensive region, the Southern Capital was responsible for the integration of differentiations between people from ethnic groups, tribes primarily living in the forests, mountains or steppe areas and people living in the farm land. Ethnic accumulations, clashes and amalgamations of different cultures were recorded in historical literatures, which help us understand history through institutions and laws used in ancient China.

The third year (1151) of Tiande reign in April, Prince Hailing murdered his brother for his seat on the throne, and issued an edict which declared to move the capital to Yanjing, the city was renamed in the first year (1153) of Zhenyuan reign to Central Capital[8]. The Xijin county was thereafter renamed to Daxing county next year, counties like Daxing and Wanping were administratively under the Central Capital, where at this time had been expanded to the northwest from the original site of Southern Capital of Khitan Liao, and to have Yangfangdian East Street and streets between Huangtingzi and Huichengmen to the south included. The rest counties within the Central Capital domain remained administratively unchanged until the end of Jurchen Jin dynasty, by then there were separately under Daxing, Wanping and Changping counties of Zhongduludaxing prefecture. Inscriptions carved on stone tablets of Liao dynasty records that current locations such as Weigongcu, Erligou west, and Gongzhufen were then under the Wanping county, Beianhe and Dajue Temple under Yuhe county[9].

The third year (1215) of Zhenyou reign, the Mongol army besieged Central Capital, "Yan was captured, Yanjing Road was constructed later on at the beginning, and the Daxing prefecture was supervised under Yan."[10] This historical record quoted from The History of Yuan Dynasty by Song Lian demonstrated the detail. A new capital was being built up in the fourth year (1267) of Zhiyuan reign on the Central Capital site

of Jin dynasty[11]. The official title of the Dynasty Dayuan, "Great Yuan", was used by the Mongols in 1271; the Central Capital was also renamed to Dadu, the "Great Capital" or the Khanbaliq in February next year[12]. Some areas in the south by east of what is now Haidian district were included within the city walls of the new capital, that is to say within the Tucheng area of present day. By the 11th year (1274) of Zhiyuan reign, two county government offices, Daxing and Wanping, were reconstructed. Finally, the construction of the capital city was completed in the 24th year of Zhiyuan reign. Most of the southern part of Haidian was under Wanping county, most of the northern under Changping County throughout the years of Yuan dynasty. Some famous Buddhist temples were also built up in the Haidian area as the most representations still existed today.

In the first year (1368) of Hongwu era August, Dadu Road was renamed to Beiping prefecture right after the seizure of Dadu by the Ming troops. In the first lunar month of 1403, the city of Beijing was established at the Shuntian prefecture site as the emperor's palace, covering the most part of what is now Beijing[13]. Beijing was renamed as Jingshi, the capital, in the first lunar month of 1421. Haidian district was still under Wanping and Changping counties during the Ming dynasty. According to the data recorded in the Shuntian Prefecture Annals from Yongle Canon, borders between Wanping and Changping counties within Haidian were in general the same as they were during Yuan dynasty. The capital of Qing was basically remained at the same are. Counties within the borders of Shuntian prefecture varied in terms of changes in administrative jurisdiction except Daxing and Wanping counties which were directly under the capital. In the 15th year (1676) of Kangxi's reign, Changping together with other 19 counties joined the capital[14]. There were four government offices were set up in four directions of east, west, south and north within the domains of Shuntian prefecture in the year of 1687. Daxing and Wanping were under the government office in the west, and Changping in the north. The southern part of Haidian district of today and Wenquan, Lengquan and Beianhe area were subjected to Wanping prefecture, most of the northern part to Changping prefecture. Followed by the construction of Jingming Garden on Yuquan Mountain and the Old Summer Palace, borders between Wanping and Changping counties had more changes after the year of 1692 in the period of Qing dynasty.

It can clearly be seen that owing to Beijing's status throughout the years in history Haidian had been developed from a local stronghold in a county to a part of the capital since the Jin dynasty. During the Qing period especially after the completion of the Old Summer Palace (the Yuanming Garden) and its surroundings this area was in fact an auxiliary or a summer resort capital. That is why the archaeological discoveries in Haidian found typically different in characters at the different stages of the empire life cycle.

II. The dawn of civilization-prehistoric cultural relics

1. Fossils sites:

Beijing area located on the plains in front of the mountains has lots of water resources, a livable place where animals and human beings adapted to dwell. A large number of fossils from prehistoric period were discovered in Haidian. For example, some elephant molars were found underground when a drilling machine reached the layer of gravel about 10 meters deep to dig a well at Heishanhu nearby Anhe Bridge on the the Qing River along an upstream alluvium in the year of 1956. The famous testing result of

6   Old Version of History of Tang Dynasty, written by Liu Xu (from Later Jin period), Vol. 39, Geography II, P. 1524, Zhonghua Book Company, 1975 edition.

7   History of Liao Dynasty, written by Toqto'a (from Yuan period), Vol. 15, Biographical Sketch on Emperor ShengZong Part Six, P. 171, Zhonghua Book Company, 1974 edition.

8   History of Jin Dynasty, written by Toqto'a (from Yuan period), Vol. 24, Geography Part One, P. 572, Zhonghua Book Company, 1975 edition.

9   Haidian District Chronicles, Composed by the Committee of Chronicles Compilation in Haidian District in Beijing, P. 50, Beijing Press, 2004.

10   The History of Yuan Dynasty, co-edited by Song Lian and others of Ming dynasty, Vol. 58, Geography I, P. 1347, Zhonghua Book Company, 1976 edition.

11   "In the year 4 of Zhiyuan period, the capital is moved from the northeast of Central Capital to the current city." quoted by Yu Minzhong (a Qing courtier) from The History of Yuan Dynasty-Geographica. A Study on the Old Events Happened During the Imperial Period, authored by Yu Minzhong, Vol. 4, P. 61, Beijing Classics Publishing House, 2000 edition.

12   The History of Yuan Dynasty, co-edited by Song Lian and others of Ming dynasty, Vol. 7, Biographical Sketches of Emperor Shizu IV, P. 140, Zhonghua Book Company, 1976 edition.

13   History of Ming Dynasty, Vol. 40, Geography I, co-edited by Zhang Tingyu and others, P. 883, published by Zhonghua Book Company, 1974 edition.

14   Draft History of Qing, Vol. 116, P. 3335, The Officials III, Zhonghua Book Company, 1976 edition.

archaeological site by Zhou Mingzhen should be assessed as the late Pleistocene period[15]. In the same year fall, another testing executed by Hu Changkang from the Institute of Vertebrate Paleontology at Social Science Academy confirmed the same result by identifying a prehistoric cow skull that was found in the gravel and sand 6.5 meters deep in the area of alluvial fans when a diversion project in Yongding River was under process in Northern Liulinguan at Yangfangdian[16]. Other discoveries proved the same conclusion as above. Like In 1957, Li Fenglin from Beijing Museum of Natural History found badger fossils existed between the fissures when he was doing a survey in the limestone field[17]. In 1976 July, anther prehistoric cow skull was found in the gravel and sand 6.8 meters deep in the area of alluvial fans Beifengwo at Yangfangdian when the people's air defense project was under construction. And this time the testing was arranged by Yan Defa from the Institute of Vertebrate Paleontology at Social Science Academy, who made the collection of specimen for the confirmation[18].In 1999, when workers were mining on the Yuquan Gravel Quarry Plant in Sijiqing (a little town), a fossilized elephant tusk (Elephas Palaeoloxodon) was found out in the riverbed sedimentary area by accident which of course belonged to the late Pleistocene period[19]. In 2005, another fossilized elephant tusk (Elephas Palaeoloxodon) was found 9 meters deep underground at Shangdi area Haidian demonstrated it belonged to the end of the late Pleistocene period[20]. In 2007, one more fossilized elephant tusk (Elephas Palaeoloxodon) was found in Zhichunli Haidiann[21]. A prehistoric fossilized elephant tusk and a fossilized ox horn unearthed at some place in southern part of Yuquan Mountain were collected by the Haidian Museum[22]. Elephas Palaeoloxodon a giant mammal lived around the end of the late Pleistocene period, 100,000 to 10,000 years ago. Many of the fossilized tusks excavated in the area of Haidian gave the evidence that rich steppe areas and plentiful forests on this land were much more abundant during the prehistoric time.

Human ancestors, represented by the Peking Man (Homo erectus pekinensis), who lived 600,000 to 700,000 years ago gave their birth to the next generations by increasing the populations gradually in number. We could still find the Pecking man fossils in Haidian area, and this demonstrates that this land was ever a vibrant homeland for animals and humans to live together.

2. Late Neolithic Period

In the late Neolithic age, human civilization has spread in Haidian. From the Haidian town extended to the Qinghe Plateau, known as the Haidian Plateau, was the place where human civilization had ever been highly developed. A stone ax collected by the Haidian Museum was excavated on the Peking University campus, which belonged to the late Neolithic period. In 1982, an ancient relics was found on the eastern side of a Brick Plant in the Suer village at the Sujiatuo town, which was dated from the late Neolithic period to the Han dynasty, but the red pieces of pottery found at this site was dated belong to the late Neolithic period[23]. In 1956, a finely designed stone ax was found in the Tofu A

No. 3 building on the Peking University campus[24], and in the same year, more than 100 stone tools and no less than 200 pieces of broken pottery sherds were excavated in front of the No. 10 building on the same campus[25]. In 1997, a number of pottery wares, stone tool and animal bones and plant specimen were found at the construction site of the Department of Science on the university campus. Potteries mainly the terracotta mixed with frail mica, next to it is the coarse pottery, and the clay pottery were all shaped in pot. According to radiocarbon dating, those man-made plain polished potteries were dated from 4300 to 4500 years old[26]. This site geographically cut through the Haidian plateau was roughly considered as the first stage of the Snow Mountain culture of the prehistoric in Beijing[27]. The similar finely designed polished stone tools were also found in some other places like Zhongguancun, Qinghe, Baijiatong, and Tian village[28]. The Neolithic period culture of Haidian in general is categorized as the Snow Mountain Culture.

III. Sunlight in the Morning-Cultural Relics of Xia, Shang and Zhou dynasties in Haidian

After entering the protohistoric period, Beijing area was the frontiers in the time of Xia and Shang, a place with civilized and barbaric in between. The vassal states Yan and Ji were conferred to the nobilities during the Zhou period. The Ji state was included into Yan, which later became the capital of Yan state, one of the Seven Warring States thereafter. Haidian area was in the northwest of the Ji city, which channeled the way between ethnic groups in the north and people living on the farm land in the central area of China with regard to economic and cultural exchange. Manufacturing industries and commercial industries were highly developed in this area during the Warring States period. Pottery workmanship and metal casting technology were well maturely developed. Pottery pieces found in an ancient city wall in Zhufang village demonstrated that the city was being built at here, probably the outskirt of the city.

What had been discovered at the stage of this time were mainly tombs and coin hoards of the Warring States period. No big geographical changes happened to the places, during this period of time, where those tombs and coin hoards were discovered. These were the places as they were in the Neolithic period just slightly extended out in the Haidian plateau and further to its surrounding areas. In 1949, two urn tombs were found at the Linglong Road Balizhuang subdistrict. The north-south oriented tombs were composed of pottery urns. A corpse of a dead person who was presumably younger than three years old child was found in the urn with its head to the north and feet to the south[29]. In 1955, an urn tomb was found at the dormitory construction site on the Peking University campus in Zhongguanyuan Zhongguan village. The north-south oriented tomb dated back to the Warring States period, was 0.5 meters long and 0.3 meters wide. The north side of the urn coffin was covered by some pieces of plain clay potteries with two tubs bound together. The tubs were painted with fishbone on its surface. The corpse

15　Tentative Discussions on the Palaeoloxodon Fossils Found in The Western Suburbs of Beijing And Elephant Fossils In The Case Of Namadicus In China, Journal of Palaeogeography, Zhou Mingzhen, 1957, the 2nd issue, PP. 283-294.

16　Bos Primigenius Skull Fossils Found in the Western Suburbs of Beijing, Vertebrate Paleontology and Paleoanthropology, Hu Changkang, 1959, the 1st issue, PP. 41-42.

17　Archaeological Discoveries in Beijing the Prehistoric Period, P. 109, co-edited by Guo Jingning and Song Dachuan, published by Shanghai Classics Publishing House, 2012.

18　Archaeological Discoveries in Beijing the Prehistoric Period, P. 109, co-edited by Guo Jingning and Song Dachuan, published by Shanghai Classics Publishing House, 2012.

19　Appreciation Of The Essence On Historical Artifacts Discovered From The Western Suburbs Of Beijing, authored by Jiao Jinlin, P. 244, published by Academy Press, Beijign, 2010.

20　Fossils Of The Tusk Of The Elephant (Palaeoloxodon) Excavated From The Mountain Area In West Beijing, authored by Dong Yugang, from the Cultural Relics and Museums in Beijing, 2nd issue, 2006, PP. 93-95.

21　Appreciation Of The Essence On Historical Artifacts Discovered From The Western Suburbs Of Beijing, authored by Jiao Jinlin, P. 244, published by Academy Press, Beijign, 2010.

22　Thousands Of Years Throughout History-Historical Relics In Haidian, edited by Li Ang PP. 2-3, Haidian Museum, Beijing, 2012.

23　An Atlas of Chinese Cultural Relics, Beijing Part Two, edited by the State Administration of Cultural Heritage, Science Press, P. 209, 2008 edition.

24　Cultural Relics Found in Peking University, authored by Yue Shengyang, and Journal of Peking University (Philosophy and Social Science)" Vol. 35, Issue No. 31, PP. 55-61, 1998.

25　Microliths Found in Haidian District Beijing, authored by Wei Xiaozu, Reference Materials for the Cultural Relics, Issue No. 7, P. 73, 1956.

26　An Investigation Report on the Historical Ruins Sites Found in Peking University, co-authored by Yue Shengyang, Archaeology and Cultural Relics, a supplementary issue on Archaeology the Pre-Qin Period, PP. 9-12, 2002.

27　Archaeology in Beijing the Prehistoric Period, P. 173, co-edited by Guo Jingning and Song Dachuan, published by Shanghai Classics Publishing House, 1st edition, December 2012.

28　Neolithic Polished Axes Found In Qing He Town In North Beijing Area, translated by Guan Chenghe, Reference Materials for the Cultural Relics, Issue No. 12, P. 109, 1953. The original paper is published in Soviet Union journal The Librarians, Issue No. 7, 1953. Microliths Found in Haidian District Beijing, authored by Wei Xiaozu, Reference Materials for the Cultural Relics, Issue No. 7, 1956.

29　An Atlas of Chinese Cultural Relics, edited by the State Administration of Cultural Heritage, Beijing Part Two, Science Press, P. 212, 2008 edition.

remained in the coffin was decayed with no burial objects in it[30]. A large number of tombs were discovered at the Haidian Shangdi Information Industry Base between 1991 and 2001 announced by the Beijing Municipal Institute of Cultural Relics. Eight of them were vertical coffin pits identified as the tombs Warring States period. Terracotta potteries, copper mirrors, copper seals, belt hooks and metal objects were found in the pits[31]. In 2007, five urn tombs were found at the construction site at Xin village Qinglongqiao. Each of the urn coffins was bound together by two plain terracotta axes with their flared blades outward. The bigger ax was about 50cm long, and the smaller one was about 30 cm long. The corpses of children were remained in the urn coffins[32].

The coin hoards of the Warring States period were very often found in the Haidian area. In 1982, some knife-shaped coins of the Warring States period were found on the eastern side of the Brick Plant at the Suer village Sujiatuo town, where dated from the late Neolithic period to the Han dynasty[33]. In 1953 June, some square folding coins were found at Zizhuqiao. The coins were shaped in a Chinese character "yan" weighted a total of about 4kg[34]. In 1976, hundreds of "yan" coins were found two meters deep underground in the Dongbutou village Wenquan commune[35]. In 1978, about 2kg "yan" coins were found in the orchard at the Xishan Farm[36]. In 1989, this kind of knife-shaped coins hoard was found many at the Guxiangyuan Food Factory, now collected by the Haidian Museum[37].

Some other relics of the Warring States period were also found in Haidian. In 1957 May, a bronze food container fu was found at the Northern Farm in the Dongbeiwang village, the bottom of it was with the inscription[38]. There were many more terracotta potteries of the Warring States period being found later on, mainly the gray pottery pots and kettles. In 1971 August, a terracotta pot was unearthed at the Bali village Haidian, which was a Warring States period pot[39]. The similar pots were also unearthed in the Peking University Yannan Garden where a pipeline was being built.

It could be interpreted that many of the cultural relics discovered in Haidian area, especially the discovery of copper coins hoards, proved that the Beijing area had been highly in growth during the period of Yan and Ji, and the Haidian region had become a well developed place with commercial, handicraft and agricultural industries burgeoning..

IV. Stronghold on the Borders-Haidian Cultural Relics of Han and Tang dynasties

Haidian area probably belonged to the Ji county of Guangyang state and the Jundu county of Shanggu prefecture during the Western and Eastern dynasties. Social economy became more prosperous than before, which indicates that the agricultural civilization had

already reached here. Beijing area had not only become a military front to defense threat from outside at the borders in the north but also an economic center at this time. Haidian was very rich in its Western and Eastern Han cultural relics, which were distinguished either from the small size of coffin pits or from a small amount of city construction sites.

In 1951, coffin pits of the Western Han and Eastern Han dynasties were found in the area between Qinghe County and Zhufang village one after another. Some gray terracotta pottery urns painted with rope pattern, pots, and ding cooking vessels as well as bricks and tiles, Banliang coins and Wuzhu money were unearthed[40]. In the winter of 1962, a tomb of Han dynasty was sorted out. This tomb was a small rectangular coffin pit and preserved in good condition. Pottery wares, Wuzhu money of Western Han and a copper mirror were found at this site[41]. In 1982, six coffin pits of Han dynasty were sorted out on an ancient relics site which is found on the eastern side of a Brick Plant in the Suer village at the Sujiatuo town. The site was roughtly dated from the late Neolithic period to the Han dynasty. The single brick-chambered tombs had been destructed, although some bronze mirrors, ornaments on bronze chariots and horses, and gray pottery pots, kettles, tubs and pottery sherds were unearthed[42]. In 1982, three coffin pits were found in an artillery command compound located near to Wukesong and Wanshoulu[43]. Some terracotta potteries and silk fabrics were unearthed. Between 2004 and 2005, seven vertical rectangular coffin pits were excavated within an area where Wukesong Basketball Hall was being constructed nearby the Fuxing Road. Two out of seven, the M3 and M5, were tombs of Han dynasty. Terracotta pottery pots, bowls, gray pottery kettles and tubs were found in the tombs. Other grave goods mainly gray pottery pots belonged to the Eastern Han dynasty[44]. Another brick-chambered tomb of Han was found in a baseball hall with single room in the front and double room in the back. Bronze coins and a bronze mirror were unearthed. This tomb dated presumably from the middle to the late Eastern Han dynasty[45].In 1984, two clay wells and three coffin pits of Western Han were found at Wanquan village subdistrict in southern Haidian. Pottery pots and bins and the Wuzhu money were unearthed at the coffin pits[46]. In 1985, a number of brick-chambered coffin pits were found in Xiyuhe area, most of them were seriously destructed, not well preserved in shape. Some pottery pots and several silver wares were found in a single chambered coffin pit[47]. More than 300 coffin pits organized by Beijing Cultural Relics Research Institute were unearthed at the Haidian Shangdi Information Industry Base through the years between 1991 and 2001[48]. In recent years, a number of tombs

30   Urn Burial Found in Zhongguanyuan the Western Suburbs of Beijing, authored by Wang Kelin: ,Reference Materials for the Cultural Relics, 1955, Issue No. 11, P. 121.

31   An Atlas of Chinese Cultural Relics, edited by the State Administration of Cultural Heritage, Beijing Part Two, published by the Science Press, P. 212, 2008; New Archaeological Achievements in Recent Years in Beijing, authored by Song Dachuan, Cultural Relics and Archaeology in Beijing Series No. 5, P. 6, Beijing Yanshan Press, 2002.

32   40 Years Archaeological Discoveries in Beijing, edited by the Beijing Municipal Institute of Cultural Relics, PP. 62-63, published by the Beijing Yanshan Press, 1990.

33   An Atlas of Chinese Cultural Relics, the State Administration of Cultural Heritage, Beijing Part Two, published by the Science Press, P. 209, 2008

34   Introduction to the Exhibition on Cultural Relics Unearthed in the City of Beijing, Reference Materials for the Cultural Relics, authored by Zhou Geng, Issue No. 8, P. 70, 1954.

35   40 Years Archaeological Discoveries in Beijing, edited by the Beijing Municipal Institute of Cultural Relics, P. 64, published by the Beijing Yanshan Press, 1990.

36   40 Years Archaeological Discoveries in Beijing, edited by the Beijing Municipal Institute of Cultural Relics, P. 64, published by the Beijing Yanshan Press, 1990.

37   Thousands Of Years Throughout History-Historical Relics In Haidian, edited by Li Ang, PP. 6-7, Haidian Museum, Beijing, 2012.

38   Bronze Wares of the Spring and Autumn Period Discovered in Haidian District, Reference Materials for the Cultural Relics, Issue No. 5, P. 72, 1958, edited by the Archaeological Work Team on Cultural Relics in Beijing.

39   40 Years Archaeological Discoveries in Beijing, edited by the Beijing Municipal Institute of Cultural Relics, P. 59, published by the Beijing Yanshan Press, 1990.

40   Introduction to the Exhibition on Cultural Relics Unearthed in the City of Beijing, Reference Materials for the Cultural Relics, authored by Zhou Geng, Issue No. 8, P. 70, 1954.

41   Tomb of the Eastern Han Dynasty at Yongding Road Beijing, authored by Yu Zhen, Archaeology, Issue No. 3, PP. 170-171, 1963.

42   An Atlas of Chinese Cultural Relics, edited by the the State Administration of Cultural Heritage, Beijing Part Two, published by the Science Press, P. 209, 2008

43   An Atlas of Chinese Cultural Relics, edited by the State Administration of Cultural Heritage, Beijing Part Two, published by the Science Press, P. 212, 2008

44   An Archaeological Report on the Excavations at the Wukesong Basketball Hall Construction Site, and A Report on the Excavations at the Olympic Gymnasiums Constructions Site, edited by the Beijing Municipal Institute of Cultural Relics, PP. 1-71, published by the Science Press, 2007.

45   An Archaeological Report on the Excavations at the Wukesong Baseball Field Construction Site, and A Report on the Excavations at the Olympic Gymnasiums Constructions Site, edited by the Beijing Municipal Institute of Cultural Relics, PP. 381-382, published by the Science Press, 2007.

46   An Atlas of Chinese Cultural Relics, edited by the State Administration of Cultural Heritage, Beijing Part Two, published by the Science Press, P. 209, 2008

47   An Atlas of Chinese Cultural Relics, Beijing Part Two, edited by the State Administration of Cultural Heritage, published by the Science Press, P. 212, 2008

48   Tomb of the Eastern Han Dynasty Found in Shangdi Village in Haidian, authored by Li Da; Chinese Archaeology Yearbook 1992, P. 146, published by Cultural Relics Press, 1994. Five tombs of the Eastern Han dynasty are announced to be discovered. New Archaeological Achievements in Recent Years in Beijing, authored by Song Dachuan, Cultural Relics and Archaeology in Beijing, Series No. 5, P. 6, Beijing Yanshan Press, 2002; An Atlas of Chinese Cultural Relics, Beijing Part Two, edited by the the State Administration of Cultural Heritage, published by the Science Press, P. 212, 2008.

were found in vegetable fields and orchards in former Shangdi village by archaeological explorations coordinated with the construction of the Shangdi Garden. This tombs area should be on a plateau more than three meters high above the ground level. Most of the 98 tombs were rectangular or polygonal vertical coffin pits, not many cubicle coffin chambers on two sides. Some coffin chambers were covered with black bricks, and some had arch to support the vault. They are all the tombs of Han dynasty[49]. In 2007, two tombs of Han, M2 and M4, were found within the Xincun development zones at Qinglongqiao. They were vertical rectangular coffin pits. Some grave goods like pottery pots, bowls, ding vessel containers and bins were unearthed[50].

In 1955, a square-shaped city site of Han dynasty was partly excavated at Zhufang village in Qinghe subdistrict in Haidian. More than ten clay wells were found at this site. Some terracotta potteries made with sand, mud-made gray potteries,plate tiles, eaves tiles and semicircle-shaped tiles were found. Moreover, a series of iron wares like iron swords, iron broad swords, iron hoes, iron mirrors and iron seals were found[51]. Some well sites of Han dynasties located in the area between what is now the Summer Palace and Yuquanshan. The Han wells were constructed with huge gray pottery rings overlapped on top of each other. Although materials about those archaeological sites have not been reported yet, we could still know that the agricultural industries were highly developed in the west part of Haidian. In addition, a kiln site of Han dynasty was found at Zhufang village Qinghe County and the foundation of it had already been sorted out[52]. These discoveries listed above interprets that the large scale manufacturing and commercialization in Haidian area had been prosperously developed. Population became at the same time nourished during the years of Western Han and Eastern Han dynasties.

During the Three Kingdoms, Jin and southern and northern dynasties period, there were basically three practical levels of local government: administrative divisions in the northern area were province, prefecture and county. The city of Ji located in the Beijing area was governed both by the You province and the Yan prefecture (the Yan State). Economic development and cultural development were much more flourished in the city which was considered as an important stronghold on the border in the north.

One of the most archaeological discoveries was the excavation of Wei tomb located in the northeast of Bali village, Yutan town in 1987. This was a north-south oriented tomb and could be regarded as a typical double brick-chambered tomb of Han. Layout of the tomb included a passage way, a door of the burial chamber, an antechamber, a long passage to the burial chamber and the back rooms. A set of yellow glazed tomb figurines and funerary objects including figurines of dancers, warehouses, kitchens, wells, mill stones, mortars, and rings in model were found. Some drinking vessels like zun, ladle, lian, ge, flat pot and tiger pot were unearthed in this tomb. This kind of glazed terracotta pottery funerary object set was very popular in the north area since Han dynasty. Green glazed funerary object figurines were popular along the areas of what is now the Yellow River. Yellow glazed set of funerary objects was widely used in north Handan Hebei province. And the set of the objects found in the Wei tomb was perfectly preserved and a representation to demonstrate that this sort of funerary objects

was widely used in the northern area. Furthermore, the Wuzhu money was also found in the Wei tomb, especially a bronze crossbow with fine carved intaglio was unearthed as well. The inscription on it said that "the crossbow is produced by Wang Zhao, Ma Guang and Zhang Xiong from Zuoshangfang (a court department of manufacture) on March 30th, 244"[53], which indicated that this tomb could be dated to the year of 244 or so. Two tombs of Jin much similar to the Wei tomb were discovered at Caochang village Sujiatuo town in 1962. They were brick-chambered tombs constructed with sloping passage and arched vault. A group of yellow glazed funerary objects like figurine of a coachman, ox cart, cattle, chicken, kitchen, bronze coins, bronze mirrors and bronze bells were also unearthed in the tombs[54].

Some other tombs of the southern and northern dynasties were sorted out in Haidian area as well. In 1953, a large brick-chambered tomb of the Wei and Jin period was excavated at Qinghe town. The corpses of the people got buried in hanging coffins in this tomb. Bronze mirrors, bronze swords, terracotta toilet articles and the Wuzhu money were unearthed from the same site. Two iron plowshares were found in a brick pit nearby[55]. In 1953, a tomb pit of Wei, Jin and southern and northern dynasties was found in the Bayi Elementary School. In 1962, two brick-chambered coffin pits were found at somewhere northwest of Jingwangfen (literately translated as the grave of Prince Jing) in Haidian[56].

The investigation of the ancient water control and conservancy project was an important work for archaeological discoveries of Jin and southern and northern dynasties period. An ancient canal was built somewhere between the southwest of Zizhuqiao and Yongding river side in Shijingshan area. According to a study by Yue Shengyang, this canal was called the trunk canal built up in the years of Wei State ruled by the Cao family. According to other discoveries happened sporadically here and there, the direction of the ancient canal had been finally confirmed. The southernmost end of the canal was roughly along the Gaoliang River side near to Zizhu Garden, the northernmost end was in somewhere between Chengfu village and Tsinghua University flowing into the Wanquan River. More or less, the southern section of the canal was paralleled with the Baishiqiao Road next to Zizhuyuan, the northern was with the Haidian Road. But it looks like that the canal goes to two different directions from the north side of what is now the Modern Plaza (a shopping mall)[57]. To what directions that the trunk canal goes helps us to get a clear picture of agricultural development and living conditions of the area near to the canal.

Beijing area got more developed during the Sui and Tang dynasties. Youzhou (You Province) was a big province and a pivotal stronghold in the north during the time of Tang dynasty, covering an area of more than 16 fangs (equals to about 26560 square meters) in total. Shi Siming took the You Province as his Yan capital at the time of An lushan-Shi siming Rebellion in 759. This was the first time in history that Beijing was called as Yanjing (Yan Capital). By the late Tang dynasty military governance system cracked down, one of the three most powerful military governors, the governor of You Capital and Lulong, who fought to have more areas under his one jurisdiction laid a good foundation later on for Beijing to be the capital of the empire.

Some important tombs of Tang dynasties were found in Beijing area, Haidian was the place where more large scale tombs were discovered. In 1980, a brick-chambered tomb pit of the middle Tang period was found at the outside of the east gate of Diaoyutai Guesthouse. The entrance of the north-south oriented tomb was facing to the south with

49   *An Archaeological Report on the Construction Site at Shangdi Jiayuan Carried by the Shichuang Real Estate Company*, authored by Guo Lizhan, edited by Song Dachuan, *A Report on Archaeological Activities in Beijing (2000-2009) Haidian*, PP. 348-349, published by the Shanghai Classics Publishing House, 2011.

50   *An Archaeological Report on the Excavations at the Qinglongqiao New Village*, authored by Guo Lizhan, edited by Song Dachuan, *A Report on Archaeological Activities in Beijing (2000-2009) Haidian*, PP. 348-349, published by the Shanghai Classics Publishing House, 2011.

51   *A Survey and Research on the City Ruins Site of the Han Dynasty*, edited by the Museum of Western Han Tombs at Dabaotai, Beijing, PP. 124-127, published by the Beijing Yanshan Press, 2009; *Archaeological Discoveries in Beijing the Han Period*, authored by Hu Chuansong,, edited by Song Dachuan, PP. 38-41, Shanghai Classics Publishing House, 2012.

52   *Introduction to the Exhibition on Cultural Relics Unearthed in the City of Beijing, Reference Materials for the Cultural Relics*, authored by Zhou Geng, Issue No. 8, P. 71, 1954.

53   *Archaeological Discoveries in Beijing the Wei-Jin, South-North, and Sui-Tang Periods*, authored by Dong Kunyu,, edited by Song Dachuan, P. 16, Shanghai Classics Publishing House, 2012.

54   *An Atlas of Chinese Cultural Relics*, edited by the State Administration of Cultural Heritage, *Beijing Part Two*, published by the Science Press, P. 213, 2008

55   *Introduction to the Exhibition on Cultural Relics Unearthed in the City of Beijing, Reference Materials for the Cultural Relics*, authored by Zhou Geng, Issue No. 8, P. 71, 1954.

56   *Archaeological Discoveries in Beijing the Wei-Jin, South-North, and Sui-Tang Periods*, authored by Dong Kunyu, edited by Song Dachuan, P. 2, Shanghai Classics Publishing House, 2012.

57   *An Ancient Canal Ruins Site at Shuangyushu and the Trunk Canal*, authored by Yue Shengyang; *Cultural Relics and Archaeology in Beijing*, Series No. 4, edited by the Beijing Municipal Institute of Cultural Relics, PP. 126-127, 1994.

arch-shaped structure formed on top inside. Some white terracotta pottery sherds, pots, bowls and tubs were found. An inscription on the memorial tablet within this tomb was also discovered[58]. In 1973, a tomb pit of Tianbao reign of Tang dynasty was discovered in Zhufang village Qinghe town. This brick-chambered coffin tomb was rectangular in shape, consisted of a passage, a door, and a chamber. Funerary objects buried with the dead were only the black pottery bowls, four series of painted pottery pots, pottery plates and an epitaph. According to the epitaph engraved on stone tablet, this tomb belonged to Wang Hui, a Taoist priest from the Kaiyuan Taoist Temple[59].

In 1985, a tomb of Tang dynasty was found in the No.14 compound at Cuiwei Road Haidian. This tomb was a single brick-chambered tomb of wood imitation structure domed on top painted with oiled ink lacquer. Wall paintings, brick carving doors and windows as well as candlestick lamps were found in this tomb. A coffin platform was set in the north side of the chamber. We knew that this tomb of Tang dynasty (in the year of 847) belonged to a head general of rangers and his wife's from a memorial tablet was found in the tomb[60]. It is demonstrated that this tomb was one of the earliest brick-chambered tombs of wood imitation structure in the northern area in the late Tang dynasty.

In 1992, a tomb of Tang dynasty was sorted out at a construction site in Balizhuang organized by the Institute of Cultural Management in Haidian. The tomb was a single chambered brick tomb in an arc square shape, consisted of a passage, a door, and a chamber. The door of the coffin chamber was found facing to the south, and a sloping passage leading to the chamber. There were not only lattice windows built with bricks found in the tomb, but also niches and walls and the top ceiling were painted with colors. A well preserved screen painting, the Peony and Wild Goose by Reed Leaves, with 2.9m long and 1.56m high was found in the tomb. What we knew from this landscape painting was about how the tombs located in the northern area were decorated and painted throughout the years of late Tang dynasty and the Five Dynasties period. The discovery of this tomb provided precious information available for the research on the history of flowers and birds painting in particular. Since the tomb had been robbed before it was excavated, only a few of artifacts debris and a memorial tablet were remained. According to the tablet, we knew that this tomb belonged to Wang Gongshu who was buried here after his death in the year of 852. He worked as a judge at the local government in You province[61].

In 1984, a tomb of Tang dynasty was found in Erligou. The north-south oriented round tomb was a single brick-chambered tomb, consisted of a passage, a door and a chamber. The tomb door was found open to the south, and the coffin platform was set in the north. Scarlet patterns were painted on the white-washed wall in the north. The only funerary objects that were found in this tomb pit were the pottery sherds and a memorial tablet. What we could get information from the tablet was that this tomb belonged to a lieutenant general from a military department. His name was Ru Hongqing who was buried here after his death in the first year (880) of Guangming reign of Tang dynasty[62]. In 1966, a tomb of Tang dynasty was found on the site where a diversion canal connecting Beijing and Miyun was then being constructed. The tomb had been destructed several times but a memorial tablet was remained, which tells us that this tomb belonged to Li Yongding, a provincial governor of Qingshan (or Jimi) Province who was buried here after

his death in the second year (759) of Qianyuan reign of Tang dynasty[63]. Other important tombs of Tang dynasty with events well recorded were discovered. For example, the tomb of Wen Lingshou was found in the Wanshou Road where he was buried in the 15th year (874) of Xiantong reign of the Emperor Yizong of Tang dynasty[64]; the tomb dated the first year (880) of Guangming reign of Tang dynasty was found in the Customs Building compound at Erligou Haidian[65]; and the tomb of Madam Yao dated the first year (888) of Wende reign of Tang dynasty was found at Baijiatong in Wenquanshan[66].

In addition, some simple and small scaled tombs were found in the northern part of You province or beyond. They were brick-chambered coffin pits with no patterns painted on walls. In 1988, a number of small scaled vertical coffin pits were found at a construction site at southeastern part of the Tsinghua University. This tomb was sorted out under the auspices of the Institute of Cultural Management in Haidian. It can be identified that the owner of the tomb was from a lower social class, but some finely well made remains were discovered. Calyxes or small cups made in the Xing Kiln of Tang dynasty, stem cups made in Gongyi Kiln and the Ryoka bronze mirrors carved with flowers and birds were found in this tomb. Now those objects are collected by the Haidian Museum[67]. Tombs, located in the Shangdi Information Industry Base under the auspices of the Beijing Municipal Institute of cultural relics, were excavated between 1991 and 2001. Two of them were dated as of Tang dynasty[68]. In 2003, a tomb of Tang dynasty in the Materials Reserves School was found. The tomb was a rectangular sloping brick-chambered tomb, 185 degrees azimuth, consisted of a passage, a door and a chamber. The passage was constructed on the southern side of the tomb. Two human skeletons were unearthed with their heads pointing to the south. Objects buried in the tomb were two terracotta pottery jars and three coffin rings[69]. A tomb of Tang dynasty was found at a construction site where a bus station at Wofosi (Temple of Sleeping Buddha) near to the Botanical Garden on the Xiangshan (Fragrant Hills) Beijing was being reconstructed in 2006. This tomb was a semi-elliptical brick chambered tomb with arch-shaped structure formed on top inside. Some terracotta pottery wares, pots and covers and two Kaiyuantongbao coins[70] were unearthed.

V. Integration and acculturation: Cultural relics of Song, Liao, Jin and Yuan dynasties

The Song, Liao, Jin and Yuan dynasties period was a time when political turmoil and military conflicts between the peoples from the north and the south of the Great Wall became influential complicated. Khitan, Jurchen, Mongolian peoples and other ethnic

58   A Number of Tombs of Tang Dynasty Discovered in Recent Years in Beijing, authored by Hong Xin, Cultural Heritage, Issue No. 12, P. 16, 1990.

59   A Number of Tombs of Tang Dynasty Discovered in Recent Years in Beijing, co-authored by The archaeological Work Team from Beijing; Archaeology, Issue No. 6, PP. 498-500, 1980.

60   A Number of Tombs of Tang Dynasty Discovered in Recent Years in Beijing, authored by Hong Xin, Cultural Heritage, Issue No. 12, 1990, P. 20.

61   The Tang Tombs Discovered in Balizhuang Haidian, edited by Management Office of Cultural Relics in Haidian; Cultural Heritage, PP. 45-53, Issue No. 11, 1995.

62   A Number of Tombs of Tang Dynasty Discovered in Recent Years in Beijing, authored by Hong Xin, Cultural Relics, Issue No. 12, 1990, P. 17.

63   An Atlas of Chinese Cultural Relics, edited by the State Administration of Cultural Heritage, Beijing Part Two, published by the Science Press, P. 213, 2008

64   Archaeological Discoveries in Beijing the Wei-Jin, South-North, and Sui-Tang Periods, authored by Dong Kunyu,, edited by Song Dachuan, P. 52, Shanghai Classics Publishing House, 2012.

65   Archaeological Discoveries in Beijing the Wei-Jin, South-North, and Sui-Tang Periods, authored by Dong Kunyu,, edited by Song Dachuan, P. 52, Shanghai Classics Publishing House, 2012.

66   Archaeological Discoveries in Beijing the Wei-Jin, South-North, and Sui-Tang Periods, authored by Dong Kunyu,, edited by Song Dachuan, P. 53, Shanghai Classics Publishing House, 2012.

67   The Haidian Museum, edited by the Haidian Museum in Beijing, PP. 12-15, P. 154, published by Cultural Relics Press, 2005.

68   40 Years Archaeological Discoveries in Beijing, edited by the Beijing Municipal Institute of Cultural Relics, PP. 62-63, published by the Beijing Yanshan Press, 1990.

69   An Archaeological Report on the Excavations at the Residential Areas Near to Beijing Material Reserves Specialized Professional School, authored by Guo Lizhan, edited by Song Dachuan, A Report on Archaeological Activities in Beijing (2000-2009) Haidian, P. 126, published by the Shanghai Classics Publishing House, 2011.

70   An Archaeological Report on the Excavations at the Construction Site of a Bus Station at Wofosi (Temple of Sleeping Buddha) near to the Botanical Garden on the Xiangshan (Fragrant Hills), authored by Guo Lizhan, edited by Song Dachuan, A Report on Archaeological Activities in Beijing (2000-2009) Haidian, PP. 280-281, published by the Shanghai Classics Publishing House, 2011.

groups who were good at horse riding attacked and dominated the Chinese territories by turn except a brief occupation of those territories by the Song power. Under the current turbulent situation, peoples living in the Beijing area which was recognized as the central core, including northern part of Shanxi and Hebei, southeastern part of Inner Mongolia and western part of Liaoning, were diverse in their customs and cultures, but at the same time integrated with each other as well. As a result of this phenomenon, the Beijing area in ancient time was very much rich in its cultural diversifications and amalgamations. The Yan capital with its unique geographical location and economic strength played a pivotal role at this time in cultural connections and communications between people who lived on the farm land in the central plains and people who lived in the steppe areas in the north. Beijing later became to be the great capital of the Chinese empire which gave us a picture of urban culture in its peculiarity..

1. Under Liao's Domination

In 936, the You prefecture was upgraded as one of the five capitals of Liao after sixteen prefectures of Yan and Yun were taken by the Khitan Liao. The capital was named as the Southern Capital but was renamed as Xijinfu thereafter. The Beijing area was developed from a "border state" of the Central Kingdom in the north to the southern frontier of a "border dynasty", a central place where cultural exchanges and integration took the role between Khitan and Han. It has been proved that the northwest corner of the Liao Nanjing was approximately the southeast corner of what is now Haidian. There some parts were overlapped with each other according to archaeological investigations that were combined with historical documents.

A number of tombs of Liao dynasty were found in Haidian, many fine artifacts were unearthed. In 1953, a tomb of Liao dynasty was discovered and sorted out under the auspices of Beijing Municipal Cultural Bureau when sewer pipes were being repaired underground at Xicui road. This tomb was a dome-shaped single brick-chambered tomb of wood imitation structure. The tomb was found rich in murals, the themes of the murals were false doors, flowers, and waterfowls. But the murals were seriously damaged, and what were painted on the walls could not be clearly figured out. No coffin was found in the tomb. What had been excavated in the tomb were Kaiyuantongbao coin, Qianyuantongbao coins, jade belt buckles in all size, thin silver sheet, a white glazed sunflower rimmed bowl made in Ding Kiln, and terracotta warriors, etc[71].

In 1985, four single brick-chambered dome-shaped tombs were found in northwest Niege village in Sujiatuo town Haidian, and sorted out under the auspices of the Institute of Cultural Management in Haidian. All four tombs had been robbed and stolen by thieves and vandals. Tomb murals could be traced at many parts on the wall, but seriously damaged. Murals showing a scene of tea-preparation had been well preserved in one of the four. The section of the murals that was painted on the wall depicted a tea cooking stove and bottles for cooking the tea or soup. The body was buried in cremation, some pottery sherds and coins of Song and Liao dynasties were discovered[72].

A rescue excavation under the auspices of the Beijing Municipal Institute of Cultural Relics took place in 1991. A rectangular single brick-chambered tomb with arch-shaped structure formed on top was excavated during the construction of a Post Office dormitory to the north at Yangfangdian in Haidian. This north-south oriented tomb was well preserved. The top of the tomb was covered with a layer of flat bricks. A sacrificial alter was found 0.4 m to the north side of the tomb. Some funerary objects like cockscomb-shaped pots, little black pottery pots, gray pottery pots, bone-made cosmetic case, and iron scissors were found near to the head of the buried body. In addition, remains of lacquer wares could be traced as well. A bronze mirror was found right on the center of chest of the buried body. And a large cattle skull was found on a supposed alter. This tomb was constructed in a special shape and plenty objects unearthed[73].

Thirty tombs of Khitan Liao and Jurchen Jin dynasties were identified when some Warring States tombs and tombs of the Ming and Qing dynasties were discovered throughout the years between 1991 and 2001 at the construction site where the Shangdi Information Industry Base was being built. The tombs were found in different types in shape. One was the brick-chambered tomb; the other was the stone coffin tomb. Bronze mirrors, terracotta pottery wares, jade objects and iron products were excavated in those tombs[74].

In 2002, a tomb of Liao dynasty was found at the construction site at the Workers' College dormitory building to the north in Zengguang road Haidian. This discovery was under the auspices of the Beijing Municipal Institute of Cultural Relics in an excavation rescue. This tomb was, a single brick-chambered tomb of wood imitation structure, dome shaped, found facing to the south, and consisted of a screen wall, a passage, and a chamber. A gray pottery basin, a gray pottery dish, a gray pottery pot and a memorial tablet were unearthed. What we knew from the inscription engraved on the tablet was that the owner of the tomb was dead in 1071. The information we got from the epitaph was rich which helped us understand the layout of the family tomb that was constructed in separated units arranged in order[75]. Three tombs of Liao and Jin were found during the construction of Olympic gyms in Wukesong ahead of the Olympics. Two of the three were identified as of Liao, all of which were oval shaped brick-chambered tombs. Pottery basins, pottery plates, pottery calyxes, and a few of ceramic wares such as porcelain bowls and plates as well as some Dark bottles were excavated in the tombs but rough in quality.

In general, the tombs of Liao dynasty discovered in Haidian include all types of Liao tombs found in other area of Beijing. Some tombs owned by the members with higher status in society identified pretty much rich in the relics were unearthed. The current studies of the tomb of Liao were narrowly focused on the date and the place of discovery, the type of the tomb, the study of murals and the study of funerary, etc. Nevertheless, comparing to the tombs of Liao found in other districts or counties, the tombs found in Haidian did not characterize any regional specifications. Therefore, the study of Liao tombs found in Haidian was taken as a typical part of the study whole to interpret the tombs located in Beijing area.

2. Prosperity of the Jurchen Jin Dynasty

In 1125, military forces of Jin attacked the Song and captured You and Yan areas, renamed Yanshan prefecture as Nanjing (the South Capital). In 1153, the Prince of Hailing Wanyan Liang moved the main capital to Nanjing and renamed it up to the Central Capital (Zhongdu). The establishment of the Central Capital not only opened up a new era for Beijing to develop but also at the same time became a great capital of the Yuan, Ming and Qing dynasties later on in the unban history. Thus we can say that the period under Jurchen Jin was an important period of time during when the city of Beijing had grown stronger. The northern walls of the Central Capital was not only overlapped with the walls of the Southern Capital of Khitan Liao but also overlapped with a small part of what is now Haidian.

A lot of tombs of Jurchen Jin dynasty were found in Haidian area. In 1956, a tomb owned by Zhang Ruyou was found at Erligou in Ganjiakou street. The tomb was destructed in its early years. According to a memorial tablet found in the tomb, we knew

71   *A Concise Archaeological Report on the Excavations of the Tombs of Khitan Liao Dynasty at Suburbs in Beijing*, authored by Su Tianjun; *Archaeology*, PP. 89-93, Issue No. 2, 1959.

72   *An Atlas of Chinese Cultural Relics*, edited by the State Administration of Cultural Heritage, *Beijing Part Two*, published by the Science Press, P. 213, 2008

73   *The Liao tombs Discovered at Yangfangdian in Haidian*, co-authored by Liu Liancheng, Li Da, quoted from the *1992-Chinese Archaeology Almanac*, P. 149, Beijing: Cultural Relics Press, 1994.

74   *Major Achievements in the Protection of Cultural Relics Preserved Underground in Beijing Area in 1998*, authored by Wang Youquan, the *Cultural Relics and Museums in Beijing*, PP. 10-12, Issue No. 1, 1999.

75   *Liao Tombs and Epitaph Tablets Discovered at the China Workers' College in Haidian*, authored by Zhu Zhigang, *Cultural Relics and Archaeology in Beijing*, Series No. 6, PP. 27-34, published by the Ethnic Publishing House, 2004.

that Zhang Ruyou was dead in the year of 1207[76]. The tomb of Pucha Huhsa was found at Niangniangfu village in the Qinglongqiao street in 1978. Pucha Husha was a nobleman wedded with the daughter of Emperor Shizong of Jin, and his elder sister got married with the emperor. This stone coffin tomb was ever robbed and stolen by thieves and vandals in its early years. The tomb was built by six slabstones with a rectangular stone bed under the coffin. Burn marks could be traced from the remains, and a memorial tablet was unearthed[77]. In 1979, a tomb of Jin was found in the south of the Banjieta village in Ganjiakou street. It was a single brick-chambered tomb which was 1.75meters long from east to west, 1.15meters wide from north to south and 0.6meters deep from top to the bottom. A narrow tomb passage was found in the northern part of the tomb but closed to the center. Cremated remains were placed in this tomb which was tapered off from bottom to the top and covered with quartzite slabs. A number of Chinese chess stones, turquoise jewelries, and bronze coins were unearthed[78].

In 1985, tombs of Jin dynasty were found and sorted out in Nanxin village in Sijiqing town under the auspices of the Institute of Cultural Management in Haidian. We found that the sarcophagi were buried in the Tombs M1 and M2. M1 was damaged and robbed by the Japanese armies in its early years. A white porcelain bowls of the Ding Kiln, melon-shaped wine vessels, plates, cases and a memorial tablet were unearthed in this tomb. The owner of the tomb was Zhang Kouzhen, a sinecure military official and a lieutenant general, and the tested date was from 1153 to 1160, the era of the Prince Hailing of Jin. M2 was a couple joint burial tomb, but had been robbed and stolen by thieves and vandals. Remains of a wooden coffin could be traced inside the tomb. A green glazed porcelain pillow painted in a pattern of broken colors, a white porcelain box of Ding Kiln, bowls, plates, wine vessels, pots, dishes, cosmetic cases, a black glazed saucer, a pottery inkstone, and a set of makeup tools kept in a paper box were unearthed. What we found in this tomb mentioned above gave us the whole knowledge about the funerary objects buried in the tombs of early Jin dynasty[79]. A group of early Ding Kiln porcelains were unearthed which reflected the differences of workmanship in good and bad quality. But in general, they had brought us the expression to the typical characters which were featured in the fine Ding Kiln white porcelains including the black glazed saucer as well. The Ding Kiln got the influence from the Cizhou Kiln in terms of what we knew about the craftsmanship and the techniques applied to the porcelain making. The green glazed porcelain pillow painted in a pattern of broken colors was a very important representation to help us know better about the porcelain manufacturing in the early years of Jin dynasty.

In 1987, a stone coffin tomb pit was found and sorted out at the foothills of the Jin Mountain in Sijiqing town. The excavation was organized by the Institute of Cultural Management in Haidian. This tomb was robbed and stolen by thieves and vandals in its early years. The stone coffin was made by mortise-tenon joints with six chiseled bluestones, which were 2.5 meter long, 1.41 meters wide and 1.2meters high. It has been identified that this tomb could be dated back to early Jin period. A Yuhu spring bottle of Jun Kiln as well as a plate and a bowl, and two lacquer box covers in interlocking flower pattern in black and red were unearthed in this tomb. In addition, some porcelain sherds

of the Jun Kiln and the Longquan Kiln were found at the entrance of the tomb[80]. A bowl of Jun Kiln is characterized by a water-caltrop flower pattern designed for the mouth rim of the bowl, and the Meiping (literally translated as plum vase) has with a narrow base, a wide body, a narrow neck, and a small opening, were unearthed. This stone coffin tomb pit dated back to the early years of the Jin dynasty was identified that it was owned by some Jurchen noble and his family. A few of pieces of porcelain of Jun Kiln unearthed in this tomb provided us the most important archaeological evidence for the confirmation of the time when the kiln was created.

In 1998, a tomb of Jin dynasty was sorted out in the Beijing Botanic Garden under the auspices of the Institute of Cultural Management in Haidian. The brick-chambered tomb was rectangular in shape and formed with arched top. A porcelain pillow of Cizhou Kiln oval in shape designed on a motif of children at play with floral pattern in black on white ground together with the Dadingtongbao bronze coins were unearthed. This tomb was dated back to the 18th year (1178) of Dading reign of Emperor Shizong of the Jurchen Jin dynasty, that is to say that the date should be pushed back after the coins were minted[81]. It could be proved from the unearthed porcelain pillow that this kind of pillows were actually produced in the year of late Jin dynasty, not as they had always been identified as the production of the Song dynasty.

Moreover, Jin tombs were also found in the Peking University[82] as well as in other areas like Beianhe[83], but no detailed information was reported. Most of the Jin tombs found in Haidian district were the stone coffin pits very much fashioned in the Jin dynasty. We knew that this type of tombs located in Beijing and its surrounding areas such as Hebei were used for burying the corpses of the dead people who were mainly the Jurchen nobles and or the Khitan nobles who had surrendered to Jurchen Jin since the Jin dynasty was established. There were some funerary objects restricted to the higher social level people more than often found in the Jin tombs as well. Such tombs were normally found in clusters in the Beijing area especially at Jinling in Fangshan county and Haidian. It seemed to indicate that Haidian was a district where many of the Jurchen nobles lived in at that time.

There was a special event happened in history in the Beijing area during the Jin dynasty. That is at the beginning of the war against Song power, two marshal-commanders of Jin, Wanyan Zonghan (Nianhan) and Wanyan Zongwang (Wolibu) had their forces stationed at Yun and Yan prefectures as a base to attack the Song armies. After the Jingkang Incident, the Jin troops commanded by the two marshals captured the two Emperors of Song to Wuguotou city in the north bypass the Yan prefecture. Military officers and soldiers under their command looted the Yun and Yan prefectures and carried off a great amount of elaborate and costly manufactured articles which were made in the late Northern Song period. Some of the articles could be found in areas around Beijing which helped us understand some political systems and manufacturing conditions existed in the second half of Song dynasty. As I mentioned above, the group of porcelain wares of Jun Kiln found in the tomb of Jin dynasty at Jinshan in Sijiqing were presumably produced in Henan area. The porcelain wares were spoiled and taken off by the Jin troops back to their military base in Yan prefecture during the Song-Jin wars, and buried with the dead later on in the tomb of Jurchen Jin period. Those wares provided us some important information that the Jun Kiln was created at the end of Song period. A Dasheng chime bell was discovered as the sand was being dredged from the waterway in Sijiqing county in 1986.

76   *An examination on the Interpretations to the Zhang Ruyou's Epitaph*, authored by Hou E, *Cultural Relics and Archaeology in Beijing*, Series No. 2, PP. 152-157. published by the Beijing Yanshan Press, 1991; *Historical Atlas of Khitan Liao and Jurchen Jin*, edited by Beijing Municipal Administration of Cultural Heritage, P. 217, published by the Beijing Yanshan Press, 2003.

77   *An examination on the Pucha's Epitaph During the Jurchen Jin Dynasty*, *Essays on the History of Bejing*, Series No. 1, PP. 101-105, edited and printed by the Research Association of the History of Beijing, 1980. See also *40 Years Archaeological Discoveries in Beijing*, edited by the Beijing Municipal Institute of Cultural Relics, P. 166, published by the Beijing Yanshan Press, 1990.

78   *An Atlas of Chinese Cultural Relics*, edited by the State Administration of Cultural Heritage, *Beijing Part Two*, published by the Science Press, P. 214, 2008

79   *A Concise Report on the Clear-up of the Tombs of Jurchen Jin Discovered in Nanxinzhuang Haidian Beijing*, edited by Haidian Bureau of Cultural Affairs, *Cultural Heritage*, Issue No. 7, PP. 56-66, 1990.

80   *Discussions on the Discovery of a Group of Jun Wares in Haidian and Related Issues*, co-authored by Qin Dashu, Wang Xiaojun,*Cultural Heritage*, Issue No. 11, PP. 80-92, 2002. See also *An Atlas of Chinese Cultural Relics*, edited by the State Administration of Cultural Heritage, *Beijing Part Two*, published by the Science Press, P. 214, 2008.

81   *A Cizhou Porcelain Pillow Unearthed in Haidian*, authored by Gao Eryue, *Cultural Relics and Museums in Beijing*, P. 76, Issue No. 1, 2000.

82   *Important Ancient Tombs and Historical Ruins Discovered in the City of Beijing Over the Past Ten Years*, authored by Su Tianjun, *Archaeology*, Issue No. 3, P. 160, 1959.

83   *40 Years Archaeological Discoveries in Beijing*, edited by the Beijing Municipal Institute of Cultural Relics, P. 167, published by the Beijing Yanshan Press, 1990.

It is now currently in the Haidian Museum[84]. A large number of new sacrificial vessels represented by the Dasheng chime bells were produced in the time of Emperor Huizong. Most of the chime bells were taken by the Jin troops and carried to Shangjing where the Jurchen Jin originally came from after the Jingkang Incident took place. The Dasheng chime bells were used for ritual ceremonies at the imperial court around the middle of Jin period. Survived chime bells had been collected by the Palace Museum in Beijing and National Palace Museum in Taipei. The discovery of the chime bell was the only case among the large number of objects excavated in the tombs of late Jin dynasty, probably they were given up by the Jurchen Jin soldiers after they looted the Song court during the wars. The discovery of the chime bell is an important significance in academic studies.

3. The Period of Mongolia Yuan

In the third year (1215) of Zhenyou reign of Jin dynasty, Mongolian troops occupied the Central Capital of Jin. The Mongols changed their policy thereafter from "to get the place but not to keep it" to take the control of the capital and to manage it. Therefore, the Central Capital was the first place to have stable development in the area where had been ever controlled by Song and Jin before. In the second year (1261) of Zhongtong reign of Yuan dynasty, Kublai Khan ordered to repair the walls of Yan Capital, but right after he abandoned the plan to reconstruct the Central Capital of Jin. A new capital was being built in the northeast Central Capital of Jin in the 4th year (1267) of Zhiyuan reign of the Yuan dynasty, the main part of the city was almost accomplished 20 years later. The construction of the new capital made Beijing developed from a core city at the local level to a center of politics, economy and culture of the Mongolian Yuan Empire. Archaeological work on Dadu of Yuan (literally the Great Capital) was the earliest to raise the concerns in academia. Efforts had been contributed to the studies by some learning communities since the Republic period. Between the years of 1964 and 1974, team members from the Institute of Archaeology at Chinese Academy of Sciences and a cultural relics work team from Beijing were joined together to form a new team to conduct exploration on the ruined city walls, streets, lakes, rivers, waterways and other relics of Dadu. There was no doubt that any archaeological achievements related to Beijing at Dadu area in Song, Yuan and Ming periods by the new team were rich and important.

The Great Capital was established in the northeast part of the Central Capital. The ruins of its walls in the northwest were scattering across the area of what is now Haidian, it was at the western part of the Beitucheng. The western gate (known as the gate of Jiande) of the city walls in the north and the northern gate (known as the gate of Suqing) of the city walls in the west snaked inside what is now Haidian district. The west section of the Dadu city wall ruins in the north and the north end of the city wall ruins in the west have survived today which could be traced in what is now Haidian from the Mingguang village in the south College Road in the Taipingzhuang North Street residential community to northward the Zhichun Road intersection and then to eastward. The wall ruins remained today is 4km long. Three culvert relics sites have been sorted out at city wall ruins in the north by the Yuan Dadu Archaeological Team, two of the culverts found at the Garden road and the College road are located within Haidian[85]. The top of the remained ruins is about 8 meters high, 22 to 24 meters wide, constructed with the rammed earth, and the rammed holes for building can be clearly seen[86]. In 1992, an anatomical excavation of the Dadu city wall ruins located to the north of Taipingzhuang under the auspices of the Beijing Municipal Institute of Cultural Relics was conducted. The excavation of the wall ruins proved that the walls were consisted of four types of soil in different layers, which tells us that the Dadu city had been repaired and constructed many times[87]. At the same time, the north section of the Dadu city walls in the west was cleared up too with the help from the Institute of Cultural Relics of Haidian when one of the Eight Great Sights of Yanjing (or Eight Sceneries of Beijing) built in the period of Emperor Qianlong, called Jimenyanshu (foggy trees of Jimen) was planned to be restored to its original state. Two bronze artillery canons made in the end of the Ming dynasty were unearthed.

In addition, a culvert relics site located on the west side of the Western Tucheng Road was found, which was under west section of the city walls in the north. The culvert site discovered in the north of the gate of Suqing was paved and covered with slabstones both on the bottom and on the walls. Three layers of bricks were laid above three arches, which was the ritual regulation for city building. The inlet and outlet in a 6.5 meter long for water runoff were built with stones inside and outside the culvert. The bottom of the stone culvert was slightly outward tilted. This culvert site was cleared up by the Yuan Dadu Archaeological Team, but was a little damaged due to the poor protection of its ruins. In 2002, the culvert site was excavated again for the second time under the auspices of the Beijing Municipal Institute of Cultural Relics in order to understand further about the structure of the whole culvert for protection. We knew from the re-excavation that the culvert was constructed before the rammed earth walls were built. The north-south oriented water culvert was 9.5 meters long and 3.45 meters high. In the center of culvert, there was a row of iron gate sticks featured in diamond shape with 10 to 15 cm spacing between the sticks. Iron ingots (wasp-waisted shape) were used for reinforcement both on the bottom and on the walls. It was significant in the discovery of the culvert site which enabled us to understand and study the drainage system built in Dadu of Yuan dynasty[88].

Not many tombs of Yuan dynasty had yet been found in Haidian area. But in 1998, a tomb with Yelü Zhu and his wife buried was excavated under the auspices of the Beijing Municipal Institute of Cultural Relics in the Summer Palace. The tomb dated back to the year of 1285 the 22nd year of Zhiyuan reign. This is a very important archaeological site of that period[89]. Yelü Zhu, the second son of Yelü Chucai, was the chancellor of the executive, examination, and legislative bureaus, with a high political status at the imperial court during the Yuan dynasty. This was a wood imitation structured brick-multichambered tomb consisted of a passage, an entrance to the coffin chamber, an antechamber with side chambers on the east side and the west side, and a rear chamber with side chambers on the east side and the west side. The tomb passage was constructed right in the center on the south side of the antechamber. There were two tombstones shaped in half round head stone were found erected side by side somewhere above the passage near to the entrance of the tomb. Murals were painted on the walls inside the tomb, but most of them were damaged except some patterns of clouds, followers and plants, and birds and animals could be seen. This tomb was robbed and stolen by vandals in its early years, but was very much rich in funerary objects unearthed, including porcelain wares, pottery wares, silver wares, stone tools and some accessories more than 180 in total. The porcelain wares included a Bluish White glazed high-footed bowl, a plate painted with double-fish pattern, and a Yuhu Spring bottle. The Bluish White glazed high-footed bowl was 12.5 cm in diameter, 4.5 cm in diameter on bottom and 9.5 cm high, wide mouth with pointed rim, swelling body tapering downwards, splayed ring foot with the foot end flared out. The body of the bowl was marked with cloud and thunder pattern engraved with two Chinese characters " 白 "and " 王 "(literally as "white" and "king"). Terracotta figurines were 48 in total very poor in quality. Most of the figurines were shaped in spiritual images appeared in mythology, for instance, the figurines carried with boards indicating the Chinese system for reckoning time, the figurines shaped in male and female servants who were carrying with all sorts of wares used in every day life, and the figurines shaped in mythical creatures and animals like dragon, phoenix, horse and

84　*The Haidian Museum*, edited by the Haidian Museum in Beijing, PP. 156-159, published by Cultural Relics Press, 2005.

85　*Exploration and Excavation Activities in Khanbaliq*, co-authored by the Yuan Dadu Archaeological Team, *Archaeology*, PP. 19 - 28, Issue No. 1, 1972; *Exploration and Excavation Activities in Khanbaliq* featuring *Critical Reviews of the Chinese Archaeology*, authored by Xu Pingfang, PP. 159-172, published by Asian Culture, Taipei, 1995.

86　*An Atlas of Chinese Cultural Relics*, edited by the State Administration of Cultural Heritage, *Beijing Part Two*, published by the Science Press, P. 209, 2008.

87　*An Atlas of Chinese Cultural Relics*, edited by the State Administration of Cultural Heritage, *Beijing Part Two*, published by the Science Press, P. 209, 2008.

88　*A Concise Report on the Exploration at the North City Wall Ruins Nearby Huayuan Road in Khanbaliq and Clear-up of the Culvert Ruins Site*, authored by Li Hua, Beijing Archaeology, Series No. 1, published by the Beijing Yanshan Press, 2008.

89　*A Introduction to the Tomb of Yelü Zhu Couple*, authored by Cheng Li, *Cultural Relics and Museums in Beijing*, Illustration 3-4, Issue No. 4, 1998; *The Tomb of Yelü Zhu Couple of Yuan Dynasty Beijing*, presented by the Beijing Municipal Institute of Cultural Relics, in the *Important Archaeological Discoveries in 1998 China*, PP. 111-115, published by the Cultural Relics Press, 2000.

camel. Figures of pegasus and dog chiseled out with white marble, a group of eight burial objects made in jade including plate, bowl, pot and saucer were found in the tomb as well. The white marble pegasus was 64 cm long, 30 cm wide, 50 cm in full length, set on a base in 55 cm long. The pegasus had a slender body with its four hoof short engraved in circus clouds as the background, a base was set underneath which was sophisticatedly carved. The tomb of Yelü Zhu was typical in its shape and rich in its buried funerary articles, the discovery of the tomb provided us indispensable information available for the study of funeral rules that took shape during the early years of Yuan dynasty.

In the year of 1971, a single brick-chambered tomb of Yuan dynasty was found at the Yongding road in Dayou village. Some ceramic wares and bronze coins were unearthed[90]. In 1985, a brick-chambered tomb of Yuan in small size was cleared up at the No2. compound in the Department of Aerospace Industry. A bluish white glazed plum bottle of Jingdezhen Kiln made in Yuan period, a set of black pottery funerary objects including a pot, a tub, a bowl, an ax, and a zun wine vessel were unearthed[91].

The tomb and the ancestral temple of Yelü Chucai as important historical relics had been remained down on the east bank of Kunming Lake in the Summer Palace. The tomb and the temple were located to the north of Wenchang Pavillion, a set of two-building double-courtyard complex with tomb and temple built together. The main house in the first building and courtyard was the ancestral hall separated into three rooms with a pottery sculpture of Yelü Chucai is worshiped inside the hall. A tombstone up to 3 meters high was erected in the courtyard. On the front side of the tablet there was an inscription of the tombstone records on Yelü Chucai written in the 15th year (1750) of Emperor Qianlong, on the back of the tablet there was another tombstone records on the Chancellor of Yuan written by the Grand Secretary Wang Youdun. A stone statue was erected near to the tablet. When we got into the second courtyard, three rooms on the north come into view, Yelü Chucai and his remarried wife from the Su family were buried in a tumulus inside one of the three rooms. According to his will before he died, the tomb of Yelü Chucai was built on the riverbank of the Wongshan Lake known as the Kunming Lake in the Yuan dynasty. Erecting of a monument on the tomb site was considered a grand ceremony at that time. The tomb complex had become a famous attractive spot in the west skirt of Dadu and a memorial site where people paid their respects and created poems to cherish the memory of the great man. The cemetery was completely destroyed at the beginning of Ming Dynasty, the tumulus and the ancestral temple were restored at the original site in the time of Emperor Qianlong of Qing at the time when the Garden of Limpid Ripples was being built. A tombstone was erected which recorded the biography of Yelü Chucai and highlighted the merits and virtues of his life. In 1860, the ancestral temple and cemetery were burned down by the Anglo-French Allied Forces. The survived ancestral temple, tumulus and other buildings were reconstructed by following the old rules for tomb building during the years of Emperor Guangxu (1875 to 1908)[92].

In addition, in the year of 1983, three kilns of Yuan dynasty were found at the south side of Gongzhufen in Yangfangdian Street. The kiln wall was about 1 meter high, 0.3 meter thick. A few of black glazed porcelain sherds, all kinds of color glazed architectural components and kiln furniture including white glazed bricks, green glazed bricks, plain glazed bricks, grooved bricks, tile-ends, pan tiles, a green glazed dome, and some kiln furniture were unearthed. In could be speculated from the location of the kilns and unearthed articles as well as the historical documents that the so-called west kiln plant was presumably built in the 4th year of the Zhiyuan reign of Yuan dynasty[93].

In general, the archaeological investigation and excavation in Yuan dynasty in the Beijing area were in fact centered in the Dadu city. A large number of important historical relics were found within the Haidian district, furthermore, quite a lot of crucial remains and written materials were discovered during the archaeological work, which developed the further study on Dadu of Yuan. About 50 Yuan tombs had been found in the Beijing area until the year of 2009. Although the Yuan tombs discovered less than the Jin tombs in number, they were widely located in many places. Yuan tombs found in Haidian were not many, but the excavation of the tomb of Yelü Zhu and his wife and the discovery of a memorial tablet provided us precious information about political participation, religious involvement, ideological thoughts and the integration of ethnic groups occurred in the Yuan dynasty. Besides, the color glazed porcelain kilns located in Yangfangdian Street were found rare in previous years which provided us an important material evidence for the study of ceramic glazing technology used in the productions for the imperial court of the Yuan dynasty.

VI. Excellent Place to Live: Cultural Relics of Ming and Qing Dynasties in Haidian

1. Haidian during Ming Dynasty[94]

The Dadu city was attacked and occupied by the Ming troops and got shrunk south by about 5 li (approximately 60 km) shortly thereafter. The change of the city boundaries finalized the layout of the inner city of Beijing in Ming and Qing dynasties. The area originally settled as a part of the city of Dadu was basically abandoned in what is now Haidian district, which later came to be the suburbs of Haidian. In the 19th year (1421) of Yongle reign, Emperor Chengzu of Ming moved his capital to Beijing, the layout of the city was maintained without any changes. The land in the Haidian area was separately under the jurisdiction of Wanping and Changping counties. Haidian district became an important burial area during the Ming dynasty. Not only were the tombs of the concubines found at the foot of the mountain where the tomb of eunuch Dongsi was located, but the tombs of princes and princesses were also found near to Wofosi (literally as Temple of Sleeping Buddha) in the Siwangzi village. The Mausoleum of Emperor Jingtai, one of the three emperors buried well away from the Ming Imperial Tombs, was found in the hills of Jinshankou located in Qinglongqiao. This mausoleum was extended and rebuilt from the tomb of Prince Cheng of Ming, where the Emperor Jintai was buried after he failed in the political struggles at the imperial court. No matter what political tricks Emperor Yingzong used for getting back to the throne, none the less, the Emperor Jintai was eventually buried here. Because of the best conditions in this place, where buildings that had been constructed were suitable with the surrounding environment, we could figure out that there was no big difference between this place and the Ming Imperial Tombs in terms of beautiful landscape and the harmonious arrangement of the place. That was why the imperial family members and the nobilities chose this place to build up their graves. There was a saying kind of popular among people that is literally as "look at the imperial palaces built at the foot of the mountains: they are actually 72 tombs there." One thing that has to be mentioned here is that the group of eunuchs who gained immense power in their political life during the Ming dynasty, most of them too preferred to be buried at a place with good environment and excellent scenery as well as with temples surrounded, because they believed that a state of perfect spiritual enlightenment could be achieved at here[95].

Tombs of Ming dynasty were found many in Haidian. Tombs that belonged to superior class were the tombs of concubines, princes, princesses, relatives of the imperial family, and the eunuchs. Many more tombs of civilians were also found in the same area. The tombs of superior class were concrete constructions a composite material composed of coarse granular material and cement widely used for buildings at that time. In addition,

90   *An Atlas of Chinese Cultural Relics*, edited by the State Administration of Cultural Heritage, *Beijing Part Two*, published by the Science Press, P. 215, 2008.

91   *Thousands Of Years Throughout History-Historical Relics In Haidian*, edited by Li Ang, PP. 45-47, Haidian Museum, Beijing, 2012.

92   *Historical Atlas of Yuan Dynasty in Beijing*, edited by the Beijing Liao and Jin Dynasty City Wall Museum, P. 283, published by the Beijing Yanshan Press, 2009.

93   *A Couple of Color-glazed Wares Kiln Found in Beijing Area in Recent Years*, authored by Zhao Guanglin, in *Archaeology*, PP. 628-631, Issue No. 7, 1986.

94   This subtitle is taken from *A Note on the Riverbank Surrounded by Beautiful Stones and Precious Trees*, authored by Wang Jiamo of Ming dynasty, in an article written by a court official from Shangdu of Yuan Empire, here goes, "the God given Hills and mountains and beautiful landscapes are the best place for us to live", featuring in the *Local Records and Chronicles*, Sun Chengze of Qing dynasty, Vol. 65, PP. 1265-1266, Beijing Classics Publishing House, 1992.

95   *The Eunuch's Funeral during the Ming Dynasty*, authored by Liu Yaohui, in *Cultural Relics and Museums in Beijing*, PP. 25-39, Issue No. 3, 2001.

a small number of stone coffin tombs with stone carvings in beautiful patterns were discovered as well[96]. The epitaph tablet found in the tightly sealed tomb was accompanied with a stone cover; characters were engraved into the face side of the cover. The tablet was secured with two wrought-iron straps. Objects buried in the tomb were usually the old money used in previous dynasties or the flowery coins known as the yasheng coins in various patterns.

There were various types of tombs for the remains of the dead in terms of shapes and materials designed and used for the construction of the tomb, mainly the vertical coffin pits were widely built at that time. Other types of tombs were categorized as the brick-chambered ones, or the cremation tombs in which pots that contain bone ashes were buried, or the concrete constructed tombs, or the octagonal or hexagonal brick or stone tombs, etc. In the vertical coffin pits, funeral utensils made of wood such as a coffin without an outer coffin were usually buried in the tomb. Depended on the number of the corpses of the dead humans that were buried, we found single-coffin tombs, double-coffin tombs and multi-coffin tombs in the burial pits, the former two kinds of tombs could be seen very often, but the multi-coffin tombs were found less[97]. The brick-chambered tombs were not same in scale but different in structure and materials. Most of the tombs were constructed with bricks for making the coffin chamber. Stones or slabstones were used to cover on the top of the coffin chamber where we could find some funeral utensils placed on the stone coffin platform. This kind of tombs were owned by the deceased who obviously came from the higher class gentry in the society, and the objects unearthed in the tombs were rich. A great amount of beautiful and exquisite Ming dynasty historical artifacts and cultural relics collected by Capital Museum and Haidian Museum were almost unearthed from this sort of tombs.

Different from the Song mausoleum, no satellite tombs were constructed beside the royal mausoleum of the Ming dynasty. The princes of the Ming dynasty were titled with nominal lordship over various fiefs throughout Ming territories and buried in their own land after death. Since we knew that the empress was usually buried together with the emperor after their death, there were no tombs in which a single member of the royal family was buried alone except the tombs of concubines. There were two ways to have the concubines buried when they were probably still alive: one was to be buried with the dead emperor, the other was not to be. Gu Yanwu in his Memoir of the Landscape Sight in Changping wrote that no maids or concubines were prohibited to be buried with the emperor after the Emperor Yingzong took the power, hence, the tombs of concubines appeared, they were buried in tombs built in mountains or other places[98]. Some tombs of concubines in Beijing area are located at the East Well and the West Well within the Ming Royal Tombs area, some others are located in Jinshan what is now the northwest of Qinglongqiao in Haidian. The mountain got its name Jinshan (literally as the Gold Mountain) in the period of Ming dynasty. Princes and princesses were buried here. The Dialogue by A Traveler from Chang'an writes that all princes and princesses were buried at the entrance of the Gold Mountain, a beautiful place where could be matched up with the Jing mausoleum, concubines were buried at the same place too[99]. Jinshan or the Gold Mountain is another place out of the Ming royal tombs that concubine tombs are mainly located in. The tombs of concubines were more than the ones found in the Ming Tombs area[100]. According to the historical documents, there had a number of 53 such tombs built in Jinshan until the 11th year of Shunzhi reign of Qing dynasty. Some villages like the East

Four Tombs and the West Four Tombs were named after the tombs.

The historically important tombs of concubines excavated in Haidian are those located in eunuch Dongsi tomb village. They are the concubines of Emperor Tianqi and Emperor Wanli. From August to November in the year of 1951, two tombs of concubines were cleared up at the Dongsi tomb village in Jinshan, ten concubines were buried in these tombs. Three concubines of Emperor Tianqi were buried in the Tomb No. 1, which were consisted of a frustum on top with the roof pommel at the apex, an entrance, an antechamber, and a coffin chamber. The dome was about 4 meters high out of rammed earth mixed up with lime. It was constructed behind the coffin chamber but not directly above the underground burial chamber. The underground chamber was a palatial architecture on the H-shaped flat plane consisted of two parts: the antechamber and the main coffin chamber. H-shaped palace was the standard model according to architectural regulations in the time of Ming, which was reflected in the construction of the tomb. Tomb chambers were separated by stone doors. Each chamber in wood imitation structure had its own roof on top. The main chamber had a double-eaved roof with one horizontal and four sloping ridges. The horizontal ridge was about 13.8 meters long and 7.2 meters high used by the glazed architectural components. At the back of the main chamber to the tomb wall there were three coffins placed on the stone coffin platform constructed in slabstones. Each one of the epitaphs to each one of the coffins was placed next to the coffin close to the back wall. The inscription was carved inside the epitaph tablet which was secured with two wrought-iron straps and covered with wooden case outside. We could know from the place where the epitaph was set next to the tomb of concubine Zhangyu of Emperor Tianqi on the left side, concubine Duanchun's tomb was in the middle, concubine Licheng was on the right. Tombs had been robbed and stolen for many times, thus the unearthed objects buried with the deceased were not many except a Chinese Blue and White porcelain inscribed with Chinese characters as Made in the year of Emperor Wanli of the Great Ming Empire, and three bluish white plum porcelain vases, hair accessories suit to the phoenix coronet including golden hairpins, jade accessories set in phoenix coronet, jade belt buckles carved in relief, different sizes of pearls probably the accessories set in the phoenix coronet too or inlaid in the gold jewelries, coins, and combs or fine-toothed combs were discovered[101]. More than thousand of the pearls were found in total.

Seven concubines of Emperor Wanli were buried in the tomb No.2, which is located 300 meters northeast of the tomb No. 1. Tomb No. 2 was consisted of a frustum on top with the roof pommel at the apex, an entrance, an antechamber, and a coffin chamber. The plane view of the tomb chamber was H-shaped constructed similar to the tomb No.1. Tomb chambers were built up with stones and bricks in cottage style bungalows. Room ridge was constructed by using the huge bricks shaped in semicircle connected together to form an arch roof. The ground of the chamber was paved with a layer of square bricks above which there were three concrete stairs on both the north and the south sides, each of the stair was about 0.5 meter high. Sacrificial articles were for the most of the time placed in the antechamber. There were two stone armchairs in front of the stone gate one on each side. The armchairs were very much like the emperors' thrones located in the three grand halls in the Forbidden City; sophisticated engraving patterns could be seen on the back and two sides of the stone armchair. Incense burners, candlesticks, vases and ever-burning lamps were placed in front of the stone chair. Two wooden frames used at the Emperor's honor guardian's ceremonial site were placed on east and west side of the chair. Two epitaph tablets were on the west side, and three on the east side. The coffin platform was in the back of the chamber, two well-preserved epitaph tablets were found in central east side to the coffin platform. Seven coffins fall scattered next to the coffin platform, three of them had not yet been stolen and robbed. The funerary objects unearthed were various in different categories. In the first category there were all kinds of daily necessities, such as, basin, compact, blusher and bronze mirror in gold or silver. Moreover, porcelain wares found in the coffin No.3 included a

96   More than 40 tombs of eunuchs or nobles have ever been cleared up under the auspices of the Haidian Institute of Cultural Heritage. In those tombs a number of Sarcophagi made of slabstones are found with fine stone carvings. The carved stones originally are hidden in the institute mentioned above, but now disappeared.

97   *Archaeological Discoveries and Studies in Beijing 1949-2009 Part Two*, edited by Song Dachuan, P. 390, published by the Science Press, 2009.

98   *Memoir of the Landscape Sight in Changping*, edited by Gu Yanwu, Vol. I, P. 18, published by the Beijing Classics Publishing House, 1982 edition.

99   *The Dialogue by A Traveler from Chang'an*, authored by Jiang Yikui of Ming dynasty, published by the Beijing Classics Publishing House, 1980 edition.

100   *Archaeological Discoveries in Beijing the Ming Period*, authored by Li Yongqiang, P. 34, published by the Shanghai Classics Publishing House, 2012.

101   *Accounts on the Tomb No. 1 Excavated at Dongsi Tomb Village in the Western Suburbs of Beijing*, co-authored by the Correspondence Unit in the Institute of Archaeology, from the *Reference Materials for the Cultural Relics*, PP. 78-87, Issue No. 2, 1952.

white porcelain plum vase with veiled ornamentation made in the year of Emperor Jiajing of the Great Ming Empire, an under-glazed blue plum vase in interlocking Indian lotus pattern made in the year of Emperor Wanli of the Great Ming Empire, and two silver ingots each weighted about 50 taels were found in the coffin No.2. We could know from the mark inscribed in the ingot that they were minted in the 15the and the 16th years of Wanli reign. The ingots were taxes levied by the local government in Fujian Province, paid by the subjects and turned into the imperial treasury at last. In the second category ritual instruments for god worshiping were presented. For example, two clock shaped ritual instruments in copper found in coffin No.2 were inscribed with incantations and signs in Sanskrit and Tibetan. Some other porcelain wares were classified in this category too. Hairpin crowns, accessories like bracelets, earrings, and phoenix coronet including some costumes were in the third category. A phoenix coronet composed of 23 hairpins with pearls set into it was found in the coffin No.2. In the category No. 4, a special sort of funerary objects which had formed since the Song dynasty were found in coffin No.2. Some wood carving figurines shaped in chariot, in horse, in maid, in servant, and in all kinds of sacrifices to serve were vividly created in small size[102]. A number of hundreds of such figurines were found at the front and the back chambers in tomb No.2, but found many in the antechamber next to the parade in mini version. By looking at the figurines sculpted in different appearances, we could figured out that they were political officials, military officials, eunuchs, yamen runners and civilians from the costumes they dressed. This sort of funerary objects should be the important objects buried with the superior deceased in the Ming tombs.

This sort of funerary objects excavated in the tomb of Emperor Wanli known as Dingling were an alloy of tin and lead, although they were not in good quality. Something appeared from the scene at the archaeological site made us understand the royal lifestyle at that time. Items unearthed in these tombs encompassed all kinds of artifacts sorted into all categories that had been found in the Ming tombs located in Haidian in general. The items from Ming dynasty on display in Haidian Museum were classified into the similar categories. According to the epitaph tablets unearthed, there were seven concubine consorts of Emperor Wanli buried in the tomb No.2. The concubine consorts were Zhang Shun, Geng Dao, Shao Jing, Wei Shen, Li Rong, Li De, and Liang He[103].

In 1963, seven tombs of concubines of the Ming Emperor Chuanghua were found in Xianghongqiying (literally as rimmed red banner camp) later renamed as Xianghongqi (literally as compartment banner camp). The north-south oriented tombs were horizontally lined up side by side on shady slope in the Gold Mountains. The roof pommel was gone, but we could know from the ruins of the tombs that they were constructed by using materials of rammed sand, lime and earth. Tomb chambers were all H-shaped built with bricks in cottage style bungalows consisted of a tomb gate, antechamber and chamber in the back. The round base of the roof pommel at the apex and pendentives in the antechamber and rear chamber were covered with square bricks, although ridge crestings were not there. A stone throne was next to the back wall at the center. Five containers including sacrificial offerings to ancestors, sacrificial utensils and ever-burning lamps were placed in front of the throne. A marble platform for the coffin was set at the center in the rear chamber. An outer coffin was rested on the coffin platform in which a square shaped hole known as the gold well filled with the first shovel of soil as the time when this place was selected to build a tomb. All tombs had been robbed and stolen, but epitaph tablets were found in three of them. According to the unearthed epitaph tablets we knew that a few of accessories, diamonds and pearls were excavated in the tombs of concubine consort Jingshun, concubine consort Zhuangyide, and

concubine consort Hehuijing of the Emperor Chenghua[104]. Other tombs like the tomb[105] of concubine consort Shenxian of Emperor Wuzong located in southern area of the Gold Mountain was excavated in the year of 1996, and the tomb of concubine consort Rongshuxian who died in the 6th year (1462) of Tianshun reign found in the Xishan Office compound of the National Government Offices Administration at the Xiangshan subdistrict Xulun Hoh Banner was excavated in the year of 1998[106]. Because the tombs were probably constructed in the early years of Ming dynasty, all consisted of double chambers at the front and the rear in rectangular shape and all with an arched roof on top of the brick chamber, but not in H-shaped like what we have known the so called veranda great hall with hipped roof and one horizontal and four sloping ridges.

A large number of tombs of princes and princesses of Ming dynasty were found in Haidian district as well as several tombs of relatives of the emperor on the side of his mother or wife. Most of the tombs were destructed or stolen throughout the years therefore could not be clearly seen in shape and structure. Thus, the funerary objects unearthed were very few in number, but a numerous epitaph tablets were excavated. Two princes' tombs through archaeological excavations were considered as the important discoveries. One was the tomb of Crown Prince Daogong (Zhu Youj)[107] the second son of Emperor Xianzong of Ming. He was buried in the 8th year (1473) of Chenghua reign. His tomb was located in in the Xishan Office compound of the National Government Offices Administration at the Xiangshan subdistrict in Haidian. This was a brick-chambered tomb found in 1998, and was stolen and seriously destructed by vandals in its early years. The tomb was 11 meters long from north to south and 4 meters wide from east to west, consisted of a tomb passage, front and rear chambers and arched roof. Two green glazed pottery containers, three green glazed pottery kettles, one white glazed pottery jars and an epitaph tablet inscribed with Chinese characters as the epitaph of Crown Prince Daogong were found. The other one was the tomb of Emperor Xianzong's eldest son Zhu Jianshen who died in the second year (1547) of Chenghua reign found in the Academy of Military Science at the Xiangshan subdistrict Haidian. In 2001, a rescue excavation was conducted on the tomb under the auspices of Beijing Municipal Institute of Cultural Relics. This brick and stone tomb was consisted of a passage, a gate, a front chamber and a rear chamber. It was stolen in its early years, an epitaph tablet, an under glazed plum vase and three gold jewelries were unearthed. The tomb was a vertical rectangular in shape with a sloping passage leading to the coffin chamber. In the end of the tomb passage there was a load bearing wall built up with wall bricks. There were two stone doors closed right at the center of the north load bearing wall. The front chamber was constructed rectangular in shape with a double hipped roof, and was floored with square bricks. A carved stone throne was placed at the center in the north; the five sacrificial utensils and ever-burning lamp were put in front of the throne. A glazed pottery lamp holder was kept on the top of the lamp. Door seal bricks and stone doors were seen along in the passageway. The rear chamber was constructed similar to the front chamber but a slightly lower than the later. A platform for placing the sarcophagus on it was put right in the middle of the coffin chamber, a hole shaped in rectangular at the center of the platform known as the gold well[108] was there. The tomb owner was Zhu Jianshen who was given the birth by the most favorite concubine consort Wan of Emperor Chenghua. Therefore, we could imagine that the uniqueness of the tomb was taken for granted.

After excavation of the tombs of princesses, two tombs were found important.

102   *The Form of Literature Works and Private Literati Etiquette*, Vol. 7, *Funeral Rites III*, vocabulary entry: *Burial Objects, Constructions Outside the Tomb, Big Dance Props, and Tablets*, edited by Sima Guang, from the *Complete Collection in Four Branches of Literature*, stored in the Wenyuan Chamber, Book 142, P. 503, a photocopy of the original, published by the Commercial Press copy Taipei: , 1983 edition.

103   *Accounts on the Tomb No. 2 Excavated at Dongsi Tomb Village in the Western Suburbs of Beijing*, co-authored by the Correspondence Unit in the Western Suburbs Excavation Group in the Institute of Archaeology, Chinese Academy of Sciences, from the *Reference Materials for the Cultural Relics*, PP. 88-100, Issue No. 2, 1952.

104   *40 Years Archaeological Discoveries in Beijing*, edited by the Beijing Municipal Institute of Cultural Relics, P. 203, published by the Beijing Yanshan Press, 1990.

105   *Archaeological Discoveries in Beijing the Ming Period*, authored by Li Yongqiang, P. 37, published by the Shanghai Classics Publishing House, 2012.

106   *Archaeological Discoveries in Beijing the Ming Period*, authored by Li Yongqiang, P. 38, published by the Shanghai Classics Publishing House, 2012.

107   *An Atlas of Chinese Cultural Relics*, edited by the State Administration of Cultural Heritage, *Beijing Part Two*, published by the Science Press, P. 215, 2008.

108   *A Concise Report on the Tomb of the Ming Crown Prince Excavated at the Academy of Military located in Xiangshan Subdistrict in Haidian*, authored by Wang Yanling, *Cultural Relics and Archaeology in Beijing*, Series No. 5, 2002.

One was the tomb of Princess Taikang the daughter of Emperor Xiaozong[109] located in the east side of the Xulun Hoh Banner village at the Xiangshan Street. She was dead in year 11 (1498) of Hongzhi era. This tomb was destructed in its early years, thus, the shape and the structure of the tomb were not in detail. There was nothing left but an epitaph tablet remained. The other one was the tomb of Princess Royal Suiping which was located in Baojiyao village in Sijiqing County[110]. This was a brick-chambered tomb rectangular in shape with an arched roof on top, found in 1999. Two bronze wares and an epitaph tablet were unearthed.

More tombs of the royal relatives were found as well. For example, father of the Empress Dowager Xiaosu the mother of Emperor Xianzong, Zhou Neng[111] was buried in the north of Houliulin village in Sujiatuo county, locally known as the Family Zhou's grave. This was a rectangular brick-chambered tomb; sit in the north facing the south, walls built on four sides around the tomb. There were stone arches, stone tablets, stone portraits, stone horses and the burial mound in the cemetery before they were all destroyed during the Cultural Revolution. Two stone horses, gravestone of the Marquise Qingyun Your Excellency Zhou buried in the Year 23 (1487) of Chenghua Era, and two monument tablets to Empress Dowager of Emperor Jiajing were currently remained. The tomb of the grandfather of Emperor Wanli on his mother's side, the Marquis Wuqing the Grand Tutor Zeng Lord of Anguo Li Wei, was located one mile northwest of the Pagoda of Cishou Temple at the Bali village subdistrict. This was a vertical tomb pit of husband and wife, north-south oriented, one coffin and one outer coffin for each of the two deceased. Li Wei's coffin and its outer coffin were destroyed by some grave robbers, but a few of silver kettle and little silver ingots were unearthed. Large silver ingots, hexagonal embossed design inlaid with gold ewer, silver basin, silver washer, gold ingots, portrait of a tortoise god, gold hairpins, gold bracelets, plates of jade belt, and two epitaph tablets were found in the tomb of His wife the Marquises Wang[112]. There is no doubt that the tombs of royal relatives found in Beijing area are much important among the Ming tombs found in everywhere in China proper. Besides of the tombs that had been cleared up in Haidian, other tombs like the tomb of father-in-law of Emperor Shizong the Marquis Anping Fang Rui was found in the People's Park at eastern suburbs. The tomb of Wan Gui and his wife[113], parents of the concubine consort Wan who lived during the Chenghua period, was also found in Pengzhuang at YouAnMen Outer Main Street. And the tomb of the parents of Empress Yi of Emperor Wuzong, was found in Weizikeng in Nanyuan. It was verified that the Empress's father Xia Ru and his wife[114] were buried in the year 10 (1515) of Zhengde era. The owners of the tombs hold similar social positions in that period of time, but their tombs found a little bit different in scale. All tombs were constructed by using rammed earth consisted of clay, sand and gravel with wooden coffins placed inside, but for the building up of the tomb walls, rubbed bricks were normally used for masonry. The top of the tomb was closed over with granite slabstones and sealed up with the rammed earth. Thanks to the well organized strict structure of the tomb, all remains were preserved in perfect condition. A large number of gold and silver wares, jewelries and jade articles weighted about 500 taels in total were unearthed in Wan Gui's tomb. A great amount of silk fabrics manufactured in sophisticated patterns in almost all styles were unearthed in Xia Ru's tomb. Most of the precious royal products were sealmarked with the title and of the period.

Ming dynasty was a period of time during which eunuchs gained and grabbed dominant power over imperial affairs. A large number of eunuchs found their ways living in Beijing the capital of the empire. After their death, most of the eunuchs were buried somewhere near to the capital. No less than one hundred tombs of Ming eunuchs according to incomplete statistics had been found and cleared up since 1950[115]. The places that had been found and cleared up like the north of Guananmen and south of Xibianmen were probably the burial areas reserved for the Ming eunuchs living in Beijing. Generally those tombs were stone or brick chambered rectangular in shape with wooden coffins inside, although the structures of the tombs were discovered different in scale and the funerary objects unearthed different in number. Some pagoda-like structures were taken into the design of tomb building. Objects buried with the deceased including porcelain wares, accessories made of jade, and epitaph tablets were unearthed. A number of tombs of eunuchs were found in Haidian district mostly dated back to the middle and late Ming period. Geographically the tombs of eunuchs were concentrated in certain area, in general, and eunuchs after their death buried in one grave seemed to be a normal way of burying at that time. The most important and luxurious tomb owned by the eunuch Liu Zhong[116] located near to the Xiangshan Hotel could be dated back to the year 33 (1554) of Jiajing era. This was a brick chambered tomb constructed against the mountain, consisted of the front chamber and the rear chamber. The rear part was a brick chambered rectangular shaped arch room. A cave for placing the coffin was carved out on natural rocks and covered with slabstones. The tomb doors were double-leaf made of white marble blocks engraved with Qixia Limestone over the lintel. There were six stone carvings found in the front chamber, including stone birds, stone animals, stone flowers and trees, stone tablet, stone incense burner and stone pier, etc. A line of Chinese characters were engraved on the stone doors in the rear chamber literally translated as a fairy place where the immortal Liu a man possessed of delicacy and elegancy lived. There were eleven brilliant stone carvings found inside the cave, including little stone attic, stone alter, stone chairs and stone piers, etc. The owner of the tomb was Liu Zhong, a B-class director of the department of imperial stables, served three emperors as the valet. The tomb gave us a glimpse of how much immense power that the eunuchs of Ming dynasty had. The tomb is very unique in the choice of the place, in the arrangement of the coffin chamber, in the wall paintings and inscriptions as well as in the stone artifacts and furnitures, all of which represent a strong influence of the Taoism.

The tomb of eunuch Yang, Keeper of the Seals in charge of the department of the emperor's crown, robes, slippers, boots and socks was found in the Haidian Geological Mechanics Institute dated back to the year 47 (1619) of Emperor Wanli's era. The tomb was cleared up in the year of 1999. A wooden coffin and a stone outer coffin as the main burial utensils carved with the sophisticated bas relief pattern placed in the tomb pit had been found well preserved. The outer coffin was rectangular in shape closed with a lid. It was a tenon-and-mortise work made of slabstones with a sumeru base as the bottom of the outer coffin. The outside of the outer coffin was carved with fancy bas relief in a line carving pattern and the floral scroll design. We could also find that some other patterns carved in the middle of the outer coffin, like the pattern of clouds and crane, of river and cliffs, of pine, bamboo and plum blossom, and of eight diagrams of Yin and Yang, etc. The wooden coffin inside was painted with red lacquer by tracing a design of clouds and crane in gold. Not many objects were unearthed except the jade belt, glazed pottery pots and, and the land purchase certificatee[117].

109 *An Atlas of Chinese Cultural Relics*, edited chiefly by the State Administration of Cultural Heritage, edited by the Beijing Municipal Administration of Cultural Heritage, *Beijing Part Two*, published by the Science Press, P. 215, 2008.

110 *An Atlas of Chinese Cultural Relics*, edited chiefly by the State Administration of Cultural Heritage, edited by the Beijing Municipal Administration of Cultural Heritage, *Beijing Part Two*, published by the Science Press, P. 216, 2008.

111 *An Atlas of Chinese Cultural Relics*, edited chiefly by the State Administration of Cultural Heritage, edited by the Beijing Municipal Administration of Cultural Heritage, *Beijing Part Two*, published by the Science Press, P. 215, 2008.

112 *An Atlas of Chinese Cultural Relics*, edited chiefly by the State Administration of Cultural Heritage, edited by the Beijing Municipal Administration of Cultural Heritage, *Beijing Part Two*, published by the Science Press, P. 217, 2008.

113 *40 Years Archaeological Discoveries in Beijing*, edited by the Beijing Municipal Institute of Cultural Relics, PP. 203-204, published by the Beijing Yanshan Press, 1990.

114 *A Concise Report on the Clear-up of the Tombs of Ming Dynasty Discovered at Weizikeng in Nanyuan Area Beijing*, co-authored by The archaeological Work Team from Beijing, *Cultural Heritage*, Issue No. 11, PP. 45 - 47, 1964.

115 *Archaeological Discoveries and Studies in Beijing 1949-2009 Part Two*, edited by Song Dachuan, P. 420, published by the Science Press, 2009.

116 *The Tomb of Ming Eunuch Liu Zhong Discovered in the Xiangshan Area Beijing*, co-authored by The archaeological Work Team from Beijing, *Cultural Heritage*, Issue No. 9, PP. 42 - 47, 1986.

117 *Tombs of The Ming Eunuchs Excavated at the Institute of Geomechanics*, authored by Cheng Li, *Cultural Relics and Museums in Beijing*, inside front cover, Color Illustration 1, 2000.

The tomb of eunuch Wang Gui located in Xishan (literally as West Mountain) had not yet been identified clear both in shape and in structure. No scientific excavation to this tomb had been done so far, except some hundred of wares in gold, silver, and jade as well as the pottery wares were unearthed. This eunuch tomb was considered more important than other eunuch tombs found in Beijing area in which a large number of artifacts were unearthed[118]. In 2005, three Ming tombs were found in the playground of the Beijing Technology and Business University located in Mashenmiao (literally as Temple of Horse God) in Haidian under the auspices of the Beijing Municipal Institute of Cultural Relics. They were tombs of eunuchs dated back to the period of Emperor Wanli[119]. Tomb No.1 was a brick-chambered tomb with an arched roof rectangular in shape, consisted of a retaining wall, a passage, and the chambers. The roof of the tomb was covered with black bricks and sealed with concrete known as the rammed earth consists of clay, sand and gravel. All tomb chambers were rectangular in shape with arched roof; the floor of the burial chamber was paved with slabstones. Two recesses carved into rectangular space were at the center part of the walls found one on each side. A double-leaf door made of two slabstones was constructed right in the middle of a wall on south side which is carved in the shape of a gatehouse. A platform for placing the coffin was constructed near to the center of the tomb chamber to the north in a form of rectangular sumeru base built up with slabstones. A bronze wine vessel, a dark yellow glazed porcelain vase and a dark brown glazed porcelain vase, a red ware tea set with two teapots and four tea cups, and 15 gray jade plates were unearthed as the funerary objects. The owner of the tomb was a royal eunuch of Ming dynasty, who was buried in the year of 1582 during the Wanli era. Tomb No.2 was a double chambered tomb rectangular in shape constructed with bricks and stones, consisted of a tomb passage, door-close wall, a tunnel, a front chamber and a rear chamber. The tomb passage was a sloping passage built up with bricks on both sides, followed by the rectangular tunnel thereafter. Walls on east and west sides were built with black bricks; the chamber roof was paved with four slabstones. The front chamber was shaped rectangular in its structure. There was a wooden imitation gatehouse built with bricks found in the north of the front chamber. Two rectangular recesses were carved in the east wall and the west wall, one on each side. A gatehouse built with polished black bricks was just above the recess. Two stone sculptures of two boys were standing against the wall at the central part of the chamber. A rectangular base together with the two sculptures under it was about 1.08 meters in height. A square black brick was placed on the southern part of the ground in the front chamber, on which some characters were engraved in cinnabar ink, identified as the land purchase certificate. There was a passage covered with slabstones connecting the front and the rear chambers. The rear chamber was rectangular shaped constructed with an arched ceiling. There was a coffin platform surrounded by slabstones rectangular shaped as sumeru base found at the center of the chamber to the north. Square bricks were used to pave the middle part of the platform, where a gourd-shaped gold well could be found at the center. Objects buried with the deceased, such as, 14 jade plates from a belt, a pair of stone portraits, jade pendant, gold accessories, and Wanli Tongbao coins were unearthed. The owner of the tomb was the eunuch Dong from the Imperial Manufacturing Department. Tomb No.3 and tomb No.2 were basically same in their shape and structure. Objects buried with the dead were 13 jade plates from a belt, a stone memorial tablet, a land purchase certificate engraved in cinnabar ink, bronze coins, jade stones, pottery jars, and copper kettles were unearthed. We knew from the land purchase certificate that the owner of the tomb No.3 was Hua Yongxing, a chief court eunuch of the Imperial Manufacturing Department, who was buried in 1595 during the Wanli period of Ming dynasty.

In 1991, a rectangular shaped stone tomb with arched roof was found at the west side of the Shangyuan Hotel in Beixiaguan subdistrict, which was sorted out under the auspices of the Administration of Cultural Relics in Haidian. Tomb chamber was 2.95 meters high, 3.6 meters long from south to north, 2.86 meters wide from east to west. Two stone doors were opened in the wall on southern side of the chamber, a pair of animal head appliques relief were engraved on the doors. Window-shaped little niches with reliefs engraved were built in the walls on east side, west side and north side. We could see that a coffin was placed carelessly on a stone platform. The objects buried with the deceased were a blue-white porcelain jar made in the year of Ming Jiajing, a bronze tablet made in the year of Wanli, jade plates in big and small sizes, and gold and silver wares. Among these objects, a bell shaped gilt waist tag attract our eyes. There were several characters found on the front of the tag, indicating that this tag belonged to a "eunuch from the Imperial Stable Department", and furthermore, identifying him as the "Loyal No. 38" on the back of the tag. In addition, two gold fortune coins were discovered. One was inscribed with the "Tianqitongbao" on the obverse of the coin, and the value of the coin was marked on the reverse, "gold five cents" or so. The other one was minted with an auspicious pattern, and an inscription both on the obverse and reverse of the coin could be cyclically read as, "namo-bhagavate bhaisajya-guru-vaidurya-prabha-rajaya". Some gemstones like opal were excavated as well[120].

In 1985, the tomb of Du Mao, one of the vice chiefs from the Imperial Household Department was cleared out at the Baihua Printing Plant in Balizhuang under the auspices of the Administration of Cultural Relics in Haidian. This discovery dated back to the first year (1620) of Taichang era of Ming dynasty, was a rectangular shaped brick-chambered stone roof tomb. A number of fine artifacts were unearthed, including a pair of gold double-ear cups designed with ganoderma lucidum pattern, a silver chiseled saucer designed with flower and bird and figure pattern, a silver flask, and a bronze jue goblet[121]. In the same year, a eunuch tomb of Ming dynasty was cleared out at the National Weather Service compound under the auspices of the Administration of Cultural Relics in Haidian. A blue-and-white big jar designed with "carrying a Chinese zither to visit a friend" pattern made in Chenghua era of Ming dynasty looked pretty much elegantly produced. This porcelain item was found in the tomb trench in front of the chamber, identified that it supposed to be some sacrificial utensil used in that time[122].

Tomb grade was obviously differentiated when we talked about the tombs of eunuch during the Ming dynasty. No less than 40 tombs of eunuchs had been cleared out over the years in Haidian. Some of the tombs were larger than the tomb of Liu Zhong in scale from which we could see the stone carvings were more elegant, but most of them were the tombs of lower ranking eunuchs. Brick chambered single room with stone arched roof were built to bury those lower ranking eunuchs, but the funerary objects in those tombs were neither many in number nor distinguished in quality. Tombs of higher ranking eunuchs were usually constructed as brick chambered with arched roof or simply stone chambered form, and the objects unearthed were made by high class craftsmanship. Basically, no set of burials were found in this sort of tombs, but a few of well made porcelain wares including, some Buddhist ritual implements, fortune necessities and some gold and silver jewelries were excavated. Many of them were well produced royal artifacts which more or less had something to do with the social specialities of the eunuchs. Besides, Laojundi at Guang'an Men was ever to be one of the burial places for Ming eunuchs, some male genitals made of ceramics were unearthed at there, presumably eunuchs wished to have their whole bodies to be put in the coffin after death and they wished to be buried with the funerary objects in the tomb[123].

118 Accounts of the Antiquities Discovered in the Mount Dazhao, from the Journal of Geography, Year Six, Issue No. 11, 1915.

119 Tombs of The Ming Eunuchs Excavated at the Beijing Technology and Business University, edited by the Beijing Municipal Institute of Cultural Relics, published by the Intellectual Property Publishing House, Co., Ltd, 2005.

120 An Atlas of Chinese Cultural Relics, edited chiefly by the State Administration of Cultural Heritage, edited by the Beijing Municipal Administration of Cultural Heritage, Beijing Part Two, published by the Science Press, P. 215, 2008. See also Thousands Of Years Throughout History-Historical Relics In Haidian, edited by Li Ang, PP. 71-73, Haidian Museum, Beijing, 2012.

121 The Haidian Museum, edited by the Haidian Museum in Beijing, PP. 106-110, published by Cultural Relics Press, 2005.

122 The Haidian Museum, edited by the Haidian Museum in Beijing, PP. 36-39, published by Cultural Relics Press, 2005.

123 Antiquities Discovered at the Construction Site of Laojundi in Guang'anmen, authored by Yang Zongan, from the Reference Materials for the Cultural Relics, PP. 103-104, Issue No. 4, 1955.

The tombs located in the north of Beijing as the central area for burial including Hebei, Henan, Shandong, and Shanxi provinces, were largely changed in terms of their structures and architectural styles during the Ming period. Comparing with the square and polygonal shaped tombs popularized in the time of Yuan, most of the tombs of high-ranking officials and wealthy people in the time of Ming were constructed differently from previous dynasties when we talked about the shapes or decorations with regard to the design of the tomb. Tombs of Ming dynasty were usually stylized with the front-and-rear double chambers rectangular in shape, or in the form of single chambered or multiple-chambered structure by using the materials like bricks or stones. Sometimes we could find that these tomb walls were decorated with murals inside the chambers, although the brick-chambered tombs of wood imitation structure were seldom found but multiple-nested coffins were very often used in this period of time. In general, tombs found in the north and south areas were constructed in different ways but later came to be consistent by borrowing the ideas from each other in terms of how a tomb was structured and what kind of construction method were taken.

The similar consideration goes to the tombs of civilians located in the northern area of Beijing. Civilian tombs are square shaped or dome shaped or polygonal shaped brick chambered tombs with some architectural elements of Yuan dynasty remained in their structures and styles. Some are brick-chambered tombs of wood imitation structure, and some are decorated with murals. Over the same period of time, the brick-chambered and rectangular shaped tombs were found among the civilian tombs as well, some of them were not decorated with anything, but the objects buried with the deceased were high class objects for sure. Some tombs were vertical stone coffin pits in which epitaph tablets were discovered. Some other small tombs were constructed either in octagonal or hexagonal shape, although not big enough in scale. A few of funerary objects were unearthed , we could detect that the architectural style of Yuan was retained in the construction of those small tombs[124].

2. Haidian during the Qing Dynasty

The Beijing area known as Shuntian Prefecture was changed in its domain during the Qing dynasty. In the year 26 of Emperor Kangxi's era (1687), four administrative divisions were setup at four places in four directions within the Shuntian Prefecture. Counties like Daxing and Wanpin were under the control of the west division, and Changping Prefecture under the north division. The southern area of what is now Haidian, Wenquan, Lengquan and Beianhe were affiliated with the Wanping County. But most part of the area in the north belonged to the Changping Prefecture. After the year 31 of Emperor Kangxi's era (1692), with the construction of the Garden of Tranquility and Brightness on the Yuquan Mountain as well as of the Old Summer Palace, the demarcation lines between Wanping and Changping were largely changed. A building boom came after the construction of the Old Summer Palace and other garden construction in its surrounding areas. Haidian district at this time actually played a role of the secondary capital or a capital of summer recess of the Qing Empire. The most important archaeological discovery in Haidian was the excavation of the ruins known as the Hanjingtang Ruins (literally as Tripataka Hall) in the Old Summer Palace.

The Hanjingtang excavation site sits in the center of the Garden of Eternal Spring section surrounded by waters and mountains in the east part of the Old Summer Palace. Beautiful landscape and elegant scenary are specifically eye-catching when we talk about this spot. The excavation site is 300 meters long from north to south; 200 meters wide from east to west, covering a total area of some 60, 000 square meters, and the construction ruins cover an area of about 30, 000 square meters. This site is close to the excavation site of the Great Waterworks to the north at the Western Building, connecting with the site of the Hall of Narcissus to the east, linking with the Bridge of Eternal Spring and the excavation site of the Danhuaitang (literally as Hall of Stoicism) to the south, and facing to each other with the excavation sites of Haiyuekaijin (literally as The Oceans and mountains opening their robes) and Siyongzhai (literally as Room of Thinking About it Forever) across the lake to the west. The building was constructed between the year

10 and the year 35 (1745-1770) of Emperor Qianlong, a complex of resting palaces in the biggest scale in the Garden of Eternal Spring, consisting of 30 groups of buildings in various architectural typology. It was one of the complexes of palaces that had the highest cultural and artistic values in the Old Summer Palace representing the highest level of construction skills in landscape architecture and royal garden design during the heyday of the Qing dynasty. It was a joyous and comfortable place where Emperor Qianlong chose to live after his retirement from the throne. Hanjingtang complex was burned down to the ground in the Second Opium War in 1860 and looted and completely destructed in 1900 by the Eight-Power Allied Forces. Between April 2001 and December 2002, systematic and scientific excavations of the palace area in the Garden of Eternal Spring and the Hanjingtang ruins under the auspices of the Beijing Municipal Institute of Cultural Relics were carried out. The whole excavation site was about a total of 32, 000 square meters in area.[125]

The Hanjingtang palace complex is consisted of two parts: the southern part and the northern part. After the excavation of the Hanjingtang ruins we found that the buildings in the southern part of the palace which sit along the central axis are archways, palace walls, corridors and tiles for paving the ground floor.), Foundations of the palace gates, courtyard buildings (including the screen wall, corridors, the main hall, the east and west wing halls, Fanxianglou (literally as Building of Hedged Fragrance), cloisters, and palace walls were discovered. Buildings complex ruins that sit in the north area along the central way are Chunhua Xuan (literally as Hall of Purity), Yunzhen Zhai (literally as Hall of Genuine), Beiyuan Men (literally as the North Gate of the Courtyard). Building ruins found in the eastern side were detected as Yuanying Zhai (literally as Hall of Shining on a Deep Pool), a dressing room, a theater, and an auditorium. Building ruins found in the western side were detected as the Hanguang Shi (literally as Room of Containing the Light), Sanyou Xuan (literally as Hall of Three Friends), Daiyue Lou (literally as Building of Waiting for the Rising Moon), Jinglian Zhai (literally as Hall of Static Lotus), and Lixin Lou (literally as Building of Adjusting the Mental State). There were no less than thousand objects with high historical values unearthed at the Hanjingtang ruins site including copper wares, iron wares, jade, ceramics, mother-of-pearl jewelries, glass wares, carved stones and a variety of construction units although most of the units were crippled..

From the Hanjingtang excavation ruins we learned about the architectural design and the construction scale of the palace complex, and the characteristic features reflected in the building structures as well as other information that told us what areas had ever been reconstructed and which buildings were somehow added to the architectural complex in the need of further development. The main buildings included in the palace complex were finished between the year 10 and the year 35 of Emperor Qianlong's era, the heyday of the Qing dynasty. Some new buildings in the north area were built up after the year 19 (1814) of Emperor Jiaqing's era. In addition, the intrepid Eight Banner soldiers were stationed around at the place of what we call the "three hills and five gardens" in the west outskirts of Beijing, therefore we could presumably deem that the important discoveries of the Manchu nobles tombs of Qing dynasty were not rarely found in this area comparing to the eunuchs tombs of Ming dynasty. Let's have a look at the following tombs that were found important:

The Qing Tomb-Suo Jia Fen (literally as tombs of Suoni and his offsprings)

In 1962, four tombs located at Suo Jia Fen of Xiaoxitian in the west outskirts of Beijing were excavated by an archaeological work team from Beijing[126]. They are brick-chambered tombs including traditional burial and cremation practices. We found that one of the deceased is buried in the tomb No.2, but the other dead three are cremated in other three tombs. It can be identified from the burial site that the dead persons buried in the tomb No.1 and tomb No.2 are the people who hold the high level social status. Tomb No.1 known as the tomb of Heseri Hala, the tomb is north-south oriented in the shape of

124   *40 Years Archaeological Discoveries in Beijing*, edited by the Beijing Municipal Institute of Cultural Relics, PP. 206-207, published by the Beijing Yanshan Press, 1990.

125   *A Concise Report on Excavations of the Hanjingtang Ruins Site in the Old Summer Palace Beijing 2001-2002*, Co-authored by the Old Summer Palace Archaeological Team sent by the Beijing Municipal Institute of Cultural Relics, *Archaeology*, PP. 41-65, Issue No. 2, 2004.

126   *A Concise Report on the Qing Tombs Discovered in Xiaoxitian in Western Suburbs of Beijing*, authored by Su Tianjun, *Cultural Heritage*, Issue No. 1, 1963.

square and constructed with triple arched roof. One side of the tomb is 1.82 meters long, and the tomb itself is 2.95 meters high. Niches are built in the walls on three directions of east, west and north except south. For each of the walls, it is designed in the shape of a saddle roof with slight overhangs, but constructed in a wood imitation structure, basically it is a brick carving gatehouse. Porcelain wares, jade, and other funerary objects are put in those niches. An arched passageway is built in the south wall. A gate made of black slabstones is opened at the southern side of the tomb. The platform for resting the coffin is set to the north of the chamber, occupying about half of the space 24 cm above the ground level of the tomb. The platform is paved with bricks, on which a wooden cinerary casket about 44 cm wide 48 cm high is placed in the center. An alter made of marbles is set up in front of the platform in the middle, on which a bronze square shaped incense burner, a candlestick and other sacrificial utensils are put. A tablet made of marbles is erected in the middle of the passageway. There is an epitaph inscribed on the tablet on which it writes "the Qing dynasty young lady of Heseri Hala family past away". A large number of distinguished funerary objects designed in royal style are unearthed, including porcelain wares, and jade, bronze wares, etc. The most precious porcelain wares are two cups made in Emperor Chenghua's era painted in contending colors with grapes pattern, a brush washer painted in five colors made in Emperor Chenghua's era, three little cups in blue-and-white made in Emperor Chenghua's era and Emperor Wanli's era, a white porcelain pot decorated in veiled colors, and a yellow glazed calyx. There are 28 jade wares in total, including jade vases, jade cups, jade brush washers, jade inkstones, and all sorts of jade accessories. Most of the jade artifacts are made with a high level of craftsmanship in the Ming dynasty. In addition, 6 bronze wares, including a bronze kettle, a square shaped bronze pot, a bronze incense burner, a bronze mirror, and two bronze candlesticks are found as well. Among the bronze wares, the bronze kettle is a Song-made copy of the same shape of kettle made in the Warring States period. We could know from the unearthed tablet inscription that Heseri Hala is the granddaughter of Suoni (Sonin), who is a duke and a senior regent of the Four Regents during the Emperor Kang'xi's period, and a daughter of Songgotu, who is an educator of the crown prince and a grand secretary of the imperial central government. Heseri Hala is dead at the age of seven. Tomb No.2 is a rectangular shaped brick-chambered tomb, 5.4 meters long, 2.5 meters wide and 1.4 meter high. Walls on four sides are built by laying black bricks up to the top covered with slabstones, the floor of the chamber is paved with the black bricks as well. Two wall niches are built into the east and the west chamber walls, and one on each side. A little blue-and-white porcelain bottle and a little blue-and-white porcelain pot are put in each one of the niches. A coffin platform is set up at the end of the tomb, and a rectangular shaped coffin made of Acacia wood is placed in the chamber. The corpse is in dresses, garments, and cotton-padded clothes, seven layers in total, and finally wrapped up with a quilt. The head of the corpse is dressed up with gold hair accessories, two gold bracelets are found on both wrists. Most of the funerary objects unearthed are gold jewelries including bracelets, phoenix pendants, all kinds of hairpins, ear pick (curette), and buttons, 39 pieces in total. Some superb skills and techniques are well used in making those artifacts, such as, the filigreeing technique, wire plating, carving in a floral design, openwork carving, gems inlaying, etc. Besides, two "Kang'xi Tongbao" bronze coins are found in the tomb. Tomb No. 3 and No.4 are simply constructed rectangular shaped brick-chambered cremation tombs. The "Kang'xi Tongbao" bronze coins are found in both tombs as well[127].

Yongtai village cemetery is located in the Yongtai village, Qinghe town, Haidian. In 1993, a foundation ruins site of a cemetery and 8 Qing tombs are cleared out under the auspices of the Beijing Municipal Institute of Cultural Relics[128]. M10 was a dome shaped single brick chambered tomb with arched roof on top, consisted of stone doors, a path leading to the tomb, a tomb passage and coffin chambers. The coffin chamber paved with black bricks was 3.8 meters in diameter and 3.86 meters in height. Three niches were built in the wall. The chamber was constructed in wood imitation structure with a brick carving

gatehouse. A damaged cover to the epitaph tablet was found in the tomb chamber, but no corpses, funerary utensils or other remains were found. M11 was a single brick-chambered tomb in the shape of rectangular with arched roof on top, consisted of a tomb passage, a burial chamber and an arched door. The floor of the tomb chamber paved with black bricks was 1.9 meters long and 1.6 meters wide. The top of the tomb was closed over with granite slabstones and sealed up with the rammed earth. A roof pommel constructed with the rammed earth was collapsed. Two wall niches were built on east side and west side of the chamber, one in each wall. The chamber was also constructed in wood imitation structure with a brick carving gatehouse. A damaged pottery ware was unearthed from the chamber. M12 was a hexagonal shaped single brick-chambered tomb, presumably buried in cremation. Some articles including a bronze mirror, two iron ploughs, an inkstone, a porcelain pot, a porcelain kettle, two egg shells and more than two hundred "Shunzhi Tongbao" coins were unearthed. Other tombs such as M3 and M8 were confirmed as cremation tombs, and bones and ashes were kept in a porcelain jar. M2 and M4 were vertical coffin pits, in all of which the corpses were found buried face up lying flat with arms and legs straight or extended burial, and they were put in a coffins made of wood. Three people were buried together in M1, one among the three was buried in cremation. Some commonly worn jewelry ornaments and some "Qianlong Tongbao" coins were unearthed. It could be inferred from the rammed walls, the burials and the layout of the building that this cemetery was a family graveyard. The ancestral grave was indicated to M10. Some other tombs presumably belonged to a family cemetery and the deceased were buried in certain order. According to the cover to the epitaph tablet and some historical documents, we could speculate that the owner of the M10 was Zu Songrun, the son of Ming General Zu Dashou. The layout of this tomb was supposed to be constructed on the basis of some Qing regulation which had been restricted to the high ranking high class g ū sai (Manchurian language meaning banner) officials.

Princess Zhuang Jing's Cemetery Garden is located at the Gongzhu Fen (literally as Princess's Grave) in Yangfangdian subdistrict, popularly known as Gongzhu Fen. There are two south-facing cemetery gardens on the east and the west, one on each side. The one on the east belonged to Princess Zhuangjing Hošo (i Gungju) couple. The princess was the third daughter of Emperor Jiaqing. The one on the west belonged to Princess Zhuangjing Gurun (i Gungju), the fourth daughter of Emperor Jiaqing. Both cemetery gardens are enclosed with walls on four sides including doors to etiquette and halls for worshiping ancestors. But constructions on the ground were dismantled in 1965 when a new subway was going to be built running through the cemetery gardens. Followed by the excavations of the gardens, tomb chambers were also pulled down thereafter, and some objects buried with the deceased were unearthed including Mongolian knives, copper kettles, jade ruyi, plaques of jade, archer's thumb rings (Banzhi), snuff bottles, accessories, enamels, and gold pocket watches, etc[129].

The military commander Hong Chengchou and his wife were buried during the beginning of Qing dynasty at the Chedao Gou village in Zizhu Yuan subdistrict. The south-facing tomb of the couple excavated in 1952, was constructed with rammed earth, 2 meters high, 7 meters in diameter. Some stone portraits and tombstones were erected in front of the tomb. This was a square shaped brick chambered tomb with arched roof on top. The tomb had been robbed and stolen by vandals in its early years, nothing left but a fir wood-made coffin, some clothes, bone fragments and two epitaph tablets were remained. Hong Shiming was the son of Hong Chengchou. He was buried with his wife next to Hong Chengchou's tomb. The tomb of Hong Shiming couple had been robbed and stolen by vandals too, nothing but two epitaph tablets were unearthed.

In addition to those larger tombs, some small Qing tombs were cleared up as well.

In 1977, a Qing cremation tomb was found in the China Meteorological Administration compound located in the western suburbs of Beijing. The tomb was a single brick-chambered square shaped tomb, covered with slabstones on top. Tomb gate

127 *40 Years Archaeological Discoveries in Beijing*, edited by the Beijing Municipal Institute of Cultural Relics, PP. 209-211, published by the Beijing Yanshan Press, 1990.

128 *Archaeological Discoveries and Studies in Beijing 1949-2009 Part Two*, edited by Song Dachuan, PP. 483-484, published by the Science Press, 2009.

129 *An Atlas of Chinese Cultural Relics*, edited chiefly by the State Administration of Cultural Heritage, edited by the Beijing Municipal Administration of Cultural Heritage, *Beijing Part Two*, published by the Science Press, P. 219, 2008.

was opened right in the middle of the north wall, two wall niches were found in the east wall and the west wall, one on each side. A peanut-shaped sumeru base coffin platform was built in the chamber covered with square bricks, two of which were engraved in "Si Chu" coins pattern, literally as "Four Corner"with a square hole in the middle that had four lines on reverse radiating from the corners of the hole. A black-glazed jar for keeping bone ashes of the dead was placed on the two square bricks[130]. The Tsinghua South Road Cemetery located at the Tsinghua South Road in Yan Yuan subdistrict was excavated in the year of 2001. Thirty six Qing tombs had been cleared out; most of the tombs were found vertical rectangular-shaped coffin pits. The entrance of the tomb was about one meter deep under the surface of the earth. The bottom of the tomb was around 3 to 4 meters deep under the ground. Some pottery wares, blue-and-white porcelain wares, bronze coins and jade wares were unearthed[131]. In 2004, twenty five Qing tombs located at the Wukesong Basketball Hall construction site in Fuxing Road in Haidian were excavated and cleared up under the auspices of the Beijing Municipal Institute of Cultural Relics. All tombs were vertical coffin pits. There were 9 tombs, in each of which one single corpse was buried; 11 tombs two corpses were buried, 4 tombs three corpses were buried, but 9 tombs no human remains were found. Most of the bone remains were well preserved, the bodies were normally buried face up lying flat with arms and legs straight (extended burial). A minority of tombs in each of which a secondary burial practices were carried out. Wooden coffins and funerary utensils could be found in most of the tombs, but one tomb with no funerary utensils inside. Pottery wares, gold and silver wares, copper and jade artifacts were unearthed[132]. . In 2007, eight Qing tombs were cleared up at the southern part of the Beijing Material Reserves Specialized Professional School. Six of the tombs were vertical coffin pits, the other two were brick-chambered tombs. Bones of the deceased were found face up lying flat with arms and legs straight (extended burial). Bone ashes were buried in three tombs, but wooden coffins were found in other five, in each of which one corpse was put. Burial urns were used for keeping bone ashes in four of the five. Objects unearthed included porcelain urns, blue-and-white helmet-shaped pots, gold and silver wares, copper accessories, jade, corals, and bronze coins, etc. These tombs looked large in scale more or less; relics unearthed were well designed and exquisitely made, especially the official hat and the court beads which demonstrated that the owners of the tombs were probably government officials all of whom had a corresponding rank before their death[133]. In 2007, twenty eight Qing tombs were cleared up at the construction site of the Qinglongqiao village development zone under the auspices of the Beijing Municipal Institute of Cultural Relics. All tombs were vertical coffin pits among which single-burials were found in nine tombs, double-burials were found in fifteen tombs, and triple-burials were found in four tombs. Most of the corpses were laid down in extended position, except one corpse was in flexed position. All corpses were put in wooden coffins, and some funerary objects buried together with the dead including pottery wares, porcelain wares, copper and silver made artifacts as well as some bronze coins were unearthed[134].

What we have teased out above from prehistoric period to Ming and Qing is the cultural relics in Haidian district Beijing. Here are some sum-ups from my point of view:

First, Haidian district is located in the plain area of low mountains and hills, a livable environment for human life. Since early times, humans had settled in this place which later came to be a well-developed region in agriculture during Warring States period though out the years up to Qin and Han dynasties. Diverse and abundant historical relics from ancient times are left behind.

Second, the Beijing area has become a cross-border stronghold to protect and a communication channel to access between agricultural areas and steppe areas under the governance of dynasties in the Central Plain since the Han dynasty due to the rapid development of agriculture and handicraft industry. To establish a provisional capital in Beijing during the Liao period is actually to contact the Chinese central plain. Thus, characteristics in regional culture are distinctive and are expressed and appeared in all its diversity and enrichment. A place we should pay more attentions on.

Third, ethnic minorities during the Jin and Yuan dynasties such as the Jurchens and Mongolians from North China pushed all the way to the south and built their capitals in Beijing. By doing in this way, they could base in the north from where they rose to power in one hand and at the same time be able to control the Chinese central plain areas in the other hand. The cultural characteristics of Beijing show a mode of integration and acculturation. Therefore, as a part of the capital or the suburb there is no surprise that the historical artifacts with elegant design and magnificent craftsmanship which significantly reflect the royal might are discovered in Haidian district.

Fourth, Beijing is officially designated and continued to be the capital of Ming and Qing Dynasties. One of the important changes that different from the past is that Haidian is developed to be the major water resource of the imperial households. Beautiful landscapes become more comfortable to live that makes this "geomantic treasure ground" be famous in this city. Therefore, not only do the royal family members choose here to be their grave after death, but a large number of powerful dignitaries and eunuchs of Ming dynasty prefer to be buried in this resting place after they pass away. Hence, a great number of fancy objects specially created for the royal family are found matchless and unique in quality and design comparing to other treasures unearthed in surrounding areas of Beijing and even in the whole country. A plenty of gardens are built in Haidian during the Qing period especially the splendid Old Summer Palace used to serve as a summer capital or a detached palace for the Imperial Family. Because the military men of Eight Banners are quartered in the Western hills imperial gardens known as the "three hills and five gardens", numerous tombs of the Manchurian nobles are discovered. As a result of discoveries, many historical artifacts with superior features are unearthed. With the increasing attentions on archaeological findings related to the Manchu period, more historical treasures would finally see the light of day.

130   *40 Years Archaeological Discoveries in Beijing*, edited by the Beijing Municipal Institute of Cultural Relics, P. 213, published by the Beijing Yanshan Press, 1990.

131   *An Atlas of Chinese Cultural Relics*, edited chiefly by the State Administration of Cultural Heritage, edited by the Beijing Municipal Administration of Cultural Heritage, *Beijing Part Two*, published by the Science Press, P. 218, 2008.

132   *An Archaeological Report on the Excavations at the Wukesong Basketball Hall Construction Site*, and *A Report on the Excavations at the Olympic Gymnasiums Constructions Site*, co-edited by Beijing Municipal Administration of Cultural Heritage and Beijing Municipal Institute of Cultural Relics, PP. 1-73, published by the Science Press, 2007.

133   *Archaeological Discoveries and Studies in Beijing 1949-2009 Part Two*, edited by Song Dachuan, P. 488, published by the Science Press, 2009.

134   *A Concise Report on the Excavations at the New Village in Qinglongqiao in Haidian Beijing*, edited by the Beijing Municipal Institute of Cultural Relics, *Cultural Relics and Museums in Beijing*, Issue No. 2, 2010.

中国是世界上较早开始制作和使用陶器的国家之一。已知考古资料表明，我国新石器时期的早期人类就开始了陶器制作的不断摸索和创新。随着制陶技术的不断提高，中国古代陶器在胎质、器型、纹饰、釉等各个方面都取得了不小的成就，不仅满足了当时人们的生活需要，也为此后闻名世界的中国瓷器的出现和发展准备了坚实的物质和技术条件。

海淀博物馆藏陶器主要是本地区出土的灰陶、黑陶及部分低温釉陶，其中海淀区大批出土的两汉时期灰陶数量尤其可观，器型也十分丰富多样；1987年海淀区八里庄地区一座三国时期墓葬出土的低温釉陶明器，涵盖了人们生活中的盘、壶、灶、仓、井、猪、鸡、俑等，堪称面面俱到；此外还有部分时代较晚的陶器，如1985年海淀区永定路地区航天部二院出土的元代黑陶。

Part 1

Pottery

According to the known archaeological materials, as one of the oldest civilizations producing and using pottery, Chinese people have made pottery and improved their producing method in the Neolithic Period. As the ever improving technique appeared, Chinese people made great achievements on the body, shape, design and glaze of the pottery. These experiences not only met the need of people's daily life, but also formed the basis of material and knowledge for the creation of the famous Chinese ceramics.

The pottery collections of Haidian Museum include grey pottery, black pottery and low-temperature glaze pottery unearthed in local area. The grey pottery wares of Han dynasty unearthed from Haidian District have huge amount and various shapes, such as a group of funeral pottery wares with low-temperature glaze in the period of Three Kingdoms unearthed from Balizhuang in 1987, including dish, pot, oven, granary, well, pig, chickens and figurines. Some pottery collections belong to later periods. For example, the black pottery wares of Yuan dynasty were excavated from the site in No.2 Institute of China Aerospace Science & Industry Corporation near Yongding Road in 1985.

彩绘陶鼎

汉（公元前206～公元220年）

口径17.6厘米，通高16.3厘米

Painted pottery *ding* tripod

Han dynasty (BC206 ~ AD220)

Diameter of mouth rim 17.6cm, overall height 16.3cm

深腹，双耳，三兽形足，带盖。鼎内及盖面饰有水涡纹。

彩绘陶壶

汉（公元前 206～公元 220 年）

口径 14.5 厘米，足径 8.2 厘米，高 28.8 厘米

Painted pottery pot

Han dynasty (BC206～AD220)

Diameter of mouth rim 14.5cm, diameter of base 8.2cm, height 28.8cm

折沿，长束颈，圆腹下收，矮圈足。腹部饰弦纹，近足部印有绳纹。器身用红、白两色彩绘，肩部及腰线以两道较宽白色弦纹为界，将主体纹饰分为颈部装饰和腹部装饰两部分，先用白线在陶器表面直接勾勒轮廓，再用红色朱砂填彩，绘有圆圈纹、三角纹及不规则曲线纹等多种。纹饰风格以突出线条为主，构成一幅连绵不断的神秘云气纹图案。

灰陶弦纹盖罐

汉（公元前 206 ～公元 220 年）

口径 12.4 厘米，底径 7.5 厘米，高 16 厘米

1998 年北京市海淀区八一中学内出土

Grey pottery covered jar with string pattern

Han dynasty (BC206 ~ AD220)

Diameter of mouth rim 12.4 cm, diameter of base 7.5 cm, height 16 cm

Unearthed from Bayi Mid-school, Haidian district in 1998

　　泥质灰陶，溜肩，弧腹，平底，带盖。罐身、盖上均饰弦纹，盖顶带一圆钮，周围有珠状凸起，且有不规则片状凸起一周。

灰陶印纹罐

汉（公元前 206 ～公元 220 年）

口径 15.6 厘米，底径 15 厘米，高 33.5 厘米

Grey pottery jar with stamped pattern

Han dynasty (BC206 ~ AD220)

Diameter of mouth rim 15.6 cm, diameter of base 15 cm, height 33.5 cm

　　泥质灰陶，侈口，口沿向外微卷，丰肩，鼓腹，平底。肩、腹部各饰印纹一周，近底部饰较细绳纹。

灰陶网纹罐

汉（公元前 206 ～公元 220 年）
口径 13.5 厘米，底径 12 厘米，高 27 厘米

Grey pottery jar with net pattern

Han dynasty (BC206 ~ AD220)

Diameter of mouth rim 13.5 cm, diameter of base 12 cm, height 27 cm

　　泥质灰陶，盘口，丰肩，鼓腹，平底。肩、腹部
饰有网纹带两周，网纹带内不均匀点缀"8"形双连环
纹，近底部饰有较细绳纹。

灰陶方格印纹罐

汉（公元前 206 ～公元 220 年）
口径 18 厘米，底径 18 厘米，高 38 厘米
1995 年北京林业大学出土

Grey pottery jar with stamped square pattern

Han dynasty (BC206 ~ AD220)

Diameter of mouth rim 18cm, diameter of base 18 cm, height 38 cm

Unearthed from Beijing Forestry University in 1995

　　泥质灰陶，口沿外卷，丰肩，弧腹，平底。肩部饰
有方格状印纹两周，近底部饰较细绳纹。

灰陶灶

汉（公元前 206 ～公元 220 年）
长 20.5 厘米，宽 16 厘米，高 7 厘米

Grey pottery kitchen range

Han dynasty (BC206 ~ AD220)
Length 20.5cm, width 16cm, height 7cm

　　泥质灰陶，双锅灶。整体呈马蹄形，灶面前
方后圆，灶前壁有方形火门，灶面上置有高隆的
前大后小两个圆形釜，灶体内空，灶台后端贴塑
兽头，火膛左右对称印有菱形几何纹。

灰陶灶

汉（公元前 206 ～公元 220 年）
长 25.5 厘米，宽 15.5 厘米，高 9.5 厘米

Grey pottery kitchen range

Han dynasty (BC206 ~ AD220)
Length 25.5cm, width 15.5cm, height 9.5cm

　　泥质灰陶、双锅灶。胎体较为粗糙，灶呈长方形，前壁有方形灶门，灶门上部有灶墙，灶台面正中置两个圆形陶釜，灶体内空，灶后方有一烟囱。灶台面上装饰有多组凸起三角纹、菱形纹及三条鱼纹图案。

灰陶弦纹兽足奁

汉（公元前 206 ~ 公元 220 年）

口径 19 厘米，底径 19 厘米，高 18.5 厘米

北京市海淀区万泉庄出土

Grey pottery case with string pattern and animal-shaped feet

Han dynasty (BC206 ~ AD220)

Diameter of mouth rim 19 cm, diameter of base 19 cm, height 18.5 cm

Unearthed from Wanquanzhuang, Haidian district

泥质灰陶，直筒腹，三兽形足。腹部上下各有深刻双弦纹一组。

灰陶弦纹谷仓罐

汉（公元前 206 ～公元 220 年）

口径 11.2 厘米，底径 23 厘米，高 28.5 厘米

Grey pottery granary jar with string pattern

Han dynasty (BC206 ~ AD220)

Diameter of mouth rim 11.2 cm, diameter of base 23 cm, height 28.5 cm

泥质灰陶，唇口，斜肩，直筒腹，平底。肩部至足部自上而
下饰有五组双弦纹。

青釉陶男立俑

三国·魏（220～265 年）

长 5 厘米，宽 3.5 厘米，高 19.2 厘米

1987 年北京市海淀区八里庄出土

Celadon pottery standing male figure

Wei, Three Kingdoms period (220 - 265)

Length 5cm, width 3.5cm, height 19.2cm

Unearthed from Balizhuang, Haidian district in 1987

青釉陶，明器。陶俑静静站立，双臂自然下垂，面部用浅浮雕手法表现，五官刻画的比较清晰，轮廓分明，表情略带微笑。通体施青釉，釉层有多处剥落，露出红色胎体，足底不施釉。

陶舞俑

三国·魏（220～265 年）

底径 11.4 厘米，高 24.8 厘米

1987 年北京市海淀区八里庄出土

Pottery dancing figure

Wei, Three Kingdoms period (220～265)

Diameter of base 11.4cm, height 24.8cm

Unearthed from Balizhuang, Haidian district in1987

　　泥质红陶，明器。面部五官清晰，身着长裙，发髻高耸，双臂微扬，翩翩起舞，姿态优美，系起舞人物俑。

釉陶仓

三国·魏（220 ～ 265 年）

仓身：长 11 厘米，宽 8.1 厘米，高 12 厘米

仓顶：长 12 厘米，宽 10 厘米，高 5.8 厘米

1987 年北京市海淀区八里庄出土

Glazed pottery granary

Wei, Three Kingdoms period (220 ~ 265)

Body: length 11cm, weight 8.1cm, height 12cm

Roof: length 12cm, weight 10cm, height 5.8cm

Unearthed from Balizhuang, Haidian district in1987

　　青釉陶，明器。仓呈上小下大的喇叭形，由仓身和仓顶两个独立部分构成，仓身前方中部开有一方形窗口，下方线刻有阶梯状图形，仓顶上起多棱，脊两端上翘。

青釉陶井

三国·魏（220～265年）

口径9.4厘米，底径8.2厘米，高5.5厘米

1987年北京市海淀区八里庄出土

Glazed pottery well

Wei, Three Kingdoms period (220 ~ 265)

Diameter of mouth rim 9.4cm, diameter of base 8.2cm, height 5.5cm

Unearthed from Balizhuang, Haidian district in 1987

　　青釉陶，明器。圆形井圈，口沿
平折，一侧贴塑有一头盔式隆起。通
体施青釉，釉层大片剥落，露出红色
胎体。

青釉陶榼盒

三国·魏（220～265 年）
长 28 厘米，宽 17.8 厘米，高 6.1 厘米
1987 年北京市海淀区八里庄出土

Celadon pottery box with compartments

Wei, Three Kingdoms period (220 ~ 265)

Length 28cm, width 17.8cm, height 6.1cm

Unearthed from Balizhuang, Haidian district in1987

青釉陶，明器。呈长方形，共分为十个大小不等的格子。底部有座，附有四个直角矮足，两足之间呈联弧形垂帐状，该器物是魏晋南北朝时期的典型随葬器物之一。

榼盒又名多子盒，是三国两晋时期模仿漆榼制成的。最早的榼是平底足，后足壁下部切割成花座，形制变得既美观又方便拿取。至东晋以后长方榼渐为圆形榼所代替。

釉陶灶

三国·魏（220 ～ 265 年）

长 15.6 厘米，宽 12.3 厘米，高 6 厘米

1987 年北京市海淀区八里庄出土

Glazed pottery kitchen range

Wei, Three Kingdoms period (220 ~ 265)

Length 15.6cm, width 12.3cm, height 6cm

Unearthed from Balizhuang, Haidian district in1987

青釉陶，明器。单锅灶，灶台呈长方形，台面四边饰有两圈凸起的棱线，灶台前开一个方形火口，灶门上部有挡火墙，灶后有烟囱。灶台正面施青釉，四侧面不施釉，露出红色胎体。

釉陶磨

三国·魏（220 ~ 265 年）
直径 7.3 厘米，通高 1.8 厘米
1987 年北京市海淀区八里庄出土

Glazed pottery millstone

Wei, Three Kingdoms period (220 ~ 265)
Diameter 7.3cm, overall height 1.8cm
Unearthed from Balizhuang, Haidian district in 1987

　　青釉陶、明器，圆形。釉陶磨由上下两扇磨盘
组成，磨盘相交面刻有凹凸纹路，上下呈锯齿状对应。

釉陶猪圈

三国·魏（220 ~ 265 年）

直径 11.8 厘米，高 2.9 厘米

1987 年北京市海淀区八里庄出土

Glazed pottery pigsty

Wei, Three Kingdoms period (220 ~ 265)

Diameter 11.8cm, height 2.9cm

Unearthed from Balizhuang, Haidian district in 1987

　　青釉陶，明器。圆形、直口、内塑家猪一头，
并立有一长条形挡墙，除底部外通体施青釉，釉面
较薄，底部露红色胎体。

釉陶虎子

三国·魏（220～265 年）

长 12.8 厘米，宽 6 厘米，高 9 厘米

1987 年北京市海淀区八里庄出土

Glazed pottery *huzi*

Wei, Three Kingdoms period (220 ~ 265)

Length 12.8 cm, width 6 cm, height 9 cm

Unearthed from Balizhuang, Haidian district in 1987

青釉陶，明器。直筒口，颈部微向下弯曲，茧形扁圆腹，背部有带状提梁，虎状圆臀有尾，四条形矮足。圆形器口外部饰两道弦纹。

虎子是形若伏虎的一种器物，用途有水器、溺器两种说法。

釉陶臼

三国·魏（220 ～ 265 年）

总长 15 厘米，宽 4.8 厘米

1987 年北京市海淀区八里庄出土

Glazed pottery mortar

Wei, Three Kingdoms period (220 ~ 265)

Overall length 15cm, width 4.8cm

Unearthed from Balizhuang, Haidian district in1987

　　青釉陶，明器。臼由舂杆和底座两个独立部分构成，底座呈长方形，座上有支架以支起舂杆、舂杆与底座相合，完整表现了实用器的原貌。臼为稻谷脱壳的工具，大约发明于西汉时期。

青釉双系陶扁壶

三国·魏（220 ~ 265 年）
口径 4 厘米，底径 7.7 厘米，高 12.5 厘米
1987 年北京市海淀区八里庄出土

Glazed pottery flask with two rings

Wei, Three Kingdoms period (220 ~ 265)

Diameter of mouth rim 4 cm, diameter of base 7.7 cm, height 12.5 cm

Unearthed from Balizhuang, Haidian district in1987

　　青釉陶，明器。直口、短直颈，斜肩，扁方形腹，条形双足。
颈部饰弦纹一周，肩部有对称双系。

青釉水波纹辅首耳陶奁

三国·魏（220 ～ 265 年）

口径 14.2 厘米，底径 14.2 厘米，高 10 厘米

1987 年北京市海淀区八里庄出土

Glazed pottery case with wave pattern, animal masks and three feet

Wei, Three Kingdoms period (220 ~ 265)

Diameter of mouth rim 14.2 cm, diameter of base 14.2 cm, height 10 cm

Unearthed from Balizhuang, Haidian district in1987

　　青釉陶，明器。直筒腹，三
兽形足。器身外侧饰三个兽面辅
首，器身内外均以水波纹、弦纹
间隔装饰。

釉陶奁

三国·魏（220 ~ 265 年）
口径 9.2 厘米，底径 10 厘米，高 9 厘米
1987 年北京市海淀区八里庄出土

Glazed pottery case

Wei, Three Kingdoms period (220 ~ 265)
Diameter of mouth rim 9.2 cm, diameter of base 10 cm, height 9 cm
Unearthed from Balizhuang, Haidian district in1987

　　青釉陶，明器。微束腰，三乳足，除足底外其余均施青釉。

陶砚

金（1115 ～ 1234 年）

长 10.7 厘米，宽 8 厘米，厚 1.7 厘米

1985 年北京市海淀区南辛庄出土

Pottery inkslab

Jin dynasty (1115 ~ 1234)

Length 10.7cm, width 8cm, thickness 1.7cm

Unearthed from Nanxinzhuang, Haidian district in 1985

　　泥质灰陶，正面呈梯形，由灰陶砖改造磨
制而成，斜坡状墨池，其内残存有墨迹、砚底
背面饰细绳纹。

黑陶双耳瓶（两件）

元（1271 ~ 1368 年）

左：口径 4.8 厘米，足径 6.8 厘米，高 16.8 厘米

右：口径 4.8 厘米，足径 6.4 厘米，高 16.2 厘米

1985 年北京市海淀区永定路出土

Black pottery vases with two ears (two)

Yuan dynasty (1271 ~ 1368)

Left: diameter of mouth rim 4.8cm, diameter of base 6.8cm, height 16.8cm

Right: diameter of mouth rim 4.8cm, diameter of base 6.4cm, height 16.2cm

Unearthed from Yongdinglu, Haidian district in 1985

泥质黑陶，直口，口部呈椭圆形，微垂腹，圈足，口外有对称双耳。

黑陶六扳锅

元（1271 ～ 1368 年）

口径 10.4 厘米，底径 5.3 厘米，高 4.9 厘米

1985 年北京市海淀区永定路出土

Black pottery cauldron with six handles

Yuan dynasty (1271 ~ 1368)

Diameter of mouth rim 10.4cm, diameter of base 5.3cm, height 4.9cm

Unearthed from Yongdinglu, Haidian district in 1985

　　泥质黑陶，子母口，深腹，平底。锅沿有凹凸不平的
锯齿状纹饰，并有扳手六个，底部装饰有水波纹。

黑陶碗

元（1271 ～ 1368 年）

口径 7.8 厘米，底径 2.8 厘米，高 3 厘米

1985 年北京市海淀区永定路出土

Black pottery bowl

Yuan dynasty (1271 ~ 1368)

Diameter of mouth rim 7.8cm, diameter of base 2.8cm, height 3cm

Unearthed from Yongdinglu, Haidian district in 1985

泥质黑陶、口部微敛、深腹、平底、底部印有水波纹装饰。

黑陶盆

元（1271 ～ 1368 年）

口径 13.2 厘米，底径 4.7 厘米，高 4.5 厘米

1985 年北京市海淀区永定路出土

Black pottery basin

Yuan dynasty (1271 ~ 1368)

Diameter of mouth rim 13.2cm, diameter of base 4.7cm, height 4.5cm

Unearthed from Yongdinglu, Haidian district in 1985

泥质黑陶、折沿、深腹、平底。盆底印有水涡状纹饰。
胎质较粗、胎体较厚。

黑陶罐

元（1271 ~ 1368 年）

口径 12.1 厘米，底径 6.7 厘米，高 14.8 厘米

1985 年北京市海淀区永定路出土

Black pottery jar

Yuan dynasty (1271 ~ 1368)

Diameter of mouth rim 12.1cm, diameter of base 6.7cm, height 14.8cm

Unearthed from Yongdinglu, Haidian district in 1985

泥质黑陶，敞口，弧腹，平底，胎质细腻，烧结程度较高。

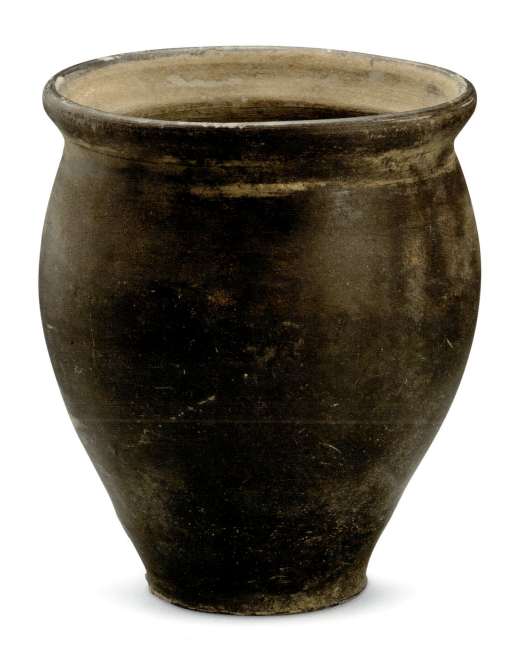

瓷器

中国古代瓷器肇始于商代的原始青瓷，因瓷釉中无法避免地含较多的铁元素，其后相当长的时期内青瓷都占据着绝对的统治地位。直至隋唐时期，以北方邢窑为代表的窑厂烧制出类银似雪的白瓷，才开创了一个『南青北白』的崭新局面。在此基础上，辽、宋、金、元、明、清时期的瓷器在装饰技法上取得了长足的进步；同时，绚丽多姿、相互争艳的颜色釉瓷和彩瓷的逐步发展也使得中国古代瓷器尤为引人注目。

海淀博物馆藏瓷器从年代看，涵盖了隋唐以降北方瓷器发展的绝大多数历史时期。1988年清华大学校内唐墓出土的玉璧底白釉碗，是北京地区出土的唐代邢窑白瓷的代表；南辛庄村发现的有墓志金代贵族墓，出土了一批造型精美、装饰技法成熟、具有典型定窑特征的白釉瓷以及少量黑釉瓷，如白釉瓜棱执壶、鸳鸯荷莲纹菊瓣盘等；1987年中国林业科学研究所出土的钧窑胆式瓶，造型端庄秀美，釉色古朴，是宋金时期钧窑的重要参考文物。

瓷的精品之作；1990年八里庄出土的嘉靖时期甜白釉罐，是明代白釉瓷的佳品；此外，海淀区范围内还出土了大量明清时期的青花瓷、粉彩瓷、五彩瓷等，如明正德时期的青花缠枝牡丹纹罐、明嘉靖时期的青花岁寒三友罐、明成化时期的青花携琴访友罐、清顺治时期的青花麒麟芭蕉图罐、清康熙时期的五彩鱼藻纹将军罐等。

更加难能可贵的是，海淀博物馆藏瓷器，绝大多数是具有明确出土时间、地点、伴出遗物的文物，因此具有极高的资料性和研究价值，部分出土文物甚至对特定历史时期的文物研究具有不可替代的作用和意义，如1985年白石桥出土的明成化时期的青花携琴访友图罐，造型端庄大方，釉色细润洁白，青花发色浓淡得当，是以玲珑秀巧著称的成化时期不多的『大型』精美瓷器，与此类似之器存世量极少，又因其具有明确的出土信息，成为研究明代成化时期青花瓷器的重要参考文物。

Part 2

Porcelain

Ancient Chinese porcelain were originated from the proto-porcelain in the Shang dynasty. Because there are the many iron in the combination of glaze, most porcelain wares show the celadon color in a long history. Just during Sui and Tang dynasties, Xing kiln in the Northern China created a new type, the white glaze porcelain and began a new phase in history. From that time, Southern China is famous for the celadon glaze porcelain and Northern China for the white glaze ones. From Liao to Qing dynasties, besides of the innovations of decoration skills for the porcelain wares, the development of colored glaze porcelain made the ancient Chinese porcelain more and more impressive.

The collections in Haidian Museum cover most kinds of porcelain wares in Northern China from Sui and Tang dynasties to this day. The white glaze bowl with jade bi shaped bottom, discovered from Tang tombs in Tsinghua University in 1988, is the representative Xing ware white porcelain. At the same year, many finest white glaze porcelain wares which are typical Ding wares and some black glaze ones were unearthed from Jin tombs in Nanxinzhuang Village. There are also white glaze melon-shaped ewer with handle and dish with the design of mandarin duck and lotus. In 1987, the Jun ware bottle vase unearthed from Chinese Academy of Forestry, which has graceful shape and elegant color, is the top-level Jun ware during Song and Jin dynasties. The sweet white glaze pot of Jiajing reign unearthed from Balizhuang in 1990 is one of the finest works of white glaze of the time. Moreover, there are many blue-and-white, famille rose and wucai wares of Ming and Qing dynasties excavated from Haidian District, such as, the blue-and-white jar with peony scrolls of Ming Zhengde Reign, the blue-and-white jar with design of pine tree, bamboo and plum of Ming Jiajing Reign, the blue-and-white jar with scene of visiting friend of Ming Chenghua Reign, the blue-and-white jar with design of qilin and Chinese banana leaf of Qing Shunzhi Reign and the wucai helmet-shaped jar with fish and waterweed pattern of Qing Kangxi Reign.

Importantly, most ceramic collections of Haidian Museum have clear excavation site, date and other concomitant evidential objects, so they are informative and of research value. Some objects even have significant value for the research of certain period. For example, the blue-and-white jar with scene of visiting friend of Ming Chenghua Reign has not only dignified shape, but also the smooth white and appropriate underglaze blue. The porcelain wares in Chenghua reign are famous for small and exquisite, and the wares of relative large body, just like this pot, are very rare. Based on the clear unearthed information, this pot becomes an important standard reference of Chenghua blue-and-white wares.

（底部）

邢窑白釉碗

唐（618 ~ 907 年）

口径 15.7 厘米，足径 6.6 厘米，高 4.3 厘米

1988 年清华大学校内出土

White-glazed bowl, Xing kiln

Tang dynasty (618 ~ 907)

Diameter of mouth rim 15.7cm, diameter of base 6.6cm, height 4.3cm

Unearthed from Tsinghua University in1988

　　敞口，口沿卷唇外折，斜腹，玉璧底，底部不施釉。器身施白釉，釉层较厚，釉色洁白纯净，素面无纹饰，体现了质朴素净的美感。

　　唐代是邢窑白瓷烧制的成熟期，结束了南方青瓷一统天下的局面，形成"南青北白"的制瓷新格局，为宋以后定窑系白瓷的形成和繁荣打下了基础。

磁州窑白釉黑彩婴戏图枕

宋（960～1279 年）

长 25 厘米，宽 18.5 厘米，高 10 厘米

1998 年北京植物园内出土

White-glazed pillow with black design of playing children, Cizhou kiln

Song dynasty (960 ~ 1279)

Length 25cm, width 18.5cm, height 10cm

Unearthed from Beijing Botanical Garden in 1998

腰圆形，枕面中凹，四边出沿，前低后高，卷边圈足。除底部外，通体施白釉。枕面外周以双线勾勒如意形开光及双弦纹，开光与弦纹间饰四组写意卷草纹，开光内绘婴戏图，稚童手牵四轮鸭形玩具木车在户外嬉戏，透射出天真可爱的童趣，画笔简练，画面生动，枕四壁绘卷草纹。枕后壁正中偏上有气孔，枕底有竖式长方形"张家造"戳记。

磁州窑是我国北方的一个著名古代瓷窑，窑址位于今河北磁县观台镇和彭城镇一带，因磁县宋代属磁州，故名。它始烧于北宋中期，一直延续到清代。因其烧造的器形和纹饰多为民间喜闻乐见，受到了普遍的欢迎，也影响了当时北方的其他窑场，形成了一个庞大的磁州窑体系。磁州窑以生产白釉黑彩瓷器而著称，黑白对比，强烈鲜明，图案十分醒目，并且创造性地将中国绘画技法应用于瓷器装饰，引人入胜，为宋代以后景德镇青花及彩绘瓷器的发展奠定了基础。

磁州窑绿釉刻花如意头形枕

宋（960 ～ 1279 年）

长 33.5 厘米，宽 25.5 厘米，高 15.7 厘米

1985 年北京市海淀区南辛庄出土

Green-glazed pillow in shape of *ruyi* head and carved with floral design, Cizhou kiln

Song dynasty (960 ~ 1279)

Length 33.5cm, width 25.5cm, height 15.7cm

Unearthed from Nanxinzhuang, Haidian district in1985

枕呈如意云头形，除底部外均施绿釉，露胎处显红褐色，两端稍高、中部略凹、底部有气孔。枕面勾勒与边缘形状相同之如意云头形轮廓，其内刻折枝花卉纹。

定窑白釉盖罐（两件）

宋（960 ~ 1279 年）

口径 3.9 厘米，足径 2.7 厘米，通高 5.8 厘米

1985 年北京市海淀区南辛庄出土

White-glazed covered jars, Ding kiln (two)

Song dynasty (960 ~ 1279)

Diameter of mouth rim 3.9cm, diameter of base 2.7cm, overall height 5.8cm

Unearthed from Nanxinzhuang, Haidian district in 1985

　　子母口，鼓腹，矮圈足，带圆形盖，盖顶中部内凹。罐均为白胎，质细腻，体轻薄。除底足、近足腹部露胎外，均施白色透明釉，施釉均匀；盖外侧施白釉，内侧露胎不施釉。整器端庄稳重，釉色洁白莹润，光洁素雅，给人一种宁静典雅之美。

定窑白釉瓜棱执壶

宋（960 ～ 1279 年）

口径 1.6 厘米，足径 4.5 厘米，通高 16 厘米

1985 年北京市海淀区南辛庄出土

White-glazed ewer with melon-shaped ridges, Ding kiln

Song dynasty (960 ~ 1279)

Diameter of mouth rim 1.6cm, diameter of base 4.5cm, overall height 16cm

Unearthed from Nanxinzhuang, Haidian district in 1985

　　蘑菇形盖，小口，葫芦形壶身，下腹部呈七瓣瓜棱状，短流，流口高度仅达壶身腹部，三棱形曲柄，极矮圈足。胎质细腻，通体施白釉，釉色莹润光亮。

　　定窑是我国宋代五大名窑之一，窑址位于今河北曲阳县辖区内，因曲阳县宋属定州，故名。定窑是中国历史上贡御时间最长、文献记载最多的窑址，其最重要的产品是精细的不施化妆土的白瓷，成为宋元时期士大夫清雅艺术取向的典型代表。

定窑白釉瓜棱壶

宋（960 ~ 1279 年）

口径 2.4 厘米，足径 5.5 厘米，通高 12.3 厘米

北京市海淀区南辛庄张□震墓出土

White-glazed pot with melon-shaped ridges, Ding kiln

Song dynasty (960 ~ 1279)

Diameter of mouth rim 2.4cm, diameter of base 5.5cm, overall height 12.3cm

Unearthed from the tomb of Zhang at Nanxinzhuang, Haidian district

荷叶形盖，小口，直颈，折肩，腹部呈六瓣瓜棱状，短流，三棱形曲柄，矮圈足。白瓷胎，釉色白中略闪黄。

钧窑胆式瓶

宋（960 ～ 1279 年）

口径 5 厘米，足径 7 厘米，高 28.8 厘米

1987 年原中国林业科学研究所院内出土

Gall-shaped vase, Jun kiln

Song dynasty（960 ~ 1279）

Diameter of mouth rim 5cm, diameter of base 7cm, height 28.8cm

Unearthed from Chinese Academy of Forestry in 1987

　　长颈下收，悬胆形腹，矮圈足。胎体轻薄，除底部外，均施天青色釉，釉层有细密开片。造型端庄秀丽，古朴中透出玄秘感，似有仿汝窑之痕迹。

　　钧窑是我国北方的一个著名古代瓷窑，其窑址位于今河南禹县，因古属钧州，故名。钧窑也是我国宋代五大名窑之一，以烧造色彩艳丽的钧釉瓷著称于世，因其"入窑一色，出窑万彩"的独特工艺，备受赞誉，北宋末年甚至一度为官府垄断为御用官窑厂，禁止民间私用，于是又有"纵有家财万贯，不如钧瓷一片"之说，其珍贵可见一斑。元、明、清时期钧窑瓷仍有烧造。

（底部）

钧窑月白釉洗

宋（960 ～ 1279 年）

口径 18.7 厘米，足径 11.9 厘米，高 2.7 厘米

1987 年原中国林业科学研究所院内出土

Writing-brush washer in light blue glaze, Jun kiln

Song dynasty (960 ~ 1279)

Diameter of mouth rim 18.7cm, diameter of base 11.9cm, height 2.7cm

Unearthed from Chinese Academy of Forestry in 1987

折沿，浅弧腹，矮圈足，通体施月白色乳浊釉。底心微塌，足底有五枚分布均匀的支钉痕。整器规整精细，大方简洁。釉层薄厚稍欠均匀，在素净的釉面上这种胎釉的不均，反而使器物在崇尚自然朴素的风格中彰显出创作的灵感和韵味。

（内壁）

定窑白釉刻莲纹洗

宋（960～1279年）

口径11.2厘米，底径8.4厘米，高2.1厘米

北京市海淀区南辛庄张□震墓出土

White-glazed writing-brush washer carved with lotus pattern, Ding kiln

Song dynasty (960 ~ 1279)

Diameter of mouth rim 11.2cm, diameter of base 8.4cm, height 2.1cm

Unearthed from the tomb of Zhang at Nanxinzhuang, Haidian district

斜直壁，平底，芒口。内心釉下刻折枝莲花纹，刻工流畅，寥寥几笔即将莲花的高洁气质展现出来。

定窑白釉盘

宋（960 ~ 1279 年）

口径 12.8 厘米，足径 4.8 厘米，高 2.2 厘米

1985 年北京市海淀区南辛庄出土

White-glazed dish, Ding kiln

Song dynasty (960 ~ 1279)

Diameter of mouth rim 12.8cm, diameter of base 4.8cm, height 2.2cm

Unearthed from Nanxinzhuang, Haidian district in 1985

　　浅腹，矮圈足，芒口。胎体细薄，线条优美。

定窑白釉小碟（九件）

宋（960 ~ 1279 年）
口径 7.2 厘米，底径 5.7 厘米，高 0.9 厘米
1985 年北京市海淀区南辛庄出土

Small white-glazed plates, Ding kiln (nine)

Song dynasty (960 ~ 1279)
Diameter of mouth rim 7.2cm, diameter of base 5.7cm, height 0.9cm
Unearthed from Nanxinzhuang, Haidian district in 1985

　　浅腹，平底，芒口。胎体坚实，釉层略闪黄。

定窑白釉印盒

宋（960 ～ 1279 年）

口径 7.8 厘米，通高 2.2 厘米

1985 年北京市海淀区南辛庄出土

White-glazed seal box, Ding kiln

Song dynasty (960 ~ 1279)

Diameter of mouth rim 7.8cm, overall height 2.2cm

Unearthed from Nanxinzhuang, Haidian district in 1985

　　子母口，极矮圈足，带盖。除盒底、口沿无釉外，皆施白釉。整器造型规整，精致小巧。

定窑白釉小碗

宋（960～1279 年）

口径 7.8 厘米，足径 3.3 厘米，高 4.5 厘米

1985 年北京市海淀区南辛庄出土

Small white-glazed bowl, Ding kiln

Song dynasty (960～1279)

Diameter of mouth rim 7.8cm, diameter of base 3.3cm, height 4.5cm

Unearthed from Nanxinzhuang, Haidian district in 1985

　　直口、深腹、圈足。碗内外均施白釉，底足露胎不施釉，釉色白中略闪暗黄，通体光素无纹饰。整器端庄稳重，简洁俊秀，落落大方，但造型相对较小，胎质亦略显疏松。

定窑白釉葵口碗

宋（960～1279 年）

口径 10.3 厘米，足径 3.7 厘米，高 4.5 厘米

1985 年北京市海淀区南辛庄出土

White-glazed bowl with okra-shaped mouth, Ding kiln

Song dynasty (960～1279)

Diameter of mouth rim 10.3cm, diameter of base 3.7cm, height 4.5cm

Unearthed from Nanxinzhuang, Haidian district in 1985

　　芒口微侈，唇部饰六个对称削口，碗口俯视呈六瓣葵花形，深腹微鼓，矮圈足，内外均施白釉。胎体较薄，釉面肥润光亮，造型小巧美观，为难得的珍品。

　　葵口碗是北宋以来常见碗式之一，碗口沿作四、六、八瓣葵花式，宋器常为六瓣葵花式。器口作葵花式，主要是吸收了植物形象，以丰富器物形制的表现力。

定窑白釉碗

宋（960 ~ 1279 年）

口径 8 厘米，足径 3.1 厘米，高 2.7 厘米

北京市海淀区南辛庄张□震墓出土

White-glazed bowl, Ding kiln

Song dynasty (960 ~ 1279)

Diameter of mouth rim 8cm, diameter of base 3.1cm, height 2.7cm

Unearthed from the tomb of Zhang at Nanxinzhuang, Haidian district

　　芒口微撇，腹壁渐内收，矮圈足。器身施白釉，
釉面光亮，胎质略显粗糙。

定窑白釉碗

宋（960 ~ 1279 年）

口径 7 厘米，足径 2 厘米，高 3.2 厘米

1985 年北京市海淀区南辛庄出土

White-glazed bowl, Ding kiln

Song dynasty (960 ~ 1279)

Diameter of mouth rim 7cm, diameter of base 2cm, height 3.2cm

Unearthed from Nanxinzhuang, Haidian district in 1985

　　侈口微撇，深腹，矮小圈足。器身施白釉，足底不施釉，
胎白质薄，釉面明亮，釉色柔和洁净。

定窑白釉碗

宋（960 ~ 1279 年）

口径 10.8 厘米，底径 5.9 厘米，高 4.6 厘米

北京市海淀区南辛庄张□震墓出土

White-glazed bowl, Ding kiln

Song dynasty (960 ~ 1279)

Diameter of mouth rim 10.8cm, diameter of base 5.9cm, height 4.6cm

Unearthed from Jin tomb of Zhang at Nanxinzhuang, Haidian district

　　斜直腹，平底，芒口。外壁近口处凸起一周，整器胎体轻薄，胎质细腻，施釉洁白均匀。

定窑白釉洗

宋（960 ~ 1279 年）

口径 13 厘米，底径 9.6 厘米，高 3 厘米

1985 年北京市海淀区南辛庄出土

White-glazed writing-brush washer, Ding kiln

Song dynasty (960 ~ 1279)

Diameter of mouth rim 13cm, diameter of base 9.6cm, height 3cm

Unearthed from Nanxinzhuang, Haidian district in 1985

深腹，平底，芒口。胎质细白，釉调润泽。

磁州窑白釉板沿盆

宋（960 ～ 1279 年）

口径 24.5 厘米，底径 16.4 厘米，高 5.8 厘米

1985 年北京市海淀区南辛庄出土

White-glazed basin with folded border, Cizhou kiln

Song dynasty (960 ~ 1279)

Diameter of mouth rim 24.5cm, diameter of base 16.4cm, height 5.8cm

Unearthed from Nanxinzhuang, Haidian district in 1985

　　宽板沿，浅腹，平底。胎质细腻，胎色略泛黄。盆外壁施釉不到底，底部露胎不施釉，其余皆施白釉，釉层有细密开片。器形厚重，端庄大气。

（内壁）

定窑白釉鸳鸯荷莲纹菊瓣盘

宋（960 ~ 1279 年）

口径 11.5 厘米，高 1.8 厘米

1985 年北京市海淀区南辛庄出土

**White-glazed dish shaped like chrysanthemum petals
and decorated with the pattern of mandarin birds swimming in lotus pond, Ding kiln**

Song dynasty (960 ~ 1279)

Diameter of mouth rim 11.5cm, height 1.8cm

Unearthed from Nanxinzhuang, Haidian district in 1985

　　弧腹，平底，芒口。盘壁呈菊瓣形，盘心模印鸳鸯荷莲纹，盘壁与盘心图案呈浮雕效果。

胎体坚硬，施釉均匀，整体造型十分精致美观。

黑釉托盏

宋（960～1279 年）

盏：口径 6.2 厘米，足径 2.3 厘米，高 3.1 厘米

托：直径 6.5 厘米

1985 年北京市海淀区南辛庄出土

Black-glazed cup with a saucer

Song dynasty (960 ~ 1279)

Cup: diameter of mouth rim 6.2cm, diameter of feet 2.3cm, height 3.1cm

Saucer: diameter 6.5cm

Unearthed from Nanxinzhuang, Haidian district in 1985

盏，直口微敛，深腹，饼形实足；托，中空，圆盘形，中间有凸起托口，中心下凹，小圈足。盏内、托面均施黑釉，外壁施釉不到底，黑白对比效果鲜明。

盏是盛装茶的小碗或杯，盏托是放置茶盏的托盘，又称"茶托"、"茶船"，两者配套使用。宋人把饮茶看做是一种高雅的享受，茶具盛行，式样繁多，因黑釉盏最便于衬托和观察茶色，因而受到斗茶者的喜爱。

（内壁）

兔毫盏

宋（960～1279 年）

口径 9.5 厘米，足径 3.2 厘米，高 4.1 厘米

Porcelain teacup with hare's hair pattern

Song dynasty（960～1279）

Diameter of mouth rim 9.5cm, diameter of base 3.2cm, height 4.1cm

　　口部微敛，弧腹，斜壁较深，小圈足。茶盏内部及外壁施酱釉，外壁近足部及足底无釉，露出铁锈色胎体。盏内流釉痕迹明显，黑色条形斑纹如万千雨丝，漂洒自如地覆盖于碗壁，状如兔毫，故称"兔毫斑"。

　　兔毫盏有"兔褐金丝"之美称，是建窑创烧的一种独特产品。这种特殊釉色是胎中的氧化铁，在焙烧中将铁元素带到釉面，后经高温流成长短不一的条状细丝纹。兔毫是黑釉的名贵品种，盏是宋代典型的斗茶用具。

（内壁）

黑釉褐斑碗

金（1115 ～ 1234 年）

口径 12 厘米，足径 4.2 厘米，高 7.5 厘米

Black-glazed bowl with brown spot pattern

Jin dynasty (1115 ~ 1234)

Diameter of mouth rim 12cm, diameter of base 4.2cm, height 7.5cm

　　圆口微敛，深腹，小圈足。内壁及外侧均施黑釉，圈足及底部露胎不施釉。釉色黑亮如漆，内壁饰有褐色斑点，恰与黑釉相间辉映，构思巧妙。黑釉、褐斑均是铁的呈色，通过对胎釉中铁元素的精准控制，使此碗在装饰技法上尤为独特。

白釉高足碗

辽（916 ~ 1125 年）

口径 10 厘米，足径 4.4 厘米，高 6.8 厘米

White-glazed bowl with high stem

Liao dynasty (916 ~ 1125)

Diameter of mouth rim 10cm, diameter of base 4.4cm, height 6.8cm

　　口沿微侈，深腹，高足平底。外壁施白釉，施釉不均，碗口有流釉、积釉痕迹，内壁近口沿处施白釉，其余均不施釉，露白胎。整体造型端庄大方，全器为素身，更显高贵雅洁。

黑釉双系罐

金（1115 ~ 1234 年）

口径 5.5 厘米，足径 5 厘米，高 12.7 厘米

Black-glazed jar with two rings

Jin dynasty (1115 ~ 1234)

Diameter of mouth rim 5.5cm, diameter of base 5cm, height 12.7cm

　　盘口，短颈，弧腹下收，圈足矮小外撇。口部及上腹部均施黑釉，内腹内底、外腹近足部及足底均露胎不施釉，露胎处呈灰白色，且有拉坯时形成的明显螺旋纹。肩部塑有扁形对称双系。器物胎质坚硬，釉层光泽匀亮润滑，釉色黑亮如漆，造型工整美观。

青白釉梅瓶

元（1271～1368 年）

口径 5.8 厘米，底径 10.3 厘米，高 28.8 厘米

1985 年北京市海淀区永定路出土

Bluish-white-glazed *meiping* vase

Yuan dynasty (1271 - 1368)

Diameter of mouth rim 5.8cm, diameter of base 10.3cm, height 28.8cm

Unearthed from Yongdinglu, Haidian district in 1985

唇口，短颈，丰肩，敛腹，矮圈足微外撇，平底。肩部及近足部各刻划双弦纹一周。除底足外，瓶内外满施青白色釉，釉色青中泛白，白中闪青，如青白玉。造型修长典雅，端庄朴素，美观大方。

梅瓶又称"经瓶"，创烧于北宋时期，因口之小仅容梅枝而得名。

白釉三足炉

元（1271 ~ 1368 年）

口径 10.5 厘米，高 11.5 厘米

White-glazed tripod incense burner

Yuan dynasty (1271 ~ 1368)

Diameter of mouth 10.5cm, height 11.5cm

　　侈口，扁圆形腹，三足。炉身施青白色釉，底部及下半
足部不施釉，釉色白中泛青，较不纯净，黑色斑点较多。整
体造型较为粗犷。

青花携琴访友图罐

明·成化（1465～1487年）

口径15厘米，底径15.3厘米，高24.2厘米

1985年北京市海淀区白石桥出土

Blue and white jar decorated with bringing a *qin* (seven-stringed plucked instrument) to visit a friend

Chenghua reign, Ming dynasty (1465～1487)

Diameter of mouth rim 15cm, diameter of base 15.3cm, height 24.2cm

Unearthed from Baishiqiao, Haidian district in 1985

　　直口，短颈，丰肩，腹部下收，平底无釉。颈、肩部依次为朵云纹、变形莲瓣纹、覆蕉叶纹各一周，腹部绘携琴访友图、高士奕局图，并以松竹梅三友图、祥云纹共同营造出恬淡、宁静的世外悠闲之感，近底部饰以仰莲瓣纹一周。整体造型大气端庄，画工精细，青花色泽淡雅美观，胎质细腻洁白，堪为明成化时期景德镇官窑青花瓷器的一件精品。

青花缠枝牡丹纹罐

明·正德（1506～1521年）

口径 6.1 厘米，底径 7 厘米，高 13.8 厘米

1984 年北京市海淀区钓鱼台出土

Blue and white jar with entwined peony sprays

Zhengde reign, Ming dynasty (1506 ~ 1521)

Diameter of mouth rim 6.1cm, diameter of base 7cm, height 13.8cm

Unearthed from Diaoyutai, Haidian district in 1984

直口微敛、短颈、丰肩、鼓腹下收、平底无釉。通体绘四层纹饰，层间隔以双弦纹：颈部绘连续回纹一周，肩部饰如意云纹，云纹轮廓内绘制朵莲纹，腹部饰缠枝牡丹纹，近足部饰以变形仰莲瓣纹。整器形制小巧，制作规整，青花发色略显灰暗，并有晕散。

缠枝纹又名"万寿藤"，寓意吉庆，是瓷器上常见的吉祥纹样，盛行于元代以后，明代称为转枝，以植物的枝干或蔓藤作骨架，向上下、左右延伸、循环往复、宛转流动、变化无穷，因其结构连绵不断，故又具有"生生不息"之意。

甜白釉罐

明·嘉靖（1522～1566年）

口径 9.5 厘米，底径 11 厘米，高 21.7 厘米

1990 年北京市海淀区八里庄出土

Jar in sweet white glaze

Jiajing reign, Ming dynasty (1522～1566)

Diameter of mouth rim 9.5cm, diameter of base 11cm, height 21.7cm

Unearthed from Balizhuang, Haidian district in1990

直口，短颈，丰肩，腹部下收，平底无釉。胎质细腻，釉色洁白，造型端庄，是一件明嘉靖时期的白釉佳品。

甜白釉瓷是明永乐年间景德镇官窑创烧的一种精致白釉瓷器。匠人们通过精细的制釉工艺，使得原有釉料中铁的含量极低，烧造出的白釉瓷釉色极其莹润，且具有明显的乳浊感，给人以温柔甜静之感，故得甜白之名。

青花岁寒三友图罐

明·嘉靖（1522 ~ 1566 年）

口径 8 厘米，底径 8.5 厘米，高 14 厘米

1991 年北京市海淀区北下关出土

Blue and white jar decorated with "three friends of winter"

Jiajing reign, Ming dynasty (1522 ~ 1566)

Diameter of mouth rim 8cm, diameter of base 8.5cm, height 14cm

Unearthed from Beixiaguan, Haidian district in 1991

直口，短颈，圆腹，矮圈足。罐外自上至下有四层纹饰，层间隔以双弦纹，依次为：颈部饰回纹一周，肩部绘如意云纹，腹部绘岁寒三友图（松、竹、梅），近底部绘仰莲瓣纹，底部有青花双圈双行竖写款"大明嘉靖年制"。整体纹饰构图精致，规矩而丰富，层次分明，青花色泽鲜艳浓烈，具有明嘉靖时期青花瓷器的典型特征。

青花百鸟朝凤图大罐

明·万历（1573 ～ 1620 年）

口径 15.7 厘米，底径 16.5 厘米，高 35 厘米

1985 年国家气象局院内出土

Blue and white jar decorated with myriads of birds hailing the phoenix

Wanli reign, Ming dynasty (1573 ~ 1620)

Diameter of mouth rim 15.7cm, diameter of base 16.5cm, height 35cm

Unearthed from China Meteorological Administration in1985

唇口、短颈、丰肩、弧腹、平底无釉。颈部饰缠枝花卉纹，肩部饰以锦地纹，并有四海棠式开光，内绘牡丹花卉纹，腹部绘百鸟朝凤图，并间饰以山石及多种奇花异草，近足部饰仰莲瓣纹一周。在肩、腹、胫三层纹饰之间留出两条空白带，使主题纹饰更醒目。器型高大、胎白质坚、画面生动清晰，但略显繁缛，具有明万历时期的典型特征。

百鸟朝凤纹，又名凤仪图，是瓷器装饰的典型纹样之一，是一种具有吉祥寓意的风俗图案。构图方式为画面显要位置画凤凰、梧桐、四周配画百鸟，仿佛向凤凰朝觐。凤凰为百鸟之长，百鸟朝凤象征明君威德，君臣有序，天下归附，寓意江山社稷太平、祥瑞。

青花瓜瓞绵绵瓜棱罐

明·万历（1573～1620 年）

口径 8.7 厘米，底径 12 厘米，高 18.6 厘米

1988 年北京市海淀区万寿寺出土

Blue and white jar with melon motif

Wanli reign, Ming dynasty (1573～1620)

Diameter of mouth rim 8.7cm, diameter of base 12cm, height 18.6cm

Unearthed from the Longevity Temple, Haidian district in 1988

花口，短颈，丰肩，瓜棱状腹部，极矮圈足。口沿饰以花叶纹，肩部以覆莲瓣纹装饰，腹部满绘瓜瓞绵绵纹，近足部饰仰莲瓣纹一周。青花色泽鲜艳，有晕散，具有明万历时期青花民窑瓷器的典型风格。

瓜瓞绵绵，是中国古代传统纹饰之一，即瓜始生时常小，但其蔓不绝，会逐渐长大、绵延滋生，表达了人们祈求多子多福的美好愿望。

青花缠枝灵芝纹罐

明·万历（1573～1620 年）

口径 7.4 厘米，底径 8.6 厘米，高 10.8 厘米

Blue and white jar with entwined magic fungus pattern

Wanli reign, Ming dynasty (1573 ~ 1620)

Diameter of mouth rim 7.4cm, diameter of base 8.6cm, height 10.8cm

直口、短颈、溜肩、圆腹、极矮圈足。纹饰共三层：肩部及近足腹部为变形灵芝纹，腹部为缠枝带叶灵芝纹，层间以双弦纹为界，底部有青花"福"字款。

青花山水海兽纹缸

明·崇祯（1628 ~ 1644 年）

口径 22 厘米，底径 13 厘米，高 17.8 厘米

Blue and white jar with the pattern of landscape and sea animals

Chongzhen reign, Ming dynasty (1628 ~ 1644)

Diameter of mouth rim 22cm, diameter of base 13cm, height 17.8cm

直口、深腹、平底。内外壁均施透明白釉，但釉层中夹杂有大量黑色斑点，且底部露胎不施釉。外壁近口沿及近底部分别饰有弦纹两道，腹部绘青花山水、海兽纹，并辅以祥云红日。整件器物胎釉不甚精细，装饰图案具有明显的民窑风格。

青花人物纹笔筒

明·崇祯（1628 ~ 1644 年）

直径 8.3 厘米，高 13.6 厘米

Blue and white writing brush pot with figure pattern

Chongzhen reign, Ming dynasty (1628 ~ 1644)

Diameter 8.3cm, height 13.6cm

　　直筒形，平底无釉。浅刻边饰，近口沿、底部装饰有一条釉下暗刻花纹带，上条为缠枝花卉纹，下条为草叶纹一周，腹部通绘庭院人物故事图。整器采用刻划、绘画相结合的技法，线条简约流畅，画面层次分明，构图疏朗清逸，具有明崇祯时期青花笔筒的典型特征。

青花人物罐

明中晚期

口径 6.4 厘米，足径 8.6 厘米，高 11.9 厘米

Blue and white jar with figure pattern

Mid to late Ming dynasty

Diameter of mouth rim 6.4cm, diameter of base 8.6cm, height 11.9cm

　　唇口、短颈、溜肩、鼓腹、矮圈足。颈部绘有花叶纹，其下有双弦纹一周；肩部饰青花如意云头纹；腹部为人物故事图，或持扇徐行，或手捧飞禽，或坐于回廊内，似赏庭院风景，背景配以山石、花叶、亭台，给人一种恬淡悠闲之感。

青花花鸟纹罐

明晚期

口径 6.3 厘米，足径 8 厘米，高 14 厘米

1995 年北京市海淀区西八里庄出土

Blue and white jar with flower-and-bird pattern

Late Ming dynasty

Diameter of mouth rim 6.3cm, diameter of base 8cm, height 14cm

Unearthed from Xibalizhuang, Haidian district in 1995

　　唇口、短颈，肩部微折，弧腹下收，矮圈足。外壁自上至下有三层纹饰，层间隔以弦纹，依次为：颈部绘花叶纹，肩部绘锦地开光花果纹，腹部绘有花鸟、山石、昆虫。画面构图合理，青花色泽鲜艳明快。

青花麒麟纹罐

明晚期

口径 6.2 厘米，足径 7.8 厘米，高 13.5 厘米

1985 年北京市海淀区太平庄出土

Blue and white jar with *kilin* pattern

Late Ming dynasty

Diameter of mouth rim 6.2cm, diameter of base 7.8cm, height 13.5cm

Unearthed from Taipingzhuang, Haidian district in 1985

唇口，短颈，溜肩，深腹，矮圈足。颈部饰草叶纹，肩部绘如意云纹，腹部绘麒麟戏球图，麒麟后肢屈蹲，前蹄抬起，瞠目张口，气势凶猛，形象生动。以瑞兽麒麟为主题纹饰，具有明显的吉祥寓意。

青花淡描牡丹纹瓜棱罐

明晚期

口径 7.2 厘米，足径 8.8 厘米，高 11.9 厘米

Blue and white melon shaped jar with light-colored peony pattern

Late Ming dynasty

Diameter of mouth rim 7.2cm, diameter of base 8.8cm, height 11.9cm

直口，短颈，丰肩，瓜棱状腹部，矮圈足。口沿外侧饰有青花弦纹两道，肩部勾绘花瓣形轮廓，内绘锦地开光花叶纹，腹部青花淡描牡丹花卉纹，并有蜜蜂飞于花间，圈足处饰青花双弦纹。纹饰繁密，画风较随意奔放。

龙泉窑青釉菊花纹印花盘

明（1368 ~ 1644 年）
口径 32.6 厘米，足径 15.6 厘米，高 5.8 厘米

Green-glazed dish with chrysanthemum pattern, Longquan kiln

Ming dynasty (1368 ~ 1644)
Diameter of mouth rim 32.6cm, diameter of base 15.6cm, height 5.8cm

折沿，弧腹，圈足。除底部外，均施青釉。整体呈菊瓣形，盘心有印花花卉纹。

龙泉窑是中国古代重要的青瓷窑场，其窑址位于今浙江龙泉市境内。烧瓷时间从宋至清，有七八百年的历史，具有广泛而深远的影响。当时福建、江西等地窑场，先后仿烧其产品，形成了一个庞大的龙泉窑系。

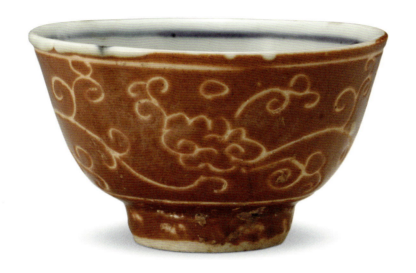

酱釉缠枝花卉纹杯

明（1368 ~ 1644 年）

口径 6.5 厘米，足径 2.7 厘米，高 2.8 厘米

Brown-glazed cup with entwined floral pattern

Ming dynasty (1368 ~ 1644)

Diameter of mouth rim 6.5cm, diameter of base 2.7cm, height 2.8cm

侈口，深腹，较高圈足。内壁及外底施白釉，外壁施酱釉，圈足露胎不施釉。该器采用刻划、绘画相结合的装饰技法，外壁釉下刻缠枝花卉纹，内壁近口沿处饰弦纹一道，杯心双圈内绘青花人物图，杯底有青花双行竖款"大明年造"。

白釉炉

清初期

口径 13 厘米，足径 9.8 厘米，高 8.5 厘米

White-glazed censer

Early Qing dynasty

Diameter of mouth rim 13cm, diameter of base 9.8cm, height 8.5cm

　　侈口，扁圆形腹，圈足。炉外侧及口沿内侧均施白釉，内腹部
及内底不施釉，釉色洁白细润，有甜腻感，底部有方形篆字戳记"子
孙永铭"。整体造型稳重大方。

青花太平有象尊

清早期

长 13 厘米，宽 11 厘米，高 11.2 厘米

1986 年北京市海淀区板井村出土

Blue and white elephant carrying a *zun* on its back, symbolizing peaceful prosperity

Early Qing dynasty

Length 13cm, width 11cm, height 11.2cm

Unearthed from Banjingcun, Haidian district in 1986

　　整体呈卧伏象形，背部出喇叭形瓶口，头部望向尾部。喇叭口处饰以青花蕉叶纹，象头及背部有青花饰件。以瓶谐意太平，象代表气象，整体寓意太平有气象，是典型的吉祥纹饰陈设摆件。其造型精巧秀美，形象生动，具有清代早期的典型特征。

青花麒麟芭蕉图罐

清·顺治（1644 ～ 1661 年）
口径 22 厘米，底径 21.5 厘米，高 38.8 厘米

Blue and white jar decorated with *kilin* and plantain leaves

Shunzhi reign, Qing dynasty (1644 ~ 1661)

Diameter of mouth rim 22cm, diameter of base 21.5cm, height 38.8cm

　　唇口微外撇，短颈，溜肩，腹部下收，平底无釉。纹饰自上至下分四层，层间以双弦纹分隔，依次为：颈部饰花卉纹，肩部饰缠枝花纹一周，腹部绘凤凰、麒麟、山石、芭蕉图，麒麟形象生动，昂头回首望天，祥云似火，凤凰展翅而下，预示好运从天而降。近足部饰变形火焰纹。整器青花发色清脆艳丽，纹饰优美流畅。

　　麒麟为古代传说中的仁兽，是"四灵"之一，虽形象凶猛，但被赋予仁厚贤德之意。芭蕉是清顺治时期瓷器中常与麒麟配用的纹饰。

青花四美十六子图大罐

清·顺治（1644～1661 年）

口径 23.5 厘米，底径 24 厘米，通高 49 厘米

Blue and white jar decorated with four beauties and sixteen boys

Shunzhi reign, Qing dynasty (1644～1661)

Diameter of mouth rim 23.5cm, diameter of base 24cm, overall height 49cm

子母口，短颈，溜肩，弧腹，带高圆盖，平底无釉。盖上绘山石、婴戏纹，口外饰弦纹一道，颈、肩部分饰变形莲瓣纹、几何纹一周，腹部绘四美十六子图，辅以山石、花草、祥云纹，近底部饰变形莲瓣纹、弦纹。绘画技法娴熟，用笔流畅细腻，人物形象生动，具有清顺治时期青花瓷器的典型特征。

四美十六子，亦名四妃十六子，是一种传统的吉祥纹饰，具有祈求国运昌盛、政通人和、家庭幸福、多子多孙的美好寓意。

青花云肩莲纹大罐

清·康熙（1662 ～ 1722 年）

口径 22.5 厘米，底径 25 厘米，通高 57 厘米

Blue and white jar with pattern of lotus and cloud shoulder

Kangxi reign, Qing dynasty (1662 ~ 1722)

Diameter of mouth rim 22.5cm, diameter of base 25cm, overall height 57cm

子母口、短颈、溜肩、腹部下收，平砂底，带高圆盖（盖钮佚失）。盖面以圆钮为中心，勾勒出以四相连云肩纹组成的如意花瓣形轮廓，其内填充花卉，颈部饰青花莲纹一周，肩、腹部亦以四相连云肩纹为轮廓，云肩内部饰缠枝花卉纹，近底部均匀绘制三瓣莲花八朵。胎质洁白，釉汁肥润，青花呈色稳定艳丽，构图严谨，层次疏密有致。

五彩开光鱼藻纹将军罐

清·康熙（1662 ～ 1722 年）

口径 13 厘米，底径 14.5 厘米，通高 38.5 厘米

1997 年北京市海淀区马甸西村路甲 5 号出土

Polychrome jar with a lid shaped like a general's helmet and decorative patterns of fish and algae in panels

Kangxi reign, Qing dynasty (1662 ~ 1722)

Diameter of mouth rim 13cm, diameter of base 14.5cm, overall height 38.5cm

Unearthed from A-5, Xicunlu, Madian, Haidian district in 1997

　　子母口，丰肩，腹部下收，平底，带纽盖。盖上饰以飞凤纹，罐颈部以山石、八宝纹装饰，肩部则饰以水波纹一周，并有四片倒覆莲瓣均匀散布，莲瓣内填以锦纹，腹部正中为四相连菱花形开光，内绘鱼藻图，其下为与肩部对应的四片仰莲瓣，内部亦填以锦纹，罐身空白处皆以红彩花卉纹填充。整体画面主次分明，色彩鲜艳活泼。

五彩花卉人物小将军罐 （八件）

清·康熙（1662 ～ 1722 年）
口径 3.9 厘米，足径 4 厘米，通高 12.5 厘米
1997 年北京市海淀区马甸西村路甲 5 号出土

Small polychrome jars with floral and figure design and lids shaped like general's helmets (eight)

Kangxi reign, Qing dynasty（1662 ~ 1722）

Diameter of mouth rim 3.9cm, diameter of base 4cm, overall height 12.5cm

Unearthed from A-5, Xicunlu, Madian, Haidian district in 1997

　　直口，短颈，丰肩，圆腹，腹下敛收，圈足稍外撇，带盔式盖。通体以红、绿、黄、褐、紫诸彩施绘，七件腹部绘花草、山石，余一件绘婴戏图，盖上均绘花叶纹。器物造型小巧精美，整体就像戴盔披甲的将军，稳重挺拔，威猛刚健。

　　将军罐，为一种罐式，初为佛教僧侣盛敛骨灰的器物，因宝珠顶盖形似将军盔帽而得名。康熙时期，将军罐广为流行，罐体造型特点为展肩提腹，颈部拉长，圈足收紧，使其造型显得挺拔向上，气魄宏伟，深受人们的喜爱。

斗彩鹿纹盘

清·康熙（1662～1722 年）

口径 15.8 厘米，足径 10 厘米，高 3.5 厘米

Dish with deer design in contending colors

Kangxi reign, Qing dynasty（1662～1722）

Diameter of mouth rim 15.8cm, diameter of base 10cm, height 3.5cm

　　深弧腹，矮圈足。盘心以青花双圈框定，其内绘斗彩松、鹿、山石图，内壁近口沿处青花双圈内绘斗彩灵芝、飞虫、瑞猴捧寿（桃），外壁近口沿处为青花双弦纹一周，其下均匀散绘斗彩灵芝四株，圈足上有青花弦纹三道，画面题材具有明显的祈求长寿的寓意。底部有青花双圈双行竖写楷书仿款"大明成化年制"。

（内壁）

（内壁）

青花麒麟八宝折腰盘

清·康熙（1662 ～ 1722 年）

口径 15.6 厘米，足径 8.8 厘米，高 1.6 厘米

Blue and white dish with folded waist and the design of kilin and Eight Emblems

Kangxi reign, Qing dynasty (1662 ~ 1722)

Diameter of mouth rim 15.6cm, diameter of base 8.8cm, height 1.6cm

折腰，圈足。盘心绘麒麟、山石、云纹，内
壁近口沿处均匀装饰八宝纹，外壁绘有杂宝纹，
底部青花双圈内有青花双框款"五羔"。

（内壁）

墨彩山水盘

清·雍正（1723 ～ 1735 年）

口径 15.6 厘米，足径 9.7 厘米，高 3.5 厘米

Dish with ink landscape design

Yongzheng reign, Qing dynasty (1723 ~ 1735)

Diameter of mouth rim 15.6cm, diameter of base 9.7cm, height 3.5cm

　　侈口，弧腹，圈足。盘心以墨彩绘山水图，画面浓淡相宜，层次分明，较好地展现了中国传统绘画的美感。底部有青花双圈双行竖写楷书仿款"大明成化年制"。

（内壁）

青花花鸟纹浅碗

清·雍正（1723～1735 年）

口径 14.4 厘米，足径 7 厘米，高 5 厘米

Blue and white shallow bowl with floral and bird pattern

Yongzheng reign, Qing dynasty (1723～1735)

Diameter of mouth rim 14.4cm, diameter of base 7cm, height 5cm

直口，浅圆腹，圈足。除圈足外，通体施白釉。内壁满绘花鸟纹，近口沿处饰弦纹一周，外底有青花双圈双行竖写楷书款"全庆堂做古制"。

斗彩三多纹碗

清·乾隆（1736 ~ 1795 年）

口径 9 厘米，足径 3.8 厘米，高 5 厘米

Bowl with pattern in contending colors symbolizing for more blessings, more longevity and more sons

Qianlong reign, Qing dynasty (1736 ~ 1795)

Diameter of mouth rim 9cm, diameter of base 3.8cm, height 5cm

敞口，深腹，圈足。外壁近口沿处饰弦纹一道，其下绘斗彩折枝瓜果纹，以佛手、桃、石榴三果组成寓意多福、多寿、多子的纹样，釉下青花与釉上红、黄、绿、淡紫诸彩相衬斗艳，外底有青花双圈双行竖写楷书仿款"大明成化年制"。整体画面疏朗，色彩清润，釉面光润细腻。

（视图一）

（视图二）

（视图三）

（外壁）

祭红釉盘

清·乾隆（1736～1795年）

口径 16.6 厘米，足径 10.4 厘米，高 3.5 厘米

Sacrificial-red-glazed dish

Qianlong reign, Qing dynasty (1736～1795)

Diameter of mouth rim 16.6cm, diameter of base 10.4cm, height 3.5cm

侈口，弧腹，圈足。盘外壁及圈足外部施祭红釉，足部露胎，其余部分施白釉，底部有青花三行竖写篆书款"大清乾隆年制"。

祭红釉，又称"霁红釉"，烧成后釉面为失透状，呈色均匀凝厚，是清康熙、雍正、乾隆三朝盛行的红釉品种，为区别于明永乐、宣德时期的红釉，及同时代的郎窑红，习惯上称之为霁红或祭红。

（内壁）

黄釉暗龙纹小盘

清·乾隆（1736 ~ 1795 年）

口径 10.7 厘米，足径 5.5 厘米，高 2.6 厘米

2002 年北京市海淀区西上坡出土

敞口，弧腹，圈足。盘内刻弦纹一周，其内暗刻龙纹，并辅以祥云、圆日，外壁暗刻水涡纹、杂宝纹，底部有青花三行竖写篆书款"大清乾隆年制"。

Small yellow-glazed plate with veiled dragon pattern

Qianlong reign, Qing dynasty (1736 ~ 1795)

Diameter of mouth rim 10.7cm, diameter of base 5.5cm, height 2.6cm

Unearthed from Xishangpo, Haidian district in 2002

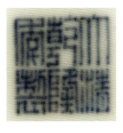

（内壁）

粉彩缠枝莲纹盘

清·乾隆（1736～1795 年）

口径 16.2 厘米，足径 9.6 厘米，高 3.5 厘米

Famille-rose dish with entwined lotus sprays

Qianlong reign, Qing dynasty (1736～1795)

Diameter of mouth rim 16.2cm, diameter of base 9.6cm, height 3.5cm

　　敞口，弧腹，圈足。盘心饰粉彩团花纹，外壁满绘缠枝莲纹，底部有青花三行竖写篆书款"大清乾隆年制"。

（内壁）

粉彩人物御制诗纹盘

清·乾隆（1736～1795 年）

口径 20 厘米，足径 11.7 厘米，高 3.6 厘米

Famille-rose dish with imperial poem and figure pattern

Qianlong reign, Qing dynasty（1736～1795）

Diameter of mouth rim 20cm, diameter of base 11.7cm, height 3.6cm

　　敞口，弧腹，圈足。盘内近口沿处饰青花双弦纹一周，其内以墨彩书乾隆咏越窑七言诗一首，并绘粉彩婴戏图，辅以山石、公鸡、花卉，画工精湛，形象鲜活生动，外壁绘粉彩灵芝、牡丹、兰花，近口沿及近足部各饰一周双弦纹，底部有青花三行竖写篆书款"大清乾隆年制"。

（内壁）

青花回纹盘

清·乾隆（1736～1795 年）

口径 15.4 厘米，足径 9 厘米，高 2.5 厘米

Blue and white dish with fret pattern

Qianlong reign, Qing dynasty（1736～1795）

Diameter of mouth rim 15.4cm, diameter of base 9cm, height 2.5cm

敞口，弧腹，矮圈足。盘心饰回纹一周，内壁近口沿处饰花卉纹，外壁均匀散绘灵芝四株，底部有青花三行竖写篆书款"大清乾隆年制"。

青花人物纹小缸

清·乾隆（1736 ～ 1795 年）

口径 9.1 厘米，底径 6.4 厘米，高 5.8 厘米

Small blue and white jar with figures pattern

Qianlong reign, Qing dynasty (1736 ~ 1795)

Diameter of mouth rim 9.1cm, diameter of base 6.4cm, height 5.8cm

板沿，深腹，隐圈足。内外壁均施透明白釉，底部露胎不施釉。口沿上有相连的小实心圈一周，腹部绘有青花持莲倚坐人物图，周围配以草叶、山石，勾勒出一幅悠然自得的赏莲画面。整器釉质细腻润洁，青花色调浓淡相宜，纹饰取材高雅古朴。

青花釉里红百鹿图鼻烟壶

清·道光 （1821 ～ 1850 年）

口径 1.1 厘米，底径 2.1 厘米，高 8.3 厘米

1987 年北京市海淀区德外沙滩北顶村出土

Underglaze blue and red snuff bottle with hundred deer pattern

Daoguang reign, Qing dynasty (1821 ~ 1850)

Diameter of mouth rim 1.1cm, diameter of base 2.1cm, height 8.3cm

Unearthed from Beiding village, Dewaishatan, Haidian district in 1987

唇口，短颈，溜肩，深腹，无盖。壶颈部饰青花回纹一周，肩、腹部细绘青花釉里红山峰、百鹿图，鹿或坐或卧，有奔跑者，有回首者，姿态各异，栩栩如生。底部有青花三行竖写篆书仿款"大清雍正年制"。

鹿，谐音禄，以百鹿图谐意禄运亨通，也是常用的吉祥纹饰。

黄釉盘

清·道光（1821～1850年）

口径 14.6 厘米，足径 9.2 厘米，高 2.4 厘米

Yellow-glazed dish

Daoguang reign, Qing dynasty (1821 ~ 1850)

Diameter of mouth rim 14.6cm, diameter of base 9.2cm, height 2.4cm

口微撇，弧腹，圈足。盘内壁及底部施白釉，外壁施黄釉，盘底有青花三行竖写篆书款"大清道光年制"。

青花淡描团花折腰盘

清中期

口径 15.7 厘米，底径 9.5 厘米，高 3.3 厘米

Blue and white dish with folded waist and the pattern of light-colored conglobate flower

Mid Qing dynasty

Diameter of mouth rim 15.7cm, diameter of base 9.5cm, height 3.3cm

　　折腰，矮圈足。盘心绘团花纹，外壁
散绘团花五组，并绘有五对石榴纹。胎质
细腻轻薄，釉色纯净洁白。

（内壁）

豆青地青花开光人物绣墩

清·同治（1862 ~ 1874 年）

面径 30 厘米，底径 28 厘米，高 46.1 厘米

Bluish green glared drum stool with underglaze blue pattern of figures

Tongzhi reign, Qing dynasty (1862 ~ 1874)

Diameter of surface rim 30cm, diameter of base 28cm, height 46.1cm

鼓式，中空，通体施豆青釉。墩面绘梅兰竹菊四君子图，并有二青花菱花形开光，内绘青花人物故事图；中心部分为镂空钱纹。墩外壁以两周乳钉纹间隔，分三层纹饰：上腹部饰有白色杂宝纹；中腹部有二青花菱花形开光，其内绘有青花人物故事图；开光外饰有花果纹及镂空双钱纹；下腹部绘有白色花叶纹。整体纹饰蓝白相间，别有一番雅致之感。

粉彩博古纹帽筒

清·光绪（1875～1908 年）

直径 12 厘米，高 27.3 厘米

Famille-rose hatstand with curio pattern

Guangxu reign, Qing dynasty (1875～1908)

Diameter 12cm, height 27.3cm

直口，筒形腹，极矮圈足。外壁近口处饰金线边纹一道，筒壁饰六个上下交错的海棠花式镂孔，系排汗气或熏香除臭之用。外壁满绘粉彩博古纹，图案绘制饱满绚丽，并题有"峨冠济济，祥钟儒雅之家；章甫煌煌，光来上国之贵"，底部有白文双行竖写篆书印款"光绪年制"。

青花勾莲八宝竹节耳盖碗尊

清·光绪（1875 ～ 1908 年）

口径 25.2 厘米，足径 24 厘米，高 55.3 厘米

Blue and white *zun* decorated with bamboo-shaped ears and design of interlacing lotus and Eight Emblems

Guangxu reign, Qing dynasty (1875 ~ 1908)

Diameter of mouth rim 25.2cm, diameter of base 24cm, height 55.3cm

敞口，束颈，折肩，弧腹，圈足微外撇，颈部对称饰竹节形贯耳。外部青花纹饰为多层主辅式构图，自上而下分绘如意云纹、蕉叶纹、团寿纹、凤纹、锦地纹、缠枝花卉纹、牡丹纹、如意云纹、缠枝莲纹（杂以吉祥八宝图案）、仰莲瓣纹、水涡纹等十一层纹饰，贯耳上饰青花竹节纹，外底有青花双圈双行竖写楷书仿款"大清康熙年制"。器型壮硕，胎体厚重坚实，青花呈色稳定艳丽，纹饰纤细繁密，构图严谨匀称。

该器形似盖碗，被称之为盖碗尊，又因颈部有对称管状贯耳，也称之为贯耳尊，其造型新颖，为难得的大型青花陈设器，是光绪时期的代表作。

（内壁）

青釉"菩萨殿茶棚"盘

清晚期

口径 13.4 厘米，足径 7.8 厘米，高 1.7 厘米

Green-glazed dish with Chinese characters

Late Qing dynasty

Diameter of mouth rim 13.4cm, diameter of base 7.8cm, height 1.7cm

　　浅弧腹、矮圈足，除口部、足部无釉外，均施青釉。盘心饰红彩楷书"菩萨殿茶棚"五字，且以稍淡红圈框定；盘内壁均匀饰红彩楷书"外馆海灯会献"六字，每字亦以红圈框定。

　　明清两代及民国时期，京西妙峰山因顶峰的碧霞元君庙而名声大噪，远近的大小香会纷纷进山朝拜，登山途中不固定地设有若干茶棚，以方便临时歇脚。菩萨殿茶棚即为众多茶棚之一，位于当时自海淀地区进山道路途中。海灯会应为当时的香会之一。

粉彩富贵牡丹纹花盆

清晚期

口径 37 厘米，足径 19.5 厘米，高 32 厘米

Famille-rose flower pot with peony pattern

Late Qing dynasty

Diameter of mouth rim 37cm, diameter of base 19.5cm, height 32cm

折沿，深腹，圈足。腹部绘粉彩富贵牡丹图，辅以蜻蜓、竹叶、花卉等纹饰，构图合理，杂而不乱。

粉彩九桃筒形花盆

清晚期

口径 40 厘米，足径 29.4 厘米，高 34.7 厘米

Famille-rose cylinder-shaped flower pot with peach pattern

Late Qing dynasty

Diameter of mouth rim 40cm, diameter of base 29.4cm, height 34.7cm

　　直口、深筒形腹、矮圈足。外壁近口处绘回纹及花卉纹一周，腹部绘粉彩九桃
纹，并以花果、灵芝、山石、双蝙蝠装饰其间，表达出祈求福寿双全的美好愿望。

青花花卉纹八方花盆

清晚期

口径 39.5 厘米，足径 25.6 厘米，高 23.6 厘米

Blue and white octagon flower pot with floral pattern

Late Qing dynasty

Diameter of mouth rim 39.5cm, diameter of base 25.6cm, height 23.6cm

倭角八方折沿花盆，八棱形深腹，正八方形圈足。花盆内壁、内底、足底均不施釉。口沿上绘花卉纹，腹部满绘莲纹，其下饰仰莲瓣纹一周，圈足外壁饰镂空云纹。整器青花发色浓艳，纹饰丰满，型体变化曲直相间，上下呼应，和谐美观。

粉彩开光龙凤纹绣墩

清晚期

面径 29.5 厘米，底径 29 厘米，高 46 厘米

Famille-rose drum stool with dragon and phoenix pattern

Late Qing dynasty

Diameter of surface rim 29.5cm, diameter of base 29cm, height 46cm

鼓式，中空。墩面近缘处以黄蓝相间的回纹圈定，四朵红莲均匀分布其上，圈内装饰以粉彩花果纹；中心部分为镂空钱纹，并点缀有花叶纹。上腹部饰以颜色各异的五层粉彩花卉纹；中腹部满绘粉彩花、蝶、桃，并有两组相对圆形开光，内绘祥云龙凤纹；另有两组相对蝠衔绶带、双钱纹，蕴含有福寿双全之美好寓意；下腹部饰以梅花纹、乳钉纹一周，及仰莲瓣纹一周。整体器形稳重大方，设色艳丽，构图疏密有致，具有浓厚的生活情趣。

釉里红钟馗打鬼鼻烟壶

清晚期

口径 1.2 厘米，足径 2.1 厘米，高 7.8 厘米

Underglaze red snuff bottle decorated with the Ghost Hunter *Zhong Kui*

Late Qing dynasty

Diameter of mouth rim 1.2cm, diameter of base 2.1cm, height 7.8cm

　　直颈，筒形腹，极矮圈足。腹部以釉里红人物图装饰，其一豹头环眼，铁面虬髯，相貌奇异，右手上指，左手持白色象牙笏板，另一神态狰狞可怖，均为钟馗形象，底部饰以青花小鬼图样。民间以这种钟馗打鬼故事为装饰题材，表达出辟邪趋吉的朴素愿望。

（视图一）　　　　　（视图二）

青花海水龙纹鼻烟壶

清末期

口径 2 厘米，底径 2.4 厘米，高 4.9 厘米

Blue and white snuff bottle with seawater and dragon design

Late Qing dynasty

Diameter of mouth rim 2cm, diameter of base 2.4cm, height 4.9cm

　　侈口，束颈，溜肩，弧腹，矮圈足。腹部绘有青花海水龙纹，并点缀有花卉纹，外底圈足内有青花双圈双行竖写楷书仿款"大清雍正年制"。

　　鼻烟壶是盛放鼻烟的器皿，其整体特征是壶口小，腹部大，壶盖带一小勺，以便伸入壶内取用。

粉彩九桃纹天球瓶

清末期

口径 13.5 厘米，底径 17 厘米，高 53 厘米

Famille-rose vault-of-heaven vase with peach pattern

Late Qing dynasty

Diameter of mouth rim 13.5cm, diameter of base 17cm, height 53cm

口微侈，长颈，丰肩，球形腹，极矮圈足。通体绘粉彩桃树一株，树干苗壮，枝上结蟠桃九个，桃树旁衬月季一簇，纹饰自腹部向上，局部延伸至长颈部。外底有青花三行竖写篆书仿款"大清乾隆年制"。

天球瓶是受西亚文化影响的器型，其造型始于明永乐时期，清雍正、乾隆时再度盛行，以"彩绘"纹者，是雍正、乾隆时期官窑的标准器物，绘九桃的，惟乾隆官窑最具代表性。

青花九老图花盆

清（1644～1911 年）

口径 36.2 厘米，足径 18.1 厘米，高 22 厘米

Black and white flower pot with pattern of Nine Elders

Qing dynasty (1644～1911)

Diameter of mouth rim 36.2cm, diameter of base 18.1cm, height 22cm

折沿，深腹，圈足。口沿内侧双弦纹内饰冰梅纹一周；外腹部绘九老图，老者或携琴会友，或坐卧闲谈，或携仗徐行，配以童子捧梅、飞雁、松石等图案，营造出一幅恬淡、悠闲的世外桃源画面。整体纹饰大气端庄，画工精细，运笔流畅有力，浓淡交织，极为精彩。

白釉罐

清（1644 ～ 1911 年）

口径 11 厘米，底径 19.8 厘米，高 23.8 厘米

1984 年北京市海淀区北安河出土

White-glazed jar

Qing dynasty (1644 ~ 1911)

Diameter of mouth rim 11cm, diameter of base 19.8cm, height 23.8cm

Unearthed from Beianhe, Haidian district in1984

直口，短颈，丰肩，圆腹，平底，素面无纹。除口沿、近足部及底部露胎无釉外，均施白釉，釉色白中泛青，釉层有细密开片。器物胎体坚实，釉层较薄，整体造型丰满。

青釉刻花卉纹胆式瓶

清（1644～1911 年）

口径 5.4 厘米，足径 12 厘米，高 39.5 厘米

Green-glazed gall-shaped vase with floral pattern

Qing dynasty (1644～1911)

Diameter of mouth rim 5.4cm, diameter of base 12cm, height 39.5cm

直口，长颈，悬胆形腹，圈足外撇，通体施青釉，呈半透明状。该瓶采用刻划装饰技法，口沿外侧暗刻回纹一周，颈部饰灵芝纹，肩部饰回纹及云纹各一周，腹部以缠枝牡丹纹、竹枝纹为饰，刻划流畅自然，自由奔放，灵活而富于节奏感。整体造型曲线优美柔和，釉质肥厚，釉色纯净莹润，有玉质美感，且刻划刀法宽阔有力，呈现明显的浮雕效果。

玉器

第三部分

玉，石之美者也。《礼记·聘义》中孔子告诫弟子说，君子应「比德于玉」，认为玉本身具备了仁、知、义、礼、乐、忠、信、天、地、德、道等特性。中国人重视玉、珍视玉远早于孔子所处的春秋时期，至少在新石器时期玉就已经受到了人们非凡的礼遇。有些玉用作装饰，但稀缺的玉更主要地还是用在了具有神秘色彩的仪式上。如著名的良渚文化，其制玉技术已经十分发达，用玉数量也极为可观。以后的历朝历代，玉器的制作和使用也从未间断，既用作礼器，也作为佩器和陈设器使用。礼器用玉器，形制相对固定，装饰方法也变化较少，据《周礼》记载，玉礼器主要指用于『礼天地四方』的六器——玉璜、玉琮、玉璧、玉圭、玉璋、玉琥。而用作佩器和陈设器的玉器则形制极其多样，富于变化，装饰方法也较为自由，在长期的发展过程中，积累了十分丰富的装饰题材。中国封建社会发展到明、清时期，玉器（尤其是作佩器和陈设器的实用玉器）发展到了空前的高度，尤其是清代的玉佩饰，堪称集古代佩玉之大成，既有仿古玉佩，也有宋元以来的各种佩，造型多变，工艺精巧。

海淀博物馆藏明、清玉器类型多样，造型丰富，以玉带饰、玉服饰、玉佩饰等为主的佩器数量尤为可观，制作也极为精巧，镂雕、巧作等技术应用十分高明。且因绝大多数具有明确出土时间、地点，对中国明、清时期玉鉴赏与研究具有重要意义。如1985年北太平庄出土的明代玉镂雕龙纹带板、1986年板井村出土的清代翠双龙戏珠纹镯、1983年皂君庙出土的玉乾隆御制诗扳指、1999年上地出土的清乾隆玉雕事事如意纹摆件等。

Part 3

Jade Wares

Jade is a kind of beautiful gem. According to the Book of Rites, Confucius once told to his disciples, a man of noble character should be inspired by the features of jade. Jade represents benevolence, wisdom, righteousness, courtesy, faith, honesty, and so on. Early in the Neolithic Period, Chinese people already considered jade as precious stone. Some jades were used as decorations, and the rare jades were used for the mysterious rites. During the period of Liangzhu Culture, the jade craft was very advanced and jade wares were widespread. In the later dynasties of Chinese history, jades were used as not only the ritual wares, but also the pendants and furnishings. According to Rites of Zhou, there are six kinds of jade ritual wares: Huang, Cong, Bi, Gui, Zhang, Hu, which are of fixed shape and less decoration. Comparing to the ritual wares, the jade pendants and furnishings have extremely various shapes and less restricted decorations. In the development of jade wares, many themes were used and innovated, especially in the Ming and Qing dynasties. Qing jade pendants, which include the pendants imitated of ancient jade wares and the jade with various shapes inherited from Song dynasty and later, are the apex of traditional Chinese jade wares.

The jade collections of Ming and Qing dynasties in Haidian Museum cover all kinds of jade wares with various shapes. Among them, the jade belt decorations, clothes decorations and pendants have great quantity and high quality. Moreover, most of them have certain excavation site and date, so they are very helpful for the research of Chinese jade of Ming and Qing dynasties. The representative ones include the jade belt board with dragon design in openwork of Ming dynasty unearthed from Beitaipingzhuang in 1985, the green jade bracelet with design of double dragons playing with a pearl of Qing dynasty unearthed from Banjingcun in 1986, jade thumb ring with Emperor Qianlong's poem inscription unearthed from Zaojunmiao in 1983, the jade carving with ruyi design of Qing Qianlong reign unearthed from Shangdi in 1999.

玉镂雕龙纹带板（十块）

明（1368 ~ 1644 年）

均宽 4 厘米

1985 年北京市海淀区西外太平庄动物园宿舍出土

Openwork jade belt decoration carved with dragon design (ten)

Ming dynasty (1368 ~ 1644)

Average width 4cm

Unearthed from the dormitory of Beijing Zoo at Xiwai Taipingzhuang, Haidian district in 1985

白玉质，晶莹剔透，边框琢磨精细，细致抛光使其带有较强的玻璃感。共十块，其中铊尾一块、圆桃一块、辅弼一块、排方七块。带板采用双层镂雕技法，龙纹为主题纹饰，并雕琢花叶纹，其底纹采用直线回转相连的横丝锦纹表现天空和云朵，用以烘托其上的龙纹，这与雕漆工艺中锦纹的运用有异曲同工之妙。

玉镂雕穿花龙纹带饰（二十块）

明（1368 ～ 1644 年）

均宽 5.5 厘米

2003 年北京市海淀区六一幼儿园出土

白玉质，质地纯净。带板形制为三台（三块）、圆桃（六块，其一残）、辅弼（两块）、排方（七块）和铊尾（两块），共二十块。采用镂雕及透雕技法，均双层镂空透雕，每块带板留有边框，带板主纹为盘曲飞舞的龙纹，空隙处间饰鸾鸟和花草纹。玉带雕刻为立体的分层镂空，花下压花，刻工精细，玲珑剔透。

Jade belt decoration carved with openwork dragon flying through flowers (twenty)

Ming dynasty (1368 ~ 1644)

Average width 5.5cm

Unearthed from Liuyi Kindergarten, Haidian district in 2003

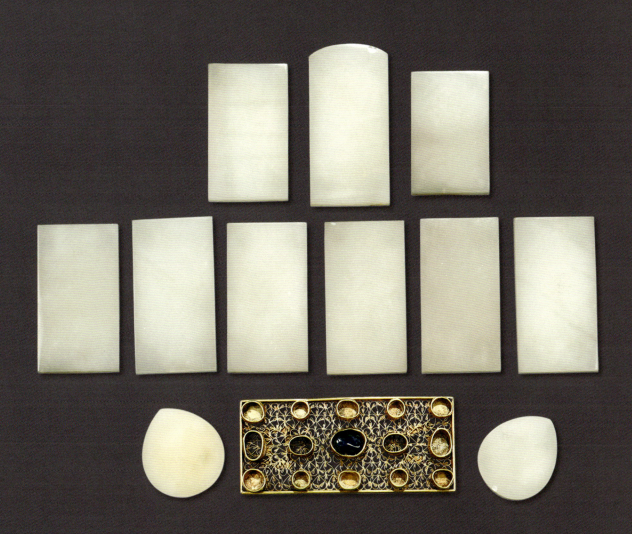

金带扣玉素带板（十二块）

明（1368 ～ 1644 年）
均宽 4.9 厘米
1990 年北京市海淀区蔡公庄出土

　　金带扣，长方形，外框简洁，表面金累丝上焊接镶嵌槽共
十五个，仅存留有一颗蓝宝石，其他缺失。玉带板，共十一块：
长方形八块，圭形一块，桃形两块。玉质温润纯净，抛光精细，
玉面光素无纹饰。

Jade belt decoration with gold buckle (twelve)

Ming dynasty (1368 ~ 1644)

Average width 4.9cm

Unearthed from Caigongzhuang, Haidian district in 1990

玉雕穿花龙纹带板（七块）

明（1368 ～ 1644 年）

均宽 5.5 厘米

Jade belt decoration carved with dragon flying through flowers (seven)

Ming dynasty (1368 ~ 1644)

Average width 5.5cm

　　白玉质，共七块，有铊尾一块，排方两块，辅弼两块，圆桃两块。带板采用剔地平雕技法，正面凸雕不高出边框的穿花龙纹，龙为四爪，龙身细长盘曲，雕工精细，纹饰及边框轮廓打磨光滑，莹润光泽。

白料带饰（二十块）

明（1368 ~ 1644 年）
均宽 3 厘米
1988 年北京市海淀区紫竹院公园出土

White-glass belt decoration (twenty)

Ming dynasty (1368 ~ 1644)

Average width 3cm

Unearthed from Purple Bamboo Park, Haidian district in 1988

料质洁白，光素无纹，正面有均匀螺钿涂层（部分剥落），边框边缘经打磨锋棱光滑，棱角分明。带饰由二十块带板按顺序排列而成，长方形八块、长条形四块、圭形两块、桃形六块，符合明代标准带板制式。

白玉素带饰（二十块）

明（1368～1644 年）

均宽 4.6 厘米

1991 年北京市海淀区北下关出土

Plain white-jade belt decoration（twenty）

Ming dynasty（1368～1644）

Average width 4.6cm

Unearthed from Beixiaguan, Haidian district in 1991

白玉质，正面及四边均打磨光滑，半透明，具有玻璃光泽。玉带板二十块，为明玉带板的标准形制，由三台、六圆桃、两辅弼、七排方和两铊尾组成。背面未抛光，其上有牛鼻穿。

白玉素带板 (十三块)

明 (1368 ~ 1644 年)

均宽 3.9 厘米

Plain white-jade belt decoration (thirteen)

Ming dynasty (1368 ~ 1644)

Average width 3.9cm

白玉质，洁白莹润，素面无纹饰。共十三块，
包括长方形带板八块，桃形带板五块。

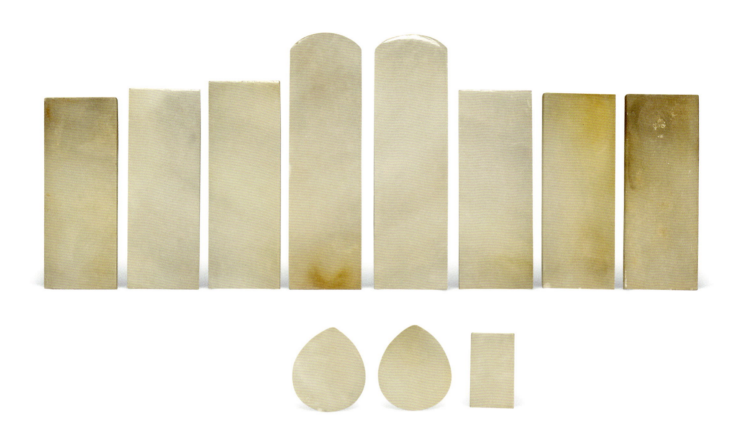

玉素带板（十一块）

明（1368 ～ 1644 年）

均宽 2.5 厘米

1994 年北京市海淀区安河桥出土

Plain jade belt decoration (eleven)

Ming dynasty (1368 ~ 1644)

Average width 2.5cm

Unearthed from Anheqiao, Haidian district in 1994

　　白玉质，微沁，素面无纹饰。共十一块，包
括铊尾两块，排方六块，辅弼一块，圆桃两块。

青玉素带板（十五块）

明（1368 ～ 1644 年）

均宽 4.2 厘米

1985 年北京市海淀区西外太平庄动物园宿舍出土

Green jade balt decoration (fifteen)

Ming dynasty (1368 ~ 1644)

Average width 4.2cm

Unearthed from the dormitory of Beijing Zoo at Xiwai Taipingzhuang, Haidian district in 1985

青玉质，玉色淡雅，玉质清莹温润，有蜡质感。带板共十五块，包括三台（缺一块），圆桃（六块），铊尾（一块），排方（六块）。玉面均光素无纹饰。

玉素带板（十块）

明（1368 ～ 1644 年）

均宽 4.5 厘米

1985 年北京市海淀区八里庄出土

Plain jade belt decoration (ten)

Ming dynasty (1368 ~ 1644)

Average width 4.5cm

Unearthed from Balizhuang, Haidian district in 1985

白玉质，洁白纯净，仅存十块，含排方五块、铊尾两块、辅弼两块、圆桃一块。

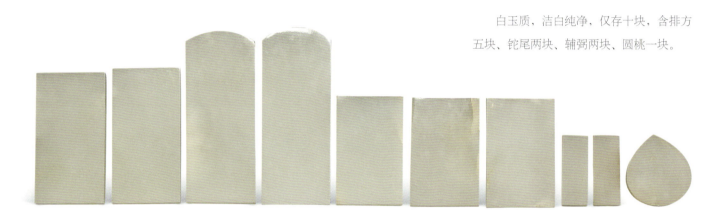

玉素带板（六块）

明（1368 ～ 1644 年）

均宽 3.2 厘米

1997 年北京理工大学院内出土

Plain jade belt decoration (six)

Ming dynasty (1368 ~ 1644)

Average width 3.2cm

Unearthed from Beijing Institute of Technology in 1997

白玉质，素面无纹饰，带黄色沁。由六块带板组成：铊尾两块、排方两块、圆桃两块。

玉素带板（十三块）

明（1368 ～ 1644 年）

均宽 3.4 厘米

Plain jade belt decoration (thirteen)

Ming dynasty (1368 ~ 1644)

Average width 3.4cm

　　白玉质，光素无纹饰，有黄色沁。共
十三块，包含排方七块，铊尾两块，圆桃两块，
辅弼两块。

玉雕龙带勾

明（1368 ~ 1644 年）

通长 12.5 厘米

1986 年北京市海淀区花园村出土

Jade belt hook carved with dragon design

Ming dynasty (1368 ~ 1644)

Overall length 12.5cm

Unearthed from Huayuancun, Haidian district in 1986

　　白玉质，洁白细腻，有油脂感，局部有黄褐色沁。带勾采用浅浮雕的制作工艺，龙首状勾首，勾腹造型若琵琶，较宽，微呈弧形，其上浮雕一螭龙，颈和背有阴刻线纹，随形延伸至尾端，尾分成两叉，纹饰凸出器表，勾背旋刻有圆形纽。龙首回望、螭龙曲身向前，颇具妙趣，寓意"苍龙教子"。

玉持莲童子

明（1368～1644 年）

高 5 厘米

1983 年北京市海淀区蔬菜公司出土

Jade boy holding lotus in his hand

Ming dynasty (1368~1644)

Height 5cm

Unearthed from the Vagetable Company of Haidian

district in 1983

　　白玉质，圆雕，童子双手持莲茎，足踏莲叶，以细阴刻线勾勒出衣纹，形象生动，栩栩如生。

　　童子持莲纹，同太子戏莲纹一样，也是婴戏纹的一种，典故亦出佛教故事之"鹿母莲花生子"，自宋代以后这种童子持莲纹十分多见。

玉雕莲鱼纹佩

明（1368 ～ 1644 年）
长 8.5 厘米，宽 6 厘米

Jade pendant with lotus and fish design

Ming dynasty (1368 ~ 1644)

Length 8.5cm, width 6cm

　　玉质、圆雕、鱼形，背部正中有穿孔。鱼鼓目厚唇，鱼鳞
脉络清晰，腹下雕荷叶莲花纹。玉呈浅褐色，增添肥腻之感。

玉雕虎摆件

明（1368 ～ 1644 年）

长 5.4 厘米，宽 3.1 厘米，高 2.3 厘米

1989 年北京市海淀区谷香园食品厂出土

Jade ornament carved with tiger design

Ming dynasty (1368 ~ 1644)

Length 5.4cm, width 3.1cm, height 2.3cm

Unearthed from the Guxiangyuan Food Factory, Haidian district in 1989

　　青玉质，圆雕卧虎，前爪相抱，交叉处有一对穿孔，虎头刻划细腻，威武略显不足，更显生动可爱。

　　古人认为白虎是代表西方的灵兽，具有辟邪消灾的神力，因此以虎形作为佩件和摆件的装饰题材十分常见。

玉雕虎摆件

明（1368 ～ 1644 年）

长 6 厘米，宽 2.5 厘米，高 3.3 厘米

1989 年北京市海淀区谷香园食品厂出土

Jade ornament carved with tiger design

Ming dynasty (1368 ~ 1644)

Length 6cm, width 2.5cm, height 3.3cm

Unearthed from the Guxiangyuan Food Factory,

Haidian district in 1989

　　青玉质，有沁，圆雕卧虎，前爪处有一对穿孔。

玉雕人物"喜"字佩

清（1644 ～ 1911 年）

长 5.8 厘米，宽 4.9 厘米，厚 1 厘米

1987 年北京市海淀区双榆树北里出土

Jade pendant carved with "*xi*" (happy) character and portraiture design

Qing dynasty (1644 ~ 1911)

Length 5.8cm, width 4.9cm, thickness 1cm

Unearthed from Shuangyushu beili, Haidian district in 1987

　　白玉质，银锭形，上下边缘雕云纹装饰，中部一面浮雕双喜字，一面浮雕红楼故事之黛玉葬花。

黄玉雕"进贤司"佩

清（1644 ~ 1911 年）

长 5.6 厘米，宽 4.2 厘米

1986 年北京市海淀区双榆树北里出土

Yellow jade pendant carved with "*jin xian si*"

Qing dynasty (1644 ~ 1911)

Length 5.6cm, width 4.2cm

Unearthed from a block north of Shuangyushu, Haidian district in 1986

　　黄玉质，如意云头形，两端带一对细小贯耳，顶端中部
有穿孔，一面雕有"进贤司"三字。

玉雕龙纹佩

清（1644 ~ 1911 年）

长 5.4 厘米，宽 5.1 厘米

1993 年北京市海淀区西翠路出土

Jade ornament carved with dragon design

Qing dynasty (1644 ~ 1911)

Length 5.4cm, width 5.1cm

Unearthed from Xicuilu, Haidian district in 1993

白玉质，圆形玉片，镂空雕出云龙纹，玉质
莹润洁白，雕工精细，腾龙形象栩栩如生。

玉雕夔龙纹佩

清（1644 ~ 1911 年）
长 5.2 厘米，宽 4.6 厘米，厚 0.5 厘米
1990 年北京市海淀区西郊粮库出土

Jade pendant with *kui*-dragon design

Qing dynasty (1644 ~ 1911)

Length 5.2cm, width 4.6cm, thickness 0.5cm

Unearthed from Granary of Western Suburbs, Haidian district in 1990

　　青白玉质，双面精雕，夔龙口衔灵芝，回首望向
尾部，有祥龙献瑞之意。镂雕出夔龙轮廓后，以阴刻、
浅浮雕手法表现出龙身及灵芝细部，极大地增强了写
实效果，使佩饰整体细腻生动。

玉镂雕太子戏莲片

清（1644～1911年）

直径5.5厘米，厚0.3厘米

1986年北京市海淀区北洼路出土

Jade carved with openwork crown prince playing with lotus

Qing dynasty (1644~1911)

Diameter 5.5cm, thickness 0.3cm

Unearthed from Beiwalu, Haidian district in 1986

青白玉质，薄片镂雕出太子戏莲纹，雕工精湛，使孩童稚气、天真的形象跃然眼前。

太子戏莲，又名太子玩莲，亦名富贵宜男，属婴戏纹之一种，源于佛教"鹿母莲花生子"的故事，是一种传统的装饰题材，被广泛使用。

玉雕葫芦坠

清（1644～1911年）

长6厘米，宽3.5厘米

1987年北京市海淀区双榆树北里出土

Jade pendant carved with gourd design

Qing dynasty (1644～1911)

Length 6cm, width 3.5cm

Unearthed from Shuangyushu beili, Haidian district in 1987

白玉质，圆雕，葫芦形，上有浮雕葫芦叶纹点缀，更增无数生机。

翠雕瓜叶纹挂件

清（1644 ~ 1911 年）

长 8 厘米，宽 4.2 厘米

1986 年北京市农林科学院出土

Jadeite pendant carved with melon design

Qing dynasty (1644 ~ 1911)

Length 8cm, width 4.2cm

Unearthed from Beijing Academy of Agriculture and Forestry Sciences in 1986

　　翠质，整体呈浅绿色，雕有扁圆形瓜一只，长圆形瓜两只，并带有多片瓜叶，顶端有穿孔，孔内附有一挂绳。整坠左右虽不对称，但平衡感很强。

（正面）　　　　　　　　　　　　　　　　（背面）

翠雕荷莲挂坠

清（1644 ～ 1911 年）
总长 11.8 厘米
1986 年北京市农林科学院出土

Jadeite pendant carved with lotus design

Qing dynasty (1644 ~ 1911)

Overall length 11.8cm

Unearthed from Beijing Academy of Agriculture and Forestry

Sciences in 1986

　　翠质，用阴刻及浮雕手法塑造出硕大的荷叶，荷叶间鹭鸶
戏游其上，背面双阴线勾勒出荷叶脉络及浑圆缠绕的茎蔓。荷
莲与鹭鸶构图紧凑，逸趣横生。荷叶上下左右均有穿，下坠翠
瓜片两枚，翠片较薄。

翠雕松鼠葫芦坠

清（1644 ～ 1911 年）

长 4.5 厘米，宽 2.7 厘米

1986 年北京电影学院出土

Jadeite pendant carved with squirrel and gourd design

Qing dynasty (1644 ~ 1911)

Length 4.5cm, width 2.7cm

Unearthed from Beijing Film Academy in 1986

翠质、圆雕，松鼠趴伏于带叶葫芦上，鼠耳贴服身体，双眼圆睁，

长尾下垂，栩栩如生。

黄晶巧作佛手坠

清（1644～1911 年）

长 5.5 厘米，宽 2.1 厘米

1986 年北京市农林科学院出土

Yellow crystal pendant carved with chagote design

Qing dynasty (1644 - 1911)

Length 5.5cm, width 2.1cm

Unearthed from Beijing Academy of Agriculture and Forestry Sciences in 1986

　　黄晶质，佛手瓜叶形。巧妙利用其上颜色的差异，雕佛手瓜叶纹，瓜叶脉络清晰，因顶端呈粉色，更突出佛手这一主题纹饰，使得整体造型生动美观，凸显工匠的技艺及妙想。

白玉扳指

清（1644 ~ 1911 年）
直径 3.8 厘米，高 2.7 厘米
1986 年北京市海淀区北洼路出土

White-jade thumb ring

Qing dynasty (1644 ~ 1911)
Diameter 3.8cm, height 2.7cm
Unearthed from Beiwalu, Haidian district in 1986

白玉质，光润细滑，呈圆筒状，一端边沿前凸，一端边沿
内凹，中部通心穿凿圆润、规整，外壁光素无纹。

玉乾隆御题诗扳指

清（1644 ~ 1911 年）

直径 2.9 厘米，高 2.4 厘米

1983 年北京市海淀区皂君庙出土

Jade thumb ring carved with the Qianlong emperor's imperial poem

Qing dynasty (1644 ~ 1911)

Diameter 2.9cm, height 2.4cm

Unearthed from Zaojunmiao, Haidian district in 1983

白玉质，筒形，轻巧精致，上下缘各饰以回纹一周，中间刻乾隆御题咏扳指诗一首："缮人规制玉人为 / 彄沓阛抨是所资 / 不称每羞童子佩 / 如磨常忆武公诗 / 底须象骨徒传古 / 恰似琼琚匪报兹 / 于度机张慎省括 / 温其德美信堪师 / 乾隆御题"。

扳指，在商周时期即已出现，是拉弓射箭时扣弦用的一种辅助工具，戴于射手右手拇指，用以扣住勾弦，防止擦伤手指，可见扳指原始是很具实用性的。清代时期的扳指，受到满汉各阶层男士的普遍喜爱，除武将外，文人亦多效此风，致使原本质地单一（骨角为主）的扳指，出现了象牙、翠、玉、碧玺等多种珍稀质地，并分化出了文扳指和武扳指两种风格。武扳指多厚重素面、文扳指则多轻巧，并于外壁精刻诗句或花纹。

白玉带皮扳指

清（1644 ～ 1911 年）

直径 3.3 厘米，高 2.8 厘米

White jade thumb ring with russet skin

Qing dynasty (1644 ~ 1911)

Diameter 3.3cm, height 2.8cm

玉质，马鞍形，上有黄色玉皮。玉质洁白温润，与黄色玉皮对比鲜明，既合理使用了玉材，也使两种颜色相得益彰。

玉扳指

清（1644 ～ 1911 年）

直径 2.6 厘米，高 1.8 厘米

Jade thumb ring

Qing dynasty (1644 ~ 1911)

Diameter 2.6cm, height 1.8cm

白玉质，中部外鼓，起棱，玉质洁白细腻、造型独特。

翠扳指

清（1644 ～ 1911 年）
直径 3 厘米，高 2.6 厘米
1987 年中国科学院院内出土

Jadeite thumb ring

Qing dynasty (1644 ~ 1911)
Diameter 3cm, height 2.6cm
Unearthed from Chinese Academy of Sciences in 1987

　　翠质，圆筒形，一端口内呈坡状，边缘内凹，由里向外逐渐趋薄，另一端边缘则向外延展少许凸出，打磨光滑，光泽莹润，青翠欲滴。筒状扳指主要流行于清代，素扳指更多凸显材质的优良。

翠扳指

清（1644 ～ 1911 年）

直径 3.2 厘米，高 2.5 厘米

1987 年北京市钢铁研究院西出土

Jadeite thumb ring

Qing dynasty (1644 ~ 1911)

Diameter 3.2cm, height 2.5cm

Unearthed from west to Beijing Central Iron and Steel Research Institute in 1987

翠质，筒形，颜色分布不均。

玉双龙戏珠镯

清（1644 ~ 1911 年）

直径 7.8 厘米

1984 年北京市海淀区太平路 14 号院出土

Jade bracelet carved with double dragons playing with a ball

Qing dynasty (1644 ~ 1911)

Diameter 7.8cm

Unearthed from the N0.14 yard at Tiapinglu, Haidian district in 1984

　　青白玉质，圆形。采用浮雕与镂空的技法，勾勒出双龙戏珠的
造型，尾部十二联珠纹，表现出双龙盘绕之感。

玉双龙戏珠镯

清（1644 ~ 1911 年）

直径 7.6 厘米

1986 年北京市农林科学院出土

Jade bracelet carved with double dragons playing with a ball

Qing dynasty (1644 ~ 1911)

Diameter 7.6cm

Unearthed from Beijing Academy of Agriculture and Forestry Sciences in 1986

　　青白玉质，扁圆形，采用阴刻与浮雕技法，呈现出双龙戏珠的造型，勾画细腻，生动传神。

玉双龙戏珠镯（一对）

清（1644 ~ 1911 年）

直径 7.2 厘米

1988 年北京市海淀区紫竹院公园出土

Jade bracelets carved with double dragons playing with a ball (pair)

Qing dynasty (1644 ~ 1911)

Diameter 7.2cm

Unearthed from Purple Bamboo Park, Haidian district in 1988

　　白玉质，弧方形，以阴刻与浮雕为主要技法。

翠雕双龙戏珠镯（一对）

清（1644 ~ 1911 年）

直径 7.2 厘米

1986 年北京市农林科学院出土

Jadeite bracelets carved with double dragons playing with a ball (pair)

Qing dynasty (1644 ~ 1911)

Diameter 7.2cm

Unearthed from Beijing Academy of Agriculture and Forestry Sciences in 1986

翠质，绿白相间。其上雕双龙戏珠纹，龙目圆睁、张嘴拱珠、
口露獠牙、甚是威猛，翠珠上刻一对团寿纹。整体采用浅浮雕
和镂空技法，将龙身和翠珠很好的串联在一起。

玉如意云纹簪

清（1644 ~ 1911 年）

长 16.8 厘米，宽 1 厘米

Jade hairpin with *ruyi*-shaped cloud design

Qing dynasty (1644 ~ 1911)

Length 16.8cm, width 1cm

　　青白玉质，簪头呈卷书式，并刻有如意云纹，
簪头与簪身之间作出较缓转折，平添几分意趣。

玉扁方

清（1644 ~ 1911 年）

长 27 厘米，宽 2.6 厘米

1984 年北京师范大学出土

Jade flat hairpin

Qing dynasty (1644 ~ 1911)

Length 27cm, width 2.6cm

Unearthed from Beijing Normal University in 1984

　　青白玉质，簪头呈卷书式，无纹饰，颇具质朴大
方之美感。

白玉翎管

清（1644 ～ 1911 年）
直径 1.7 厘米，高 7.2 厘米

**White-jade tubular ornament upon the official headgear
(used only in the Qing dynasty)**

Qing dynasty

Diameter 1.7cm, height 7.2cm

白玉质，细腻莹润，圆柱形，中空管状，上端琢出半圆形扁平钮，并置一系挂小圆穿孔，通体光素无纹。翎管是清代官员礼帽上插饰花翎的饰物。

翠翎管

清（1644 ～ 1911 年）
直径 1.7 厘米，高 6.5 厘米
1987 年北京市海淀区学院路出土

**Jadeite tubular ornament upon the official headgear
(used only in the Qing dynasty)**

Qing dynasty (1644 ~ 1911)

Diameter 1.7cm, height 6.5cm

Unearthed from Xueyuanlu, Haidian district in 1987

翠质，绿色分布不均，局部透白色，管身打磨精细，具玻璃光泽。翎管为圆柱形，中空，光素无纹，顶部出榫为半圆形钮，上有横穿。

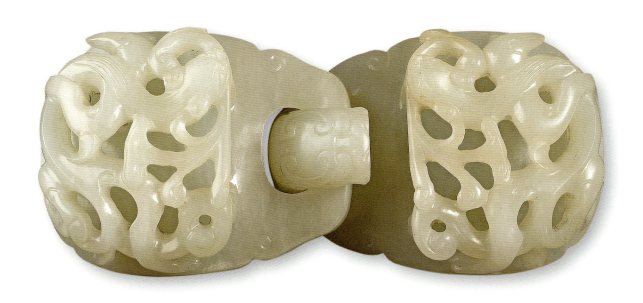

白玉雕龙纹带扣（一对）

清（1644 ~ 1911 年）
总长 12 厘米，宽 4.9 厘米
1987 年中国科学院宿舍出土

White jade belt buckles carved with dragon design (pair)

Qing dynasty (1644 ~ 1911)

Overall length 12cm, width 4.9cm

Unearthed from the dormitory of Chinese Academy of Sciences in 1987

白玉质，具有蜡质感。子、母扣均为长方形倭角，正面均雕螭龙衔灵芝图，背面各有一圆形钮，子扣榫头饰兽面纹。带扣采用高浮雕与镂空雕相结合的制作工艺，充分展示了螭龙的敏捷可爱与图案整体的空间感。

玉雕福寿纹带扣（一对）

清（1644 ~ 1911 年）

长 7 厘米，宽 5.5 厘米

1988 年北京农林科院出土

Jade belt buckles carved with felicity and longevity design (pair)

Qing dynasty (1644 ~ 1911)

Length 7cm, width 5.5cm

Unearthed from Beijing Academy of Agriculture and Forestry Sciences in 1988

白玉质，略闪青。正面中心刻团寿纹，边缘随形刻饰有张开双翅的蝙蝠，寓意福寿双全，背面各有一个凸起的铲形扣钮。整体雕琢整齐、规范、纹饰细腻生动。

玉雕万年大吉葫芦纹带板（二十块）

清（1644 ～ 1911 年）

均宽 7 厘米

1988 年北京市海淀区紫竹院公园出土

Jade belt decoration carved with gourd design (twenty)

Qing dynasty (1644 ~ 1911)

Average width 7cm

Unearthed from Purple Bamboo Park, Haidian district in 1988

　　青白玉质，共二十块。整体采用剔地平雕的技法，先在玉料表面设计主体纹饰，后把主纹外的地子均匀琢低在一定深度，进而突出主体纹饰。带板保留了四面边框，纹饰由葫芦、江崖海水、寿山、花瓣组成，带板中心葫芦上刻"大吉"，并在纹饰中间加入两个方向相反的"卍"，组成"万年大吉"的字样，以葫芦谐音福禄，蕴含吉祥寓意。

玉雕鹤鹿纹鼻烟壶

清（1644 ～ 1911 年）

长 3.8 厘米，宽 2 厘米，高 7 厘米

北京市海淀区清河出土

Jade snuff bottle carved with crane and deer design

Qing dynasty (1644 ~ 1911)

Length 3.8cm, width 2cm, height 7cm

Unearthed from Qinghe, Haidian district

　　白玉质。小口，扁方形腹，极矮圈足，带圆
形盖。腹部一面浮雕松鹿纹，一面刻画猴捧寿桃、
仙人驾云图，两侧面雕饰以夔龙纹，铜盖顶部镶
有圆形碧玺一枚，盖下连一烟勺。设计精致小巧，
实用性强。

翠鼻烟壶

清（1644 ~ 1911 年）

长 4.9 厘米，宽 2.5 厘米，高 7.2 厘米

Jadeite snuff bottle

Qing dynasty (1644 ~ 1911)

Length 4.9cm, width 2.5cm, height 7.2cm

　　翠质。直颈、斜溜肩，扁圆形腹，底部微向内凹，带馒头形象牙盖。质地光洁、种水俱佳，是一件十分难得的工艺品兼实用器。

芙蓉石挂件

清（1644 ～ 1911 年）

长 5.5 厘米，宽 4 厘米

1986 年北京市农林科学院出土

Rose quartz pendant

Qing dynasty (1644 ~ 1911)

Length 5.5cm, width 4cm

Unearthed from Beijing Academy of Agriculture and Forestry Sciences in 1986

　　芙蓉石，瓜叶形。运用圆雕手法刻出瓜叶纹。布局合理，整体
呈粉色，造型精巧美观。

水晶雕葫芦坠

清（1644～1911 年）
长 4 厘米，宽 3 厘米
1984 年中国人民大学北小区出土

Crystal pendant shaped of a cucurbit

Qing dynasty (1644～1911)
Length 4cm, width 3cm
Unearthed from a block north to the Renmin
University in 1984

　　水晶质，双联葫芦形，上有浮雕葫
芦叶，有穿孔。葫芦，谐音福禄，表达
出祝愿福禄双全的美好愿望。

茶晶雕福寿纹坠

清（1644 ～ 1911 年）

长 4 厘米，宽 3.2 厘米

1984 年中国人民大学北小区出土

Tea-color crystal pendant carved with bat design

Qing dynasty (1644 - 1911)

Length 4cm, width 3.2cm

Unearthed from a block north to the Renmin University in 1984

 茶晶质，桃形坠，上有浮雕蝠纹、桃叶纹，有穿孔。具有明显的祈愿长寿之意。

翠镶金双蝠纹坠（一对）

清（1644 ～ 1911 年）

直径 2.4 厘米，高 3.4 厘米

1986 年北京市农林科学院出土

Jadeite pendents with double bat design and gold inlay (pair)

Qing dynasty (1644 ~ 1911)

Diameter 2.4cm, height 3.4cm

Unearthed from Beijing Academy of Agriculture and Forestry Sciences in 1986

金双蝠形坠一对，内镶翠环各一，翠环
均呈不均匀浅绿色，有沁，局部呈褐色。

翠朝珠（七枚）

清（1644 ～ 1911 年）

直径 2.3 厘米

Jadeite beads of court necklace (seven)

Qing dynasty (1644 ~ 1911)

Diameter 2.3cm

翠质，光素，其一有三个穿孔，余六枚均为对穿孔。

玉蝉

清（1644 ~ 1911 年）

长 5.5 厘米，宽 2.5 厘米

Jade ornament carved with cicada design

Qing dynasty (1644 ~ 1911)

Length 5.5cm, width 2.5cm

　　青白玉质，圆雕，以简洁的阴刻线刻划出蝉形轮廓，双目突出，头部双目间有穿孔，以供佩戴。

　　蝉被古人认为是神秘而圣洁的灵物，玉蝉既作生人的佩饰，也作死者的葬玉。大体分三种用途：一种为佩蝉，头部双目间有穿孔；一种为冠蝉，用于帽饰，无穿孔；一种为含蝉（含于死者口中），一般刀法简单，无穿孔。

翠雕福寿饰件

清（1644 ~ 1911 年）

长 6.5 厘米，宽 4.5 厘米

1986 年北京市海淀区板井村出土

Jadeite ornament carved with auspicious designs
such as fingered citron, peach and pomegranate

Qing dynasty (1644 ~ 1911)

Length 6.5cm, width 4.5cm

Unearthed from Banjingcun, Haidian district in 1986

翠质。采用圆雕、镂空技法，按品字形布局刻画出石榴、佛手、桃。三果以茎叶相连，枝干短粗而有力，叶子宽大而肥硕，下方承托以一只展翅飞翔的蝙蝠。

福寿三多，以佛手谐意福，以桃子谐意寿，以石榴暗喻多子，表现多福、多寿、多子的颂祷及对幸福生活的美好期望，是常见的吉祥纹饰。

青玉雕事事如意纹摆件

清·乾隆（1736 ～ 1795 年）

长 16.5 厘米，宽 9.5 厘米，厚 6 厘米

1999 北京市海淀区上地出土

Green jade ornament carved with persimmons and *ruyi*

Qianlong reign, Qing dynasty (1736 ~ 1795)

Length 16.5cm, width 9.5cm, thickness 6cm

Unearthed from Shangdi, Haidian district in 1999

青玉质，圆雕折枝带叶双柿，并蒂突脐，下部雕一曲柄灵芝形如意，相连双柿暗指"事事"，配上如意一柄，寓意"事事如意"。整体呈深青色，色泽自然深沉，设计精巧，雕工细腻，打磨光滑。因与具有明显乾隆时期风格的铜胎画珐琅四方瓶同时出土，该摆件应是清乾隆时期具有宫廷风格的陈设器。

（正面）

（背面）

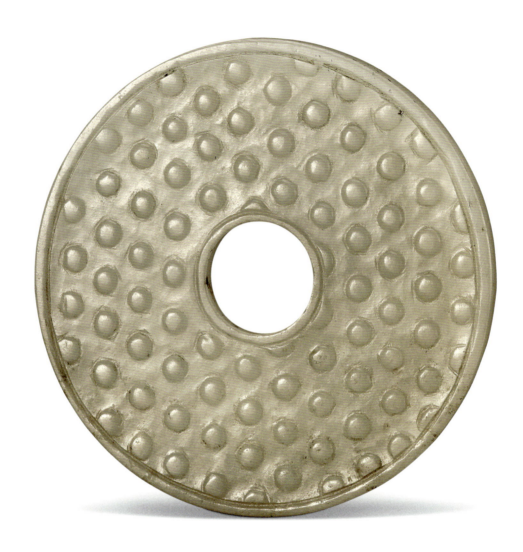

白玉谷纹璧

清（1644 ~ 1911 年）

直径 5.1 厘米，厚 0.4 厘米

1990 年北京市海淀区北医三院出土

White jade *bi* disk with grain pattern

Qing dynasty (1644 ~ 1911)

Diameter 5.1cm, thickness 0.4cm

Unearthed from Peking University Third Hospital, Haidian district in 1990

　　白玉质，两面均匀浮雕细密谷纹，造型古朴大方。

墨玉巧作雕螭龙烟嘴

清（1644 ～ 1911 年）

直径 1.3 厘米，高 5 厘米

1985 年国家图书馆出土

Black jade pipe for tobacco ingeniously carved with dragon design

Qing dynasty (1644 ~ 1911)

Diameter 1.3cm, height 5cm

Unearthed from National Library of China in 1985

　　玉质温润，呈瓶形。烟嘴采用巧作（又称俏色）工艺，利用玉石的天然色泽差异，烟嘴管部由墨玉琢磨成型，白玉则雕琢螭龙攀附其上，整件物品经过细致的镂雕、抛光、打磨，工艺精细，制作精美。

玉竹节式烟嘴

民国（1912 ～ 1949 年）

长 10 厘米

Jade pipe for tobacco with bamboo-joint design

Republic of China (1912 ~ 1949)

Length 10cm

　　青白玉，管状。管部均匀阴刻十一组双弦纹，分隔出竹节十段，并刻有竹叶纹，近口部沁蚀较严重，沁处呈牙白色。

中国已经发现的古代金银制品可上溯到商代，当时的金银制品不仅稀有，且多为简约的小型装饰物。其后伴随贵金属开采、冶炼技术的逐步提高，金银制品的使用范围不断扩大，几乎涉及了人类生活的各个方面，如器皿、服饰、钱币、工具、宗教、医药等。与铜器、玉器等不同，金银制品一开始就以具有审美价值的艺术品形式出现。商代以后的中国古代金银器以贵金属为依托，逐渐发展出了具有明显时代风格的手工业门类，虽风格多样，但多体现出造型精巧、装饰细密、工艺繁复的特征，每一件都堪称科学与艺术完美结合的佳作。

海淀博物馆藏金银器数量多、质量上乘，且大部分来源时间、地点详尽可靠，十分珍贵。尤其是宫廷气氛浓厚、华丽浓艳的明、清两代金银器，雍容华贵、色彩斑斓，龙、凤等象征权势与高贵的纹饰相当多见，有些出土于王侯、妃嫔、贵戚之墓，有些出土于特权人物（如权柄极大的明代宦官）之墓葬，这些金银器形式多样，制作精美，装饰华丽，范铸、捶揲、累丝、镶嵌、錾花等工艺样样精湛，对海淀地区、北京地区乃至整个中国明、清时代金银器的研究具有重要的资料价值。如2002年巨山农场出土的清代金嵌红宝石荷蟹纹钗、金凤钗等一组金饰，1985年八里庄明代宦官杜茂墓出土的银錾花鸟人物纹盏托，1991年北下关明代宦官墓出土的刻有『御马监太监』『忠字三十八号』的腰牌，1989年国家气象局出土的装饰极其华丽、重达500余克的一对明代金雕松竹梅镯，1986年大柳树北村出土的清代金雕莲瓣纹帽顶等。

Part 4

Gold & Silver Wares

The gold and silver wares found in China can be traced back to Shang dynasty, in which the gold and silver were very rare and used as small decorations. Due to the improvement of exploiting and smelting technology, the gold and silver wares were used for many purposes subsequently, such as utensil, clothes, coins, tools, religion and medicines. Different from bronze wares and jade, the gold and silver ones have certain aesthetic value at the beginning. After Shang dynasty, the production of gold and silver wares gradually became an important branch of Chinese traditional handicraft. Most of them have various styles, elegant shapes, fine decorations and advanced craftsmanship. It is safe in saying that every piece of them symbolizes the perfect combination of science, technology and art.

Most of the gold and silver wares collected in Haidian Museum have clear excavation site and date. Either the quality or the quantity of them is remarkable. The gold and silver wares in Ming and Qing dynasties usually have noble pattern or design of dragon and phoenix which symbolize the royal power, because they are unearthed from the tombs of royal family or some prerogative members (e.g. some high-level eunuchs in Ming dynasty). These wares are made by many traditional Chinese handicrafts, such as mold casting, hammering, filigreeing, inlaying and carving, which are very helpful for the research of ancient Chinese gold and silver objects of Ming and Qing dynasties. Some precious wares are listed as follows: the hairpins with inlaid gems and in the shape of phoenix of Qing dynasty unearthed from Jushan Farm in 2002, the dish tray carved with flower-and-bird and figure design unearthed from Du Mao's tomb of Ming dynasty in Balizhuang in 1985, the identity cards unearthed from Ming eunuch's tomb in Beixiaguan in 1991, a pair of bracelets with design of pine tree, bamboo and plum of Ming dynasty (more than 500g) unearthed from the site in State Meteorological Administration in 1989, the crown top with lotus-petal design of Qing dynasty unearthed from Daliushu Village in 1986.

鎏金镂空花卉镯

明（1368 ～ 1644 年）

直径 7.5 厘米

Gilt bracelet with openwork floral design

Ming dynasty (1368 ~ 1644)

Diameter 7.5cm

　　银质，表面鎏金，镯圈外侧为镂空十五朵相连梅花，并于开口处两端分别錾刻团寿纹一组，镯圈内侧錾刻绶带纹，谐意"寿"，表示出明确的祈愿长寿之意。镂空镯圈内藏有可滚动金珠数枚，既显示了金匠的高超技艺，也为原已精致的手镯更增意趣。

金雕松竹梅镯（一对）

明（1368 ~ 1644 年）

直径 7.4 厘米

1989 年国家气象局出土

Gold bracelets carved with pine, bamboo
and plum blossoms (pair)

Ming dynasty (1368 ~ 1644)

Diameter 7.4cm

Unearthed from China Meteorological Administration in 1989

金质，开口式镯，总重 500.6 克。镯身雕松、竹、梅，呈
十六竹节式，竹节间雕联珠纹。内侧有"中孚"戳记。

金雕二龙戏珠花卉纹项圈

明（1368～1644 年）

直径 16.7 厘米

Gold necklace carved with flowers and two dragons playing with a ball

Ming dynasty (1368～1644)

Diameter 16.7cm

　　复合质地，全器以金为皮，以象牙为骨，呈黄白相间的效果，象牙骨六段（缺失一条），以花卉形金嵌宝珠间隔（嵌物脱落）。主体纹饰以龙的刻画最为生动，戏珠龙张口拱珠、双目圆睁，角、发向后，边饰层次多，依次为绳纹、海水纹、云纹。全器运用了范铸、錾花、焊接、镶嵌等诸工艺，复杂而细腻，项圈首尾两端可自由调节。

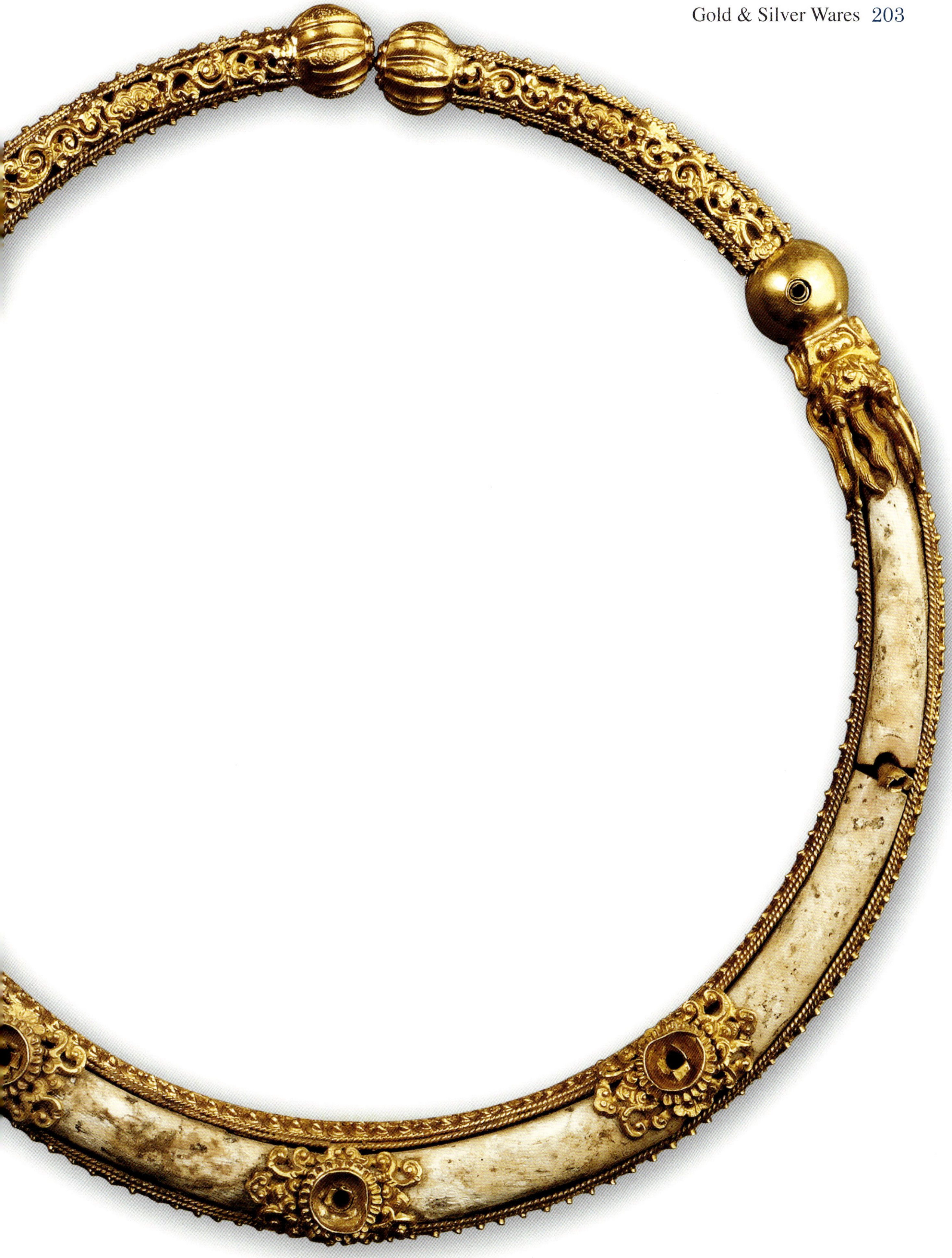

金云鹿纹簪

明（1368 ～ 1644 年）

长 8.5 厘米

1991 年北京市海淀区北下关出土

Gold hairpin with cloud and deer design

Ming dynasty (1368 ~ 1644)

Length 8.5cm

Unearthed from Beixiaguan, Haidian district in 1991

　　金针，蘑菇形簪首，顶部正中有镶嵌槽（嵌物佚失），
边缘雕灵芝、花卉、鹿纹，簪柄上部錾刻云纹、鹿纹，
纹饰凸起，呈半浮雕状。

金钱纹簪

明（1368～1644年）

长10.4厘米

1991 年北京市海淀区北下关出土

Gold hairpins with coin design

Ming dynasty (1368 ~ 1644)

Length 10.4cm

Unearthed from Beixiaguan, Haidian district in 1991

　　金质，簪首雕竹节纹，顶端以镂空钱纹装饰，外侧錾刻联珠纹，簪柄处镂刻联钱纹，底部镂刻双钱纹。

金梅花簪

明（1368 ~ 1644 年）

长 10.7 厘米

1990 年北京市海淀区蔡公庄出土

Gold hairpin with the decoration of plum blossoms

Ming dynasty (1368 ~ 1644)

Length 10.7cm

Unearthed from Caigongzhuang, Haidian district in 1990

　　金质，粗针形。簪首呈五瓣梅花形，花瓣上脉络清晰可辨。

素金簪

明（1368 ～ 1644 年）

长 6.7 厘米

1990 年北京市海淀区蔡公庄出土

Gold hairpin

Ming dynasty (1368 ~ 1644)

Length 6.7cm

Unearthed from Caigongzhuang, Haidian district in 1990

金质，钉形。

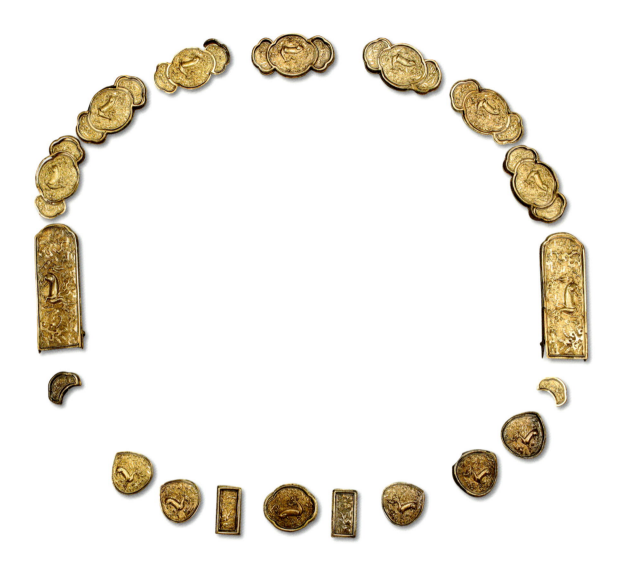

银鎏金麒麟带饰(十九块)

明（1368 ~ 1644 年）

均宽 4 厘米

1985 年北京市海淀区五塔寺东出土

Silver-gilt belt decoration with kilin design (nineteen)

Ming dynasty (1368 ~ 1644)

Average width 4cm

Unearthed from east to the Monastery of Five Stupas, Haidian district in 1985

　　银质，表面鎏金，共有带板十九块，分别为：三台（三块）、圆桃（五块，依明制应为六块，此处缺一块）、辅弼（两块）、铊尾（两块）、排方（七块），以麒麟芭蕉为主题纹饰，工艺精湛，为明代鎏金带板中的精品。

　　《明史·舆服制》有关于官员束带的明确规定，三、四品文武官朝服用金带；三、四品文武官公服用金带；三品文武官常服用金钑花带，四品文武官常服用素金带。以上不可僭越。

（正面）

（背面）

银鎏金御马监太监腰牌

明（1368 ～ 1644 年）

长 11.7 厘米、宽 5.9 厘米、厚 0.9 厘米

1991 年北京市海淀区北下关出土

**Silver-gilt waist tag inscribed with "*yumajian taijian*"
(eunuch of imperial stables)**

Ming dynasty (1368 ~ 1644)

Length 11.7cm, width 5.9cm, thickness 0.9cm

Unearthed from Beixiaguan, Haidian district in 1991

银质，通体鎏金，钟形，中空。腰牌两面边缘凸起双棱边，顶部錾刻祥云纹，云纹中有一穿孔。

腰牌是官吏悬挂于腰间，作为出入皇宫通行证件的牌子，又称"穿宫牌"。明代对官吏佩带腰牌有严格规定，不同级别、身份所用腰牌质地、形制皆不同，具有强烈的权力色彩。该腰牌一面刻"御马监太监"，一面刻"忠字三十八号"，系御马监太监出入皇宫的证件。

银錾花鸟人物纹盏托

明（1368 ～ 1644 年）

直径 15.2 厘米，高 1.2 厘米

1985 年北京市海淀区八里庄出土

Silver saucer engraved with flowers, birds and figures

Ming dynasty (1368 ~ 1644)

Diameter 15.2cm, height 1.2cm

Unearthed from Balizhuang, Haidian district in 1985

银质，通体鎏金。平折沿，浅腹，极矮圈足，整体呈菱花形。内底中央浮雕覆莲圆台，盘口折沿处以双阴线錾刻忍冬纹一周，盘内底以鱼子纹为地，錾刻以"封侯"（蜂、猴）、"福禄"（壶、鹿）、"抬头见喜"（喜鹊）三组纹饰。

银镀金灵芝双耳杯（两只）

明（1368 ～ 1644 年）

口径 5.1 厘米，底径 2.9 厘米，高 3.5 厘米

1985 年北京市海淀区八里庄出土

Silver-gilt cups with magic fungus design and two ears (two)

Ming dynasty (1368 ~ 1644)

Diameter of mouth rim 5.1cm, diameter of base 2.9cm, height 3.5cm

Unearthed from Balizhuang, Haidian district in 1985

银质，表面镀金，口部微撇，微束颈，腹部以下略鼓，矮圈足，腹部焊接有灵芝形对称双耳，造型规整，光洁素雅。

银套筷

明（1368 ～ 1644 年）

通长 19.5 厘米

1991 年北京市海淀区北下关出土

Silver chopsticks with a cover

Ming dynasty (1368 ~ 1644)

Overall length 19.5cm

Unearthed from Beixiaguan, Haidian district in 1991

银筷，带筷套。筷形呈首方足圆式，为明代流行式样，方、圆间的过渡区錾刻圆珠纹。筷套略扁，口沿凸起唇边，并有圆形挂环一个。

银壶

明（1368 ～ 1644 年）

口径 5.4 厘米，底径 12.5 厘米，通高 18.5 厘米

1985 年北京市海淀区八里庄出土

Silver pot with a lid

Ming dynasty (1368 ~ 1644)

Diameter of mouth rim 5.4cm, diameter of base 12.5cm, overall height 18.5cm

Unearthed from Balizhuang, Haidian district in 1985

银质，子母口，扁圆形腹，曲柄，曲流，高足，带喇叭形钮盖。

造型独特，实用性强。

金嵌宝石龙纹饰件（四件）

清（1644 ~ 1911 年）

长 7.5 厘米，宽 3 厘米

2002 年北京市海淀区巨山农场出土

Gold ornaments with dragon design and gem inlay (four)

Qing dynasty (1644 ~ 1911)

Length 7.5cm, width 3cm

Unearthed from Jushan Farm, Haidian district in 2002

　　金质，龙纹饰件。四爪，龙身采用累丝工艺，
并嵌宝石，作游走腾飞状，造型生动。

金嵌宝石凤纹饰件

清（1644 ~ 1911 年）

长 4.7 厘米，宽 2.5 厘米，高 2 厘米

2002 年北京市海淀区巨山农场出土

Gold ornament with phoenix design and gem inlay

Qing dynasty (1644 ~ 1911)

Length 4.7cm, width 2.5cm, height 2cm

Unearthed from Jushan Farm, Haidian district in 2002

金质，累丝凤形簪首，簪柄佚失，凤首
顶部有镶嵌槽一个（嵌物佚失）。凤昂首振翅，
口衔金珠，整体造型美观。

银鎏金蝴蝶饰件

清（1644 ～ 1911 年）

长 5.5 厘米，宽 4 厘米

2002 年北京市海淀区巨山农场出土

Silver-gilt butterfly

Qing dynasty (1644 - 1911)

Length 5.5cm, width 4cm

Unearthed from Jushan Farm, Haidian district in 2002

银质，表面鎏金，蝴蝶形饰件。

金嵌宝石扁簪

清（1644 ～ 1911 年）

长 11.6 厘米

Gold flat hairpin with gem inlay

Qing dynasty (1644 - 1911)

Length 11.6cm

兰花叶形插簪，两端共有镶嵌槽
六个，近端四个镶嵌有随形翠片，葫
芦形镶嵌槽内镶嵌物佚失，背部有对
称"甲宝成新足赤"、"福"字戳记。

金嵌宝石荷蟹纹钗

清（1644 ～ 1911 年）

长 14 厘米

2002 年北京市海淀区巨山农场出土

Gold hairpin with gem inlay and lotus and crab design symbolizing harmony

Qing dynasty (1644 ~ 1911)

Length 14cm

Unearthed from Jushan Farm, Haidian district in 2002

　　金双股针，荷叶、莲花、蟹形钗。花蕊与螃蟹背部嵌有宝石，荷叶和莲瓣采用累丝工艺，钗股之间以两个金环联接。荷、蟹谐音"和谐"，寄托了人们对美满生活的憧憬。

金雕松竹梅纹钗

清（1644 ~ 1911 年）

长 15.8 厘米

2002 年北京市海淀区巨山农场出土

Gold hairpin carved with pine, bamboo and plum blossom design

Qing dynasty (1644 ~ 1911)

Length 15.8cm

Unearthed from Jushan Farm, Haidian district in 2002

　　金双股针，上半部边缘雕竹节纹，背面捶打为扁形，其间松枝、竹叶、梅花纹饰交相缠绕，梅花正中有镶嵌槽（嵌物佚失）。金饰制作工艺复杂，手法细腻，融合捶揲、錾刻、累丝、焊接等技法，纹饰繁复，造型精美。

金嵌宝石花卉纹簪 （两支）

清（1644 ～ 1911 年）

长 11 厘米

2002 年北京市海淀区巨山农场出土

Gold hairpins with floral design and gem inlay (two)

Qing dynasty (1644 ~ 1911)

Length 11cm

Unearthed from Jushan Farm, Haidian district in 2002

　　金针，累丝花卉纹，其上各镶嵌碧玺两枚。

银鎏金松竹梅纹簪（两支）

清（1644 ～ 1911 年）

长 16 厘米

1986 年北京市海淀区羊坊店出土

Silver-gilt hairpins carved with pine, bamboo and plum blossom design (two)

Qing dynasty (1644 ~ 1911)

Length 16cm

Unearthed from Yangfangdian, Haidian district in 1986

　　银质，表面鎏金，镂空针形。簪首呈竹节状，旁出松枝、竹叶、梅花各一，花心各镶嵌宝石一枚（其一已失），花瓣内各嵌珍珠五枚（仅存三枚）。此簪汇集焊接、累丝、掐丝、鎏金等制作工艺，纹饰精细、雍容华丽。

银鎏金镶玉凤簪（两支）

清（1644～1911年）

长20厘米

1986 年北京市农林科学院内出土

**Silver-gilt hairpins with phoenix design
and jade inlay (two)**

Qing dynasty (1644 ~ 1911)

Length 20cm

Unearthed from Beijing Academy of Agriculture and
Forestry Sciences in 1986

　　银、玉复合材质，针形。银簪柄表面鎏金，
以花叶纹装饰，顶部各嵌镂雕青白玉凤一只。

金联钱纹簪（两支）

清（1644 ～ 1911 年）

长 17 厘米

1994 年北京市海淀区花园村出土

Gold hairpins with connected coin design (two)

Qing dynasty (1644 ~ 1911)

Length 17cm

Unearthed from Huayuancun, Haidian district in 1994

金质，扁针形。簪身为镂空十六联钱纹，顶端呈蘑菇形，背部有"裕通"戳记。

金嵌红宝石凤簪

清（1644 ～ 1911 年）

长 12 厘米

2002 年北京市海淀区巨山农场出土

Gold hairpin with phoenix design and ruby inlay

Qing dynasty (1644 ~ 1911)

Length 12cm

Unearthed from Jushan Farm, Haidian district in 2002

　　金质，扁长细柄，凤形簪头。凤口衔金珠一颗，凤尾
上嵌红宝石一颗。

金嵌红宝石凤簪

清（1644～1911年）

长9厘米

Gold hairpin with phoenix design and ruby inlay

Qing dynasty (1644 ~ 1911)

Length 9cm

金质，凤形簪头，凤身上嵌红宝石一颗。

金嵌红宝石花卉纹簪

清（1644 ~ 1911 年）

长 9.8 厘米

Gold hairpin with floral design and ruby inlay

Qing dynasty (1644 ~ 1911)

Length 9.8cm

金质，花瓣形簪头，花蕊中心抱嵌红宝石一颗，花瓣底部焊接有带枝花叶纹。

金"天赦"款佛手簪

明（1368～1644 年）

长 10.1 厘米

1985 年北京植物园内出土

Gold hairpin with Buddha's hand decoration and *"tian she"* inscriptions

Ming dynasty (1368 ~ 1644)

Length 10.1cm

Unearthed from Beijing Botanical Garden in 1985

　　金质，长柄，佛手形簪，佛手拇指与食指相扣，挂一钟形坠，坠上一面刻"天赦"款，一面刻花叶纹。

金如意云纹九连环簪

清（1644 ～ 1911 年）

长 12 厘米

Gold hairpin with *ruyi*-shaped cloud design and
nine interlocking rings

Qing dynasty (1644 ~ 1911)

Length 12cm

金质，细长柄，如意云纹九连环簪头，簪头顶
端为一镶嵌槽，嵌件佚失。

金凤钗

清（1644～1911 年）
长 14.2 厘米
2002 年北京市海淀区巨山农场出土

Gold hairpin with phoenix design
Qing dynasty (1644 ~ 1911)
Length 14.2cm
Unearthed from Jushan Farm, Haidian district in 2002

金镂空针，凤形簪首，昂首竖颈，口衔金珠，
双翅张开强劲有力，簪柄为镂空连续几何纹。金饰
采用累丝、焊接、镂空等工艺，技术精湛。

金累丝龙纹簪

清（1644 ~ 1911 年）

长 7.5 厘米

Gold filigree hairpin with dragon design

Qing dynasty (1644 ~ 1911)

Length 7.5cm

金质，扁针形。簪首为如意云头形金片，边缘饰以掐丝云纹，金片正中出累丝腾龙纹。造型生动逼真。

金嵌珍珠龙形簪

清（1644 ~ 1911 年）

长 11 厘米

Gold hairpin with dragon design and pearl inlay

Qing dynasty (1644 ~ 1911)

Length 11cm

金质，龙形簪头，龙身嵌珍珠五颗。

金花卉纹簪

清（1644 ~ 1911 年）

长 8.8 厘米

Gold hairpin with floral design

Qing dynasty (1644 ~ 1911)

Length 8.8cm

金针，曲柄，顶部五瓣花形，采用锤揲、錾刻、焊接等技法，花卉纹路刻划细腻顺畅，凹凸起伏，立体感强。

金梅花簪

清（1644 ～ 1911 年）

长 17.5 厘米

2002 年北京市海淀区巨山农场出土

Gold hairpin with plum blossom design

Qing dynasty (1644 ~ 1911)

Length 17.5cm

Unearthed from Jushan Farm, Haidian district in 2002

金掐丝"平安"簪

清（1644 ～ 1911 年）

长 9.5 厘米

1992 年北京市外国语大学院内出土

Gold filigree hairpin with the design wishing for peace

Qing dynasty (1644 ~ 1911)

Length 9.5cm

Unearthed from Beijing Foreign Studies University in 1992

　　金镂空针，簪首累丝梅花纹，为梅枝梅花形，簪柄镂空网格纹。金饰运用立体浮雕形凸花工艺和镂雕的装饰工艺，将器型与纹饰融为一体，体现了器物的立体感与真实感，细碾精琢，线条遒劲，刚柔相济，工艺精湛。

　　金质，针形。掐丝瓶式簪首，瓶口出"安"字，两端各出横梁，其上各坠累丝磬形饰件，有平安吉庆的美好寓意。

金竹节式扁簪

清（1644 ~ 1911 年）

长 16.5 厘米

1992 年北京市外国语大学出土

Gold flat hairpin with bamboo design

Qing dynasty (1644 ~ 1911)

Length 16.5cm

Unearthed from Beijing Foreign Studies University in 1992

  金质，雕出竹节三段，每段间以细密点状纹饰
隔开，簪中部刻有竹叶纹，簪背部有"瑞兴"款。

金簪

清（1644 ~ 1911 年）

长 18.5 厘米

Gold hairpin

Qing dynasty (1644 ~ 1911)

Length 18.5cm

  金质，扁针形，较软。簪首
两端錾刻五瓣梅花，背部有"天
祥"戳记，整体素雅大方。

金镂空五蝠纹扁方

清（1644 ~ 1911 年）

长 17.1 厘米，宽 1.8 厘米

1988 年北京市海淀区蓟门桥东出土

Gold flat hairpin with openwork bat design

Qing dynasty (1644 ~ 1911)

Length 17.1cm, width 1.8cm

Unearthed from east of Jimenqiao, Haidian district in 1988

　　金质，簪身为镂空五蝠纹，谐意五福俱全，背部有"一元足赤"款。

金联钱纹扁方

清（1644 ~ 1911 年）

长 27.6 厘米，宽 2.4 厘米

1986 年北京市农林科学院内出土

Gold flat hairpin with connected coin design

Qing dynasty (1644 ~ 1911)

Length 27.6cm, width 2.4cm

Unearthed from Beijing Academy of Agriculture and Forestry Sciences in 1986

　　金质，簪头两端呈五瓣梅花形，中部錾刻蝠纹，簪身为镂空二十七联钱纹，边缘围以回纹，背部共有五处"晋豫"戳记。

银鎏金龙凤纹扁方

清（1644～1911 年）

长 24.2 厘米，宽 2.5 厘米

1986 年北京市农林科学院内出土

Silver-gilt flat hairpin with dragon and phoenix design

Qing dynasty (1644～1911)

Length 24.2cm, width 2.5cm

Unearthed from Beijing Academy of Agriculture and Forestry Sciences in 1986

　　银质，表面鎏金，较软，簪头两端呈五瓣梅花形，簪身錾刻有腾龙、飞凤，凤尾处有大面积呈黑色，似为烧痕，背部有款"声远"。

银压兰花扁方

清（1644～1911 年）

长 29.2 厘米，宽 2.7 厘米

Silver flat hairpin with stamped orchid design

Qing dynasty (1644～1911)

Length 29.2cm, width 2.7cm

　　扁方，俗称"大扁簪"，是清代满族妇女梳两把头和大拉翅时所插饰的特殊大簪，呈扁平一字形，起到连接真、假发髻类似于"梁"的作用，多以金、银、玉等材料制成。该扁方银质，簪头两端呈五瓣梅花形，中部压印有蝠纹，谐意多福，簪身首尾两端各压印有兰花一株，边缘以小联珠纹围绕，背部戳印有"元吉足纹"。

金联钱纹扁方

清（1644 ～ 1911 年）

长 18.5 厘米，宽 2.1 厘米

Gold flat hairpin with connected coin design

Qing dynasty (1644 ~ 1911)

Length 18.5cm, width 2.1cm

　　金质，较软，簪身为镂空十七联钱纹，背部
有"文华足赤"戳记。

金錾花鸟纹扁方

清（1644 ～ 1911 年）

长 19.9 厘米，宽 1.7 厘米

1989 年北京市海淀区塔院出土

Gold flat hairpin engraved with flower and bird design

Qing dynasty (1644 ~ 1911)

Length 19.9cm, width 1.7cm

Unearthed from Tayuan, Haidian district in 1989

　　金质，簪头两端呈五瓣梅花形，中部錾刻如意云纹，
簪身两端錾刻花卉，中部刻一飞鸟，上下边缘各有弦纹双
道，背部有"天华"戳记。质地精良，美观大方。

"康宁"金镯

清（1644 ~ 1911 年）

直径 6.4 厘米

1989 年国家气象局院内出土

Gold bracelet with the inscriptions "*kangning*" (healthy and safe)

Qing dynasty (1644 ~ 1911)

Diameter 6.4cm

Unearthed from China Meteorological Administration in 1989

金质，无纹饰，镯面呈扁条形，外缘高，中部略凹，
有开口，开口两端刻有"康宁"款。

金镶玉带扣

清（1644 ～ 1911 年）

长 5.1 厘米 ，宽 3.1 厘米

1986 年北京市海淀区大柳树北村出土

Gold belt buckle with jade inlay

Qing dynasty (1644 ~ 1911)

Length 5.1cm, width 3.1cm

Unearthed from Daliushubei village, Haidian district in 1986

　　复合质地，带扣以金为皮，羊脂白玉为骨，以金镶玉，形成黄白相间的效果。玉骨有两块，一为圆日，一为月牙，以錾刻云纹间隔。制作考究，造型构思巧妙。

玳瑁包金镯

清（1644 ～ 1911 年）

直径 6.5 厘米

1988 年北京市海淀区蓟门桥东出土

Gold-covered hawksbill bracelet with floral design

Qing dynasty (1644 ~ 1911)

Diameter 6.5cm

Unearthed from east of Jimenqiao, Haidian district in 1988

　　复合质地，镯圈主体为玳瑁质，呈黑色，近半为金质薄片包裹，金片上錾刻有花卉纹。

金镯（一对）

清（1644 ～ 1911 年）

直径 6.3 厘米

1986 年北京航空航天大学出土

Gold bracelets (pair)

Qing dynasty (1644 ~ 1911)

Diameter 6.3cm

Unearthed from Beihang University in 1986

金质，开口式素镯，开口两端为球形，内侧有"宝华足赤"戳记。

金镯（一对）

清（1644 ～ 1911 年）

直径 6.8 厘米

1988 年北京市海淀区蓟门桥东出土

Gold bracelets (pair)

Qing dynasty (1644 ~ 1911)

Diameter 6.8cm

Unearthed from east of Jimenqiao, Haidian district in 1988

金质，开口式素镯，较硬。镯面呈扁条形，内侧有"一元足赤"戳记。

金镯

清（1644 ～ 1911 年）

直径 6.4 厘米

1994 年北京市海淀区花园村出土

Gold bracelet

Qing dynasty (1644 ~ 1911)

Diameter 6.4cm

Unearthed from Huayuancun, Haidian district in 1994

金质，开口式素镯，较硬。镯面呈扁条形，外侧
两端高，中部略凹。内侧有"裕通足赤"戳记。

金錾梅花耳环（一对）

清（1644 ～ 1911 年）

直径 2.1 厘米

1986 年海淀区原市政四公司出土

Gold earrings engraved with plum blossoms design (pair)

Qing dynasty (1644 ~ 1911)

Diameter 2.1cm

Unearthed from the Fourth Civil Engineering Company, Haidian district in 1986

　　金质，其上雕有带蕊花瓣，细密点状底纹上錾刻有花叶纹，内侧刻有"永□足金"。

金如意云纹耳环（一对）

清（1644 ～ 1911 年）

直径 2.5 厘米

1986 年北京市海淀区双榆树北里出土

Gold earrings with *ruyi*-shaped cloud design (pair)

Qing dynasty (1644 ~ 1911)

Diameter 2.5cm

Unearthed from a block north to the Shuangyushu, Haidian district in1986

金质，镂空如意云头形轮廓，轮廓内填以细密的点状纹饰，
环上为镂空回纹轮廓，其内亦填以点状纹饰。

（正面）

（背面）

金雕钱纹锁

清（1644 ～ 1911 年）

长 4.8 厘米，宽 3.1 厘米

1986 年北京市海淀区大柳树北村出土

Gold lock necklace carved with coin pattern

Qing dynasty (1644 ~ 1911)

Length 4.8cm, width 3.1cm

Unearthed from Daliushubei village, Haidian district in 1986

金质，轮廓呈蝙蝠形。正面深雕缠枝忍冬纹，背面镂雕钱纹，并辅以绶带纹。蝠、绶、钱，寓意福寿双全。纹饰凸起，边缘清晰，地纹整洁、融小巧、精致于一体。

金盘长纹指套

清（1644 ～ 1911 年）

长 4.5 厘米

1985 年北京市海淀区马神庙出土

Gold nail cover with pattern of auspicious knots

Qing dynasty (1644 ~ 1911)

Length 4.5cm

Unearthed from Mashenmiao, Haidian district in 1985

　　金质，较短，近指端为镂空盘长纹，内壁有"声志"款。

　　盘长，即吉祥结，是佛门八宝之一，与法螺、法轮、宝伞、白盖、莲花、宝瓶、金鱼合称"八吉祥"。由于盘长象征绵延不断，遂为民间作为吉祥纹饰而广泛使用，表达出对家族兴旺、子孙延续、富贵吉祥、世代相传的美好祈愿。

银捶揲荷叶青蛙纹指套（两件）

清（1644 ~ 1911 年）

长 8.7 厘米

Silver nail covers with lotus leaf and frog design in repoussé (two)

Qing dynasty (1644 ~ 1911)

Length 8.7cm

银质，近指端出荷叶，其上蹲伏青蛙一只，极其形象生动。

银鎏金花卉纹指套（三件）

清（1644 ~ 1911 年）

长 12.3 厘米

1986 年北京市农林科学院内出土

Silver-gilt nail covers with floral pattern (three)

Qing dynasty (1644 ~ 1911)

Length 12.3cm

Unearthed from Beijing Academy of Agriculture and Forestry Sciences in 1986

银质，表面鎏金，镂空花卉纹。

沉香木镶金"寿"字扳指

清（1644 ~ 1911 年）

直径 3.3 厘米，高 2.8 厘米

1984 年中国人民大学北小区出土

Eaglewood thumb ring inlaid with gold characters "*shou*" (longevity)

Qing dynasty (1644 ~ 1911)

Diameter 3.3cm, height 2.8cm

Unearthed from a block north to the Renmin University in 1984

　　复合质地，直筒形，金裹。外侧镶沉香木嵌金珠团寿字、长寿字，将金、木两种不同材料很好地结合在一起。

金雕莲瓣纹帽顶

清（1644 ~ 1911 年）

底径 4.3 厘米，通高 9 厘米

1986 年北京市海淀区大柳树北村出土

Gold hat finial carved with lotus petals

Qing dynasty (1644 ~ 1911)

Diameter of base 4.3cm, overall height 9cm

Unearthed from Daliushubei village, Haidian district in 1986

　　金质，以范铸为主要工艺，辅以錾刻、焊接等手法，通体纹饰凸起，呈半浮雕效果，每层纹饰间隔以圆珠纹，主体纹饰简括有力，辅助纹饰精巧细腻，整体绚丽美艳，雍容华贵。

　　帽顶即冠顶，是清代礼帽的顶饰，用以标识官员等级，可分为朝冠用和吉服冠用。朝冠顶子共有三层：上为尖形宝石，中为球形宝珠，下为金属底座；吉服冠比较简单，分为球形宝珠和金属底座两部分。此帽顶上部嵌宝石（缺失），中部为球形，亦有宝珠（缺失），下部为覆莲纹底座，通体金质，为朝服冠顶，展现了清代金银器制作的精湛技艺。

鎏金花卉纹纽扣（四枚）

清（1644 ~ 1911 年）

直径 1.8 厘米

2002 年北京市海淀区巨山农场出土

Gilt buttons with floral pattern (four)

Qing dynasty (1644 ~ 1911)

Diameter 1.8cm

Unearthed from Jushan Farm, Haidian district in 2002

　　银质，表面鎏金，镂空球形，其上镂雕花卉纹，小巧精致。

金如意纹耳环（一对）

民国（1912 ～ 1949 年）
直径 2.2 厘米

Gold earrings with *ruyi* design (pair)

Republic of China (1912 ~ 1949)

Diameter 2.2cm

金质，其上錾刻如意云头纹，内侧有"富有足金"款。

金"寿"字簪

民国（1912 ～ 1949 年）
长 10.5 厘米
1986 年北京电影学院出土

Gold hairpin with Chinese character "*shou*" (longevity)

Republic of China (1912 ~ 1949)

Length 10.5cm

Unearthed from Beijing Film Academy in 1986

金质，叶形，中间较细，两端渐宽。仅有叶轮廓，无叶脉，两端各有一寿字。背部有款"永□原金"。

金绳纹镯（一对）

民国（1912 ~ 1949 年）

直径 6.8 厘米

1985 年北京市海淀区魏公村出土

Gold bracelets with rope design (pair)

Republic of China (1912 ~ 1949)

Diameter 6.8cm

Unearthed from Weigongcun, Haidian district in1985

金质，开口式镯。镯身呈绳纹式。

造像

海淀博物馆藏的佛教造像大部分为明清时期铜造像，且主要是汉传佛教造像，时代特征鲜明，题材多样，是了解当时汉传佛教在本地传播情况的重要资料，具有重要的文物价值、艺术价值和宗教史研究价值。

此外，海淀博物馆造像类藏品中还包含一定数量的道教造像。

Part 5

Religious Statues

Most of the copper Buddhist statues of Haidian Museum are that of Chinese Buddhism and made in the Ming and Qing dynasties. They have distinctive features of the times and cover various themes. Because of their significant value of history, art and religion, people can learn the spread of Chinese Buddhism here during that time.

Furthermore, there are some Taoist statues collected in Haidian Museum.

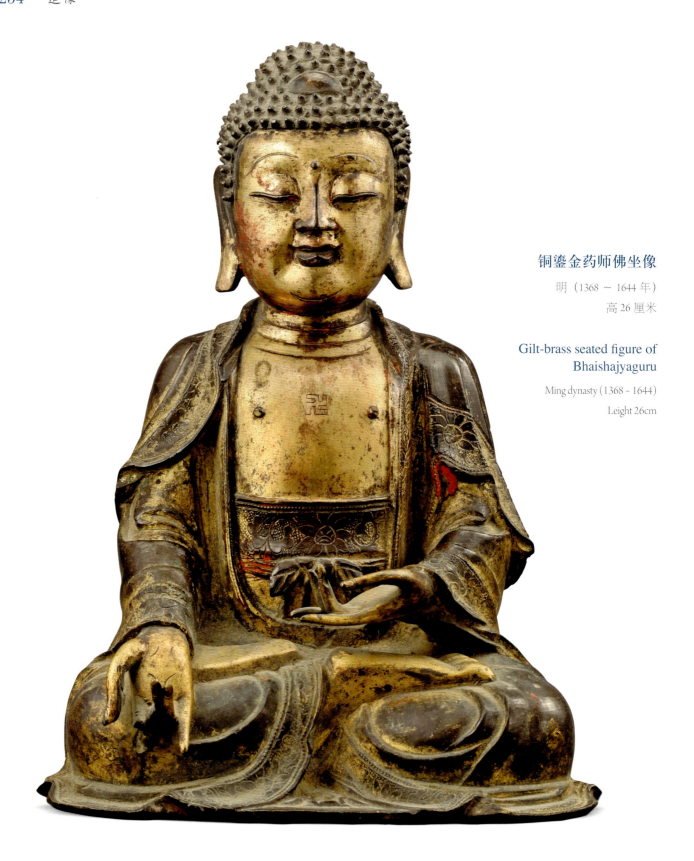

铜鎏金药师佛坐像

明（1368 ～ 1644 年）

高 26 厘米

Gilt-brass seated figure of Bhaishajyaguru

Ming dynasty (1368 ~ 1644)

Leight 26cm

　　药师佛，又称药师琉璃光王如来，为东方净琉璃世界的教主。此像螺发高髻，髻前安有宝珠。面含笑意，嘴角上扬，双目低垂，双眉间饰有白毫。身着袈裟和僧裙，胸前刻有"卍"符号，为佛的相好标志，腰间系丝带。结跏趺端坐，左手于脐前结禅定印，右手于右膝结施与印。头部较大、躯体丰肥，体现了明代晚期造像的典型特点。

铜鎏金观音菩萨坐像

明（1368 ~ 1644 年）

高 20.5 厘米

**Gilt-brass seated
figure of Avalokiteśvara**

Ming dynasty（1368 ~ 1644）

Leight 20.5cm

　　此像头戴五佛宝冠，身着天衣绸裙，胸前饰璎珞珠宝。结
跏趺端坐，左手于脐前托净瓶，右手当胸持一杨柳枝（已残）。
造型端庄、做工精细。

铜观音菩萨坐像

明（1368 ～ 1644 年）

高 39.5 厘米

Brass seated figure of
Avalokiteśvara

Ming dynasty (1368 ~ 1644)

Height 39.5cm

　　观音菩萨全称"观世音"菩萨，是印度梵语的意译名称。此像头戴五佛宝冠，头顶结高发髻，余发垂肩，面型方圆，神态沉静。身着天衣绸裙，胸前饰璎珞珠宝。结跏趺端坐，左手于脐前托净瓶，右手当胸持一杨柳枝（已残）。

铜漆金文殊菩萨坐像

明（1368 ~ 1644 年）

高 18.8 厘米

**Brass seated figure of Mañjuśrī
covered with gold lacquer**

Ming dynasty (1368 ~ 1644)

Height 18.8cm

　　文殊是印度梵语"文殊师利"的简称，意译"妙德"或"妙吉祥"，是集诸佛智慧于一身的大菩萨，也是汉传佛教尊奉的四大菩萨之一，常与普贤菩萨作为释迦牟尼佛的胁侍菩萨，合称"华严三圣"。此像头戴宝冠、面形方圆、双目垂俯、上身着僧坎、下身着裙、腰间束带、饰有项圈、璎珞和钏镯。跏趺端坐于双层莲花宝座上，双手各结说法印，并各牵一莲茎，莲花饰于双肩，左右肩花分别安经书、宝剑，是文殊菩萨形象的重要特征。

铜观音菩萨坐像

明（1368～1644 年）

高 25.6 厘米

Brass seated figure of Avalokiteśvara

Ming dynasty（1368～1644）

Height 25.6cm

观音菩萨全称"观世音"菩萨，是印度梵语的意译名称，为汉传佛教四大菩萨之一。据佛经记载，观音菩萨能随时关照众生悲苦之声而及时寻声解救，济世悲心无量，所以被世人尊为"大慈大悲救苦救难观世音菩萨"。此像头戴宝冠，顶结发髻、发辫垂肩，冠中央安有化佛阿弥陀佛，上身披袈裟，下身着僧裙，耳珰、项圈、璎珞严饰全身。结跏趺端坐，双手于脐前结定印。

铜漆金观音菩萨坐像

明（1368 ～ 1644 年）

高 32 厘米

Brass seated figure of Avalokiteśvara covered with gold lacquer

Ming dynasty (1368 ~ 1644)

Height 32cm

此像头戴宝冠，冠中央安有化佛阿弥陀佛。上身披天衣，下身着绸裙，有耳珰、项圈、璎珞和钏镯装饰。结跏趺端坐于仰莲式台座上，左右肩花上分别安有鹦鹉和净瓶，是观世音菩萨形象的重要标识。

铜罗汉像

明（1368 ~ 1644 年）

高 21.2 厘米

Brass figure of an arhat

Ming dynasty (1368 ~ 1644)

Height 21.2cm

罗汉是阿罗汉的简称，是
小乘佛教追求的最高修行果
位，大乘佛教则以修成佛果为
究竟。此像上身着僧坎和袒右
肩袈裟，下身着僧裙，双手于
胸前结说法印，跏趺端坐于方
形台座上。面相传神，衣纹刻
画细腻生动。

铜漆金持扇道教人物坐像

明（1368 ～ 1644 年）

高 20.8 厘米

Brass seated figure holding a palm-leaf fan covered with gold lacquer in Taoism

Ming dynasty (1368 ~ 1644)

Height 20.8cm

　　此像结跏趺端坐，头戴圆帽，身着宽袍，颌下长髯飘飘。右手于右侧胸前持宝扇一把，左手当胸虚拈。

铜眼光娘娘坐像

明（1368 ~ 1644 年）

高 30.5 厘米

Brass seated figure of Goddess Eyesight

Ming dynasty (1368 ~ 1644)

Height 30.5cm

眼光娘娘是道教碧霞元君的御前女仙，据说她能令众生消除眼疾，明是非、辨善恶。此像坐姿，头戴凤冠，缯带垂于双肩。身着宽大袖衫，衣缘处錾刻花卉纹。双手托金睛宝眼，为其形象主要标识。

铜文殊菩萨坐像

明（1368 ~ 1644 年）

高 24.8 厘米

Brass seated figure of Mañjuśrī

Ming dynasty (1368 ~ 1644)

Height 24.8cm

　　此像头戴宝冠，顶结高发髻，余发编成发辫垂于双肩。上身披袈裟，下身着僧裙、耳珰、项圈、璎珞严饰全身。结跏趺端坐，双手于胸前托一柄如意。面相方圆，双目微垂，神态慈祥宁静。

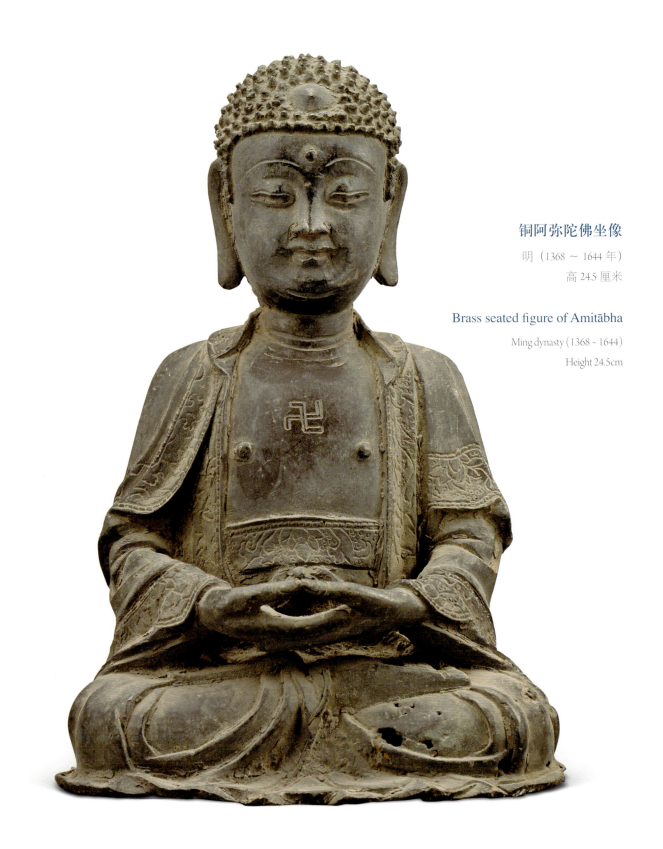

铜阿弥陀佛坐像

明（1368 ~ 1644 年）

高 24.5 厘米

Brass seated figure of Amitābha

Ming dynasty (1368 ~ 1644)

Height 24.5cm

　　此像头饰螺发、头顶正面嵌有髻珠、眉间饰白毫、眼帘低垂、　　露出蝴蝶结。衣纹写实，衣缘上刻有花纹。结跏趺端坐，双手
面含微笑。上身着双领下垂式袈裟，下身着僧裙，腰间束带并　　置于膝上结弥陀定印。

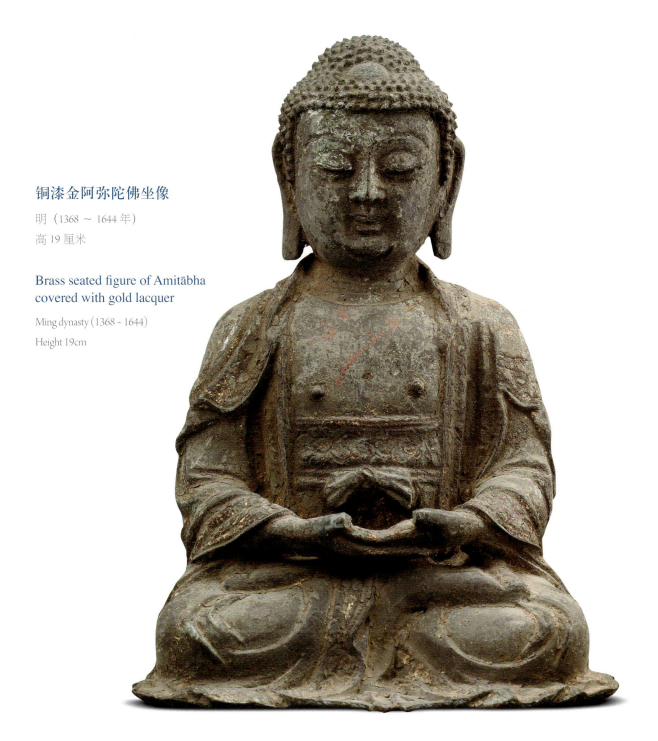

铜漆金阿弥陀佛坐像

明（1368 ~ 1644 年）

高 19 厘米

**Brass seated figure of Amitābha
covered with gold lacquer**

Ming dynasty (1368 ~ 1644)

Height 19cm

　　阿弥陀佛是佛教西方极乐世界的教主，与观音菩萨、大势至菩萨合称"西方三圣"。此像头饰螺发，头顶肉髻平缓，正面嵌有髻珠，大耳垂肩，面相宽大，眼帘低垂，神态宁静。上身着双领下垂式袈裟，右肩披袈裟边角，下身着僧裙，腰间束带并露出蝴蝶结。衣纹写实自然，衣缘上刻有立体感较强的花纹。结跏趺端坐，双手置双膝上结弥陀定印。头部偏大，躯体丰腴，具有明代晚期中原地区造像的鲜明特点。

铜观音菩萨坐像

明末清初

高 58 厘米

Brass seated figure of Avalokiteśvara

Late Ming- Early Qing

Height 58cm

　　此像为观音菩萨头陀（苦行）形象，头戴发箍，正中安有化佛阿弥陀佛，为观音菩萨形象标识。面相沉静，嘴角及下颌皆有胡须。身披袈裟和僧裙，胸前饰璎珞，腰间系丝带，衣纹流畅自然，层次分明。坐姿，左手托净瓶，右手置右膝拈一宝珠。造型独特，形象生动。

铜布袋和尚坐像

明（1368 ~ 1644 年）

高 50 厘米

Bronze seated figure of Cloth-bag Monk

Ming dynasty (1368 ~ 1644)

Height 50cm

　　布袋和尚的原型为五代时后梁浙江奉化的僧人契此，因平日常携布袋乞食，且喜与童子嬉戏玩耍，故被民间称为"布袋和尚"。契此圆寂时，自说偈曰"弥勒真弥勒，化身千百亿，时示时人，时人皆不识"，由此被后人尊为弥勒菩萨的化身。此像呈游戏坐姿，大耳垂肩，袒胸露腹，笑容可掬；右手置于右膝，左手持布袋置于左膝，是此尊的重要标识。

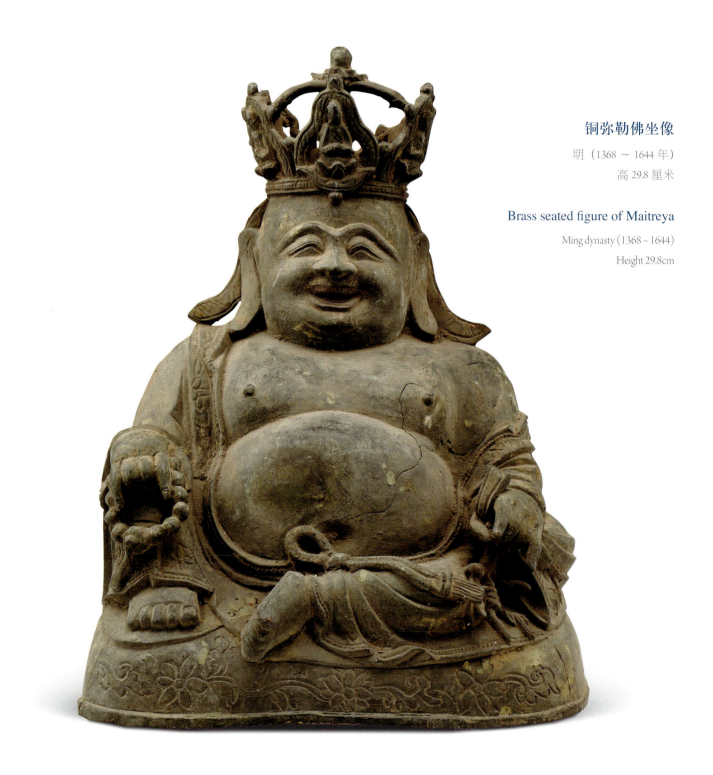

铜弥勒佛坐像
明（1368 ~ 1644 年）
高 29.8 厘米

Brass seated figure of Maitreya
Ming dynasty (1368 ~ 1644)
Height 29.8cm

　　弥勒佛是佛教宣称的未来佛，常与燃灯佛、释迦牟尼佛一起供奉，组成"竖三世佛"的固定组合。弥勒佛除了端正、庄严的形象外，还常见一种笑容可掬的大肚弥勒佛形象。此像游戏坐于椭圆形刻花台座上，头戴五佛冠，缯带飘于耳际，右手置于右膝，持念珠一串，左手持布袋置于左膝，袒胸露腹，笑容可掬，为中原地区流行的大肚弥勒佛标准形象。

铜关公坐像

明（1368 ~ 1644 年）

高 22.3 厘米

Brass seated figure of *Guan Yu*
(a hero in Three Kingdoms Period
respected as a god)

Ming dynasty (1368 ~ 1644)

Height 22.3cm

关羽为三国时蜀国大将，民间俗称"关公"。历史上广为民间崇拜，被尊为"武圣人"。因其忠诚勇敢，堪能护持佛法，佛教吸收为护法神，被尊为护法伽蓝菩萨。此像双腿下垂，正襟危坐，右手握拳置于右膝，左手扶于左膝，面部双眉上挑，双目圆睁，美髯自然垂下，身披铠甲、足蹬战靴，造型大方，形象威武生动。

铜鎏金释迦太子像

明（1368 ~ 1644 年）

高 16.6 厘米

Gilt-brass figure of
Crown-prince Sakyamuni

Ming dynasty (1368 ~ 1644)

Height 16.6cm

　　释迦牟尼佛出家前为太子，名悉达多。据佛典记载，悉达多太子降生后周行七步，步步生莲花，然后一手指天，一手指地宣称："天上天下，唯我独尊"。太子诞生像即据此而来。此像作儿童状，体态丰腴，跣足立于圆形双层仰莲台座上，胸前佩肚兜，其上錾刻花卉纹，左手上举，右手自然下垂。由于印度传统尚右，我国汉族习惯尚左，故此像为左手指天，右手指地的姿势。

铜道教护法站像（两尊）

明（1368 ~ 1644 年）

左：高 24.2 厘米，右：高 23.7 厘米

Brass standing figures of Taoist protector (two)

Ming dynasty (1368 ~ 1644)

Left: height 24.2cm, right : height 23.7cm

　　两尊像均头戴官帽，身着裙、袄，并披有云肩，两手持法器（已失），站立于方形台座上。

铜道教神像

明（1368 ~ 1644 年）

高 15.1 厘米

Brass Taoist figure

Ming dynasty (1368 ~ 1644)

Height 15.1cm

此像头戴官帽，帽翅后扬，面部轮廓清晰生动。身着铠甲，足蹬长靴，右膝跪地，左膝自然弯曲，呈半跪式。右手出双指，指向斜后方，左手微握于胸前，动感十足。

铜漆金三头六臂长者像

明（1368 ~ 1644 年）

高 24 厘米

Brass seated figure of an Elder covered with gold lacquer (a god with three heads and six hands)

Ming dynasty (1368 ~ 1644)

Height 24cm

此像结跏趺端坐，束发垂髻，面含笑意。有三头六臂，主臂合掌于胸前；其下衣袖内现出两手，左手托钵，右手虚拈；两肩各搭有一手，左手自然搁置，右手持念珠一串。造型非常奇特。

铜药王坐像

明（1368 ~ 1644 年）

高 29.2 厘米

Brass seated figure of Medicine King

Ming dynasty (1368 ~ 1644)

Height 29.2cm

　　此像头戴官帽，神态安详，身着长袍，腰间束带，端身正坐。左手当胸托一葫芦，右手自然搭于右腿。衣纹刻画精致细腻。

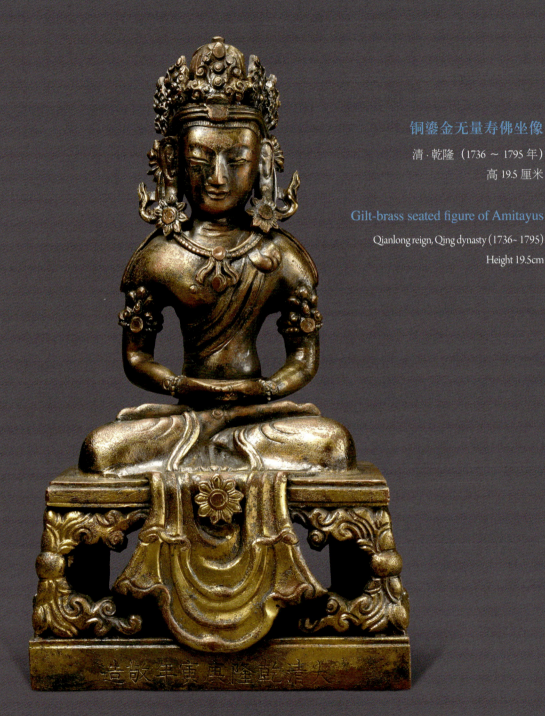

　　无量寿佛，又称"长寿佛"，是阿弥陀佛的报身形象，具有增福延寿的功用，在藏传佛教中信仰极盛。

　　此像头戴花冠，面相沉静。上身斜披络腋，下身着裙，身饰项圈、璎珞、耳珰及钏镯。全跏趺坐，双手结禅定印，手心托长寿宝瓶（已失）。身后有火焰形背光，身下为镂空形台座。台座正面垂搭坐垫，下缘阴刻"大清乾隆庚寅年敬造"铭文。应为乾隆三十五年（1770 年）由宫廷制作用于皇帝祝寿的佛像。

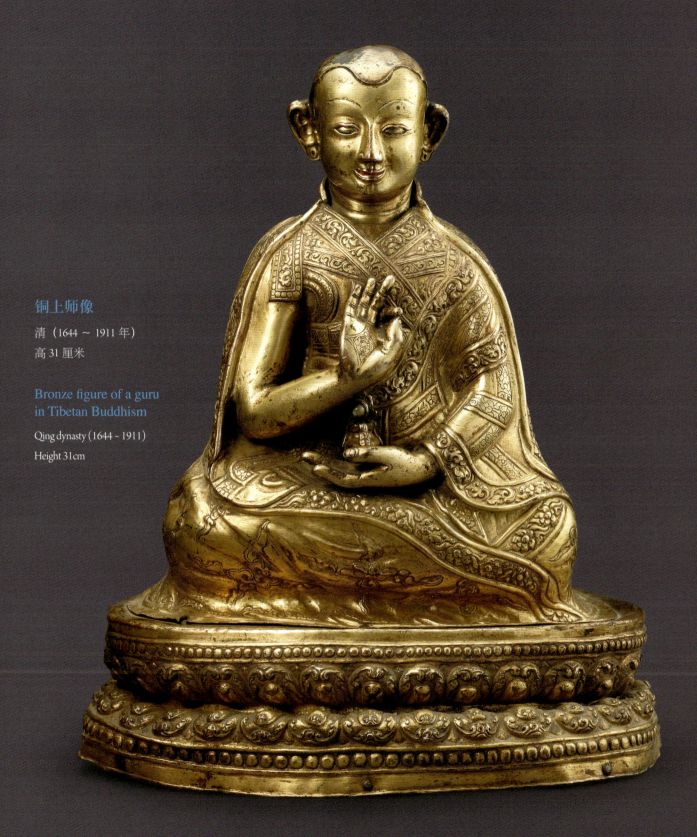

铜上师像

清（1644 ~ 1911 年）

高 31 厘米

**Bronze figure of a guru
in Tibetan Buddhism**

Qing dynasty (1644 ~ 1911)

Height 31cm

　　上师，指藏传佛教中修为高深的人物，代表人物如莲花生、米拉日巴、宗喀巴等，其造像皆根据人物原型塑造，所以具有极强的写实性。此像面形圆润，五官端庄，表情生动。上身着僧坎和袒右肩袈裟，下身着僧裙，衣缘錾刻精美花纹。跏趺端坐于双层莲座上，左手在脐前托宝瓶，右手当胸结说法印。采用打胎工艺制成，具有清代内蒙古多伦地区造像工艺特点。

第六部分

其他

海淀博物馆的藏品还包括了一定数量的石器、铜器、钱币、杂类等，虽然数量有限，但其中也不乏精品，并且对整个博物馆的藏品体系而言，具有很好的补充意义。

Part 6

Others

The collections of Haidian Museum also include stone artifacts, bronze wares, coins and objects made by other materials. There are also some fine works among them. Although their number is not large, they are the perfect supplementary objects for the whole exhibition system of the Museum.

石斧

新石器时代

长 12.1 厘米，宽 4.2 厘米，厚 1.9 厘米

Stone axe

Neolithic era

Length 12.1cm, width 4.2cm, thickness 1.9cm

　　青石质，砍砸器，整件石器两面磨制、双面刃、形状规整，
是新石器时代早期人类的典型生产、生活用具。

铜弩机

三国·魏（220 ~ 265 年）
长 14.3 厘米、宽 12 厘米
1987 年北京市海淀区八里庄出土

Brass crossbow

Wei , Three Kingdoms period (220 ~ 265)

Length 14.3cm, width 12cm

Unearthed from Balizhuang, Haidian district in1987

　　铜质，外涂朱砂红色，由郭、望山、悬刀、牙、钩几部分构成，悬刀底部有圆形穿，郭上阴刻有："正始五年三月卅日左尚方造步弩耳监作吏王昭匠马广师张雄"二十六字。正始五年即公元 244 年，该弩机铭文记录了其制作时间、管理部门、监作者、制作人等信息，这是春秋时期以来"物勒工名"制度在三国时期的延续。

　　弩是战国以来广泛使用的发箭兵器，弩机安装于弩臂后端，是弩的重要构件之一。这件弩机对研究古代兵器及管理方法都提供了极为珍贵的实物资料。

花鸟纹菱花形铜镜

唐（618 ~ 907 年）

直径 13 厘米

1988 年清华大学校内出土

Bronze mirror in shape of water chestnut
flower and with flower-and-bird pattern

Tang dynasty (618 ~ 907)

Diameter 13cm

Unearthed from Tsinghua University in1988

镜体厚实，镜面为八出菱花形，圆钮。镜背主纹为飞鸟衔绶纹，并辅以变形的荷莲纹。边缘以八组蝴蝶、折枝花纹装点。整个镜背纹饰鸟花争艳，柔美自然。

唐代是铜镜发展史上的高峰，制作打破了传统形式，较前更为精工，推出了菱花镜、葵花镜、亚字镜等创新品种，镜纹丰富绚丽，自由活泼，以花鸟植物等写实纹饰最为常见。

牡丹芦雁图壁画

唐大中六年（公元 852 年）

最长 290 厘米，最高 156 厘米

1991 年北京市海淀区八里庄王公淑墓出土

Fresco of peony and wild geese

6th year of Dazhong reign(852), Tang dynasty

Maximum length 290cm, maximum height 156cm

Unearthed from the Tang tomb of Wang Gongshu at Balizhuang, Haidian district in1991

　　唐代王公淑墓北壁壁画，略有弧度。壁画中央为一丛枝叶繁茂、色彩鲜艳的盛开牡丹花卉，花荫下芦雁悠然，花丛间彩蝶飞舞。整个壁画布局高超，动静得宜，充实而不拥挤，是北京地区已经发现的唐代晚期花鸟题材壁画的重要代表之一，是了解唐代绘画发展水平十分难得的实物资料。

（局部一）

（局部二）

"大晟"编钟

宋（960～1279年）
长 18.5 厘米，宽 14.6 厘米，高 28.5 厘米
1986 年北京市海淀区四季青出土

Bell with inscriptions *"da sheng"*

Song dynasty (960～1279)
Length 18.5cm, width 14.6cm, height 28.5cm
Unearthed from Sijiqing, Haidian district in 1986

　　钟整体呈合瓦形，甬部为双夔交接旋
钮，钟两侧有乳钉 36 枚，钲部、舞部和
篆部饰蟠虺纹，正面中部用阴线刻篆书
"大晟"二字，背面正中钲部刻"中吕中声"。
器形厚重，古朴典雅，制作规整，纹饰优美。
　　宋代大晟编钟是北宋宫廷乐府"大晟
府"的重器，是宋代仿战国风格的十分难
得的艺术珍品。它是宋徽宗赵佶崇宁三至
四年在京师所铸，今流传于世的大晟编钟
有二十余件，此为其中一件。
　　该编钟对研究宋代的庙堂乐制、青铜
乐器、仿古铸造技术及古代音乐史、工艺
史具有重要的参考价值。

蟠龙纹双环耳铜钫

宋（960～1279 年）

口部边长 11.8 厘米，底部边长 13.1 厘米，高 35.3 厘米

Bronze *fang* (a square-mouthed wine vessel) with double loops and dragon pattern

Song dynasty (960～1279)

Mouth 11.8cm, base 13.1cm, height 35.3cm

　　方口，腹部有四棱，两侧对称双耳，
耳内套一圆环，方圈足。颈部每面装饰有
两组双龙纹，其下为蟠龙纹条带，上腹部
每面饰蟠龙纹两组，其下为蟠龙纹条带，
下腹部每面有兽面纹两组。该铜钫为宋代
仿战国时期青铜器。

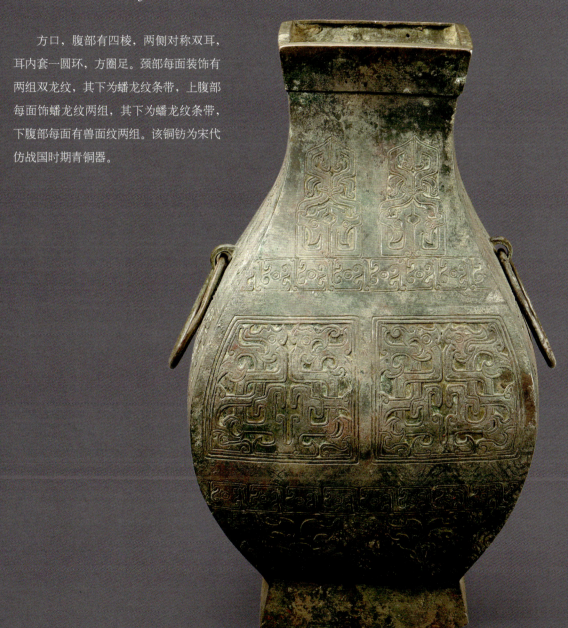

铜花卉"亚"字形镜

宋（960 ~ 1279 年）

边长 11.7 厘米

Bronze mirror in the shape of Chinese character "*ya*"
and decorated with floral pattern

Song dynasty (960 ~ 1279)

Side length 11.7cm

　　折角方形"亚"字形铜镜，中心有一桥形钮，镜背面
浅浮雕装饰以缠枝花卉纹，近外缘处饰联珠纹一周。

铜 "卍" 纹镜

金（1115 ~ 1234 年）

直径 15.6 厘米

1985 年北京市海淀区南辛庄出土

Bronze mirror with swastika pattern

Jin dynasty (1115 ~ 1234)

Diameter 15.6cm

Unearthed from Nanxinzhuang, Haidian district in 1985

圆形铜镜，镜背为素宽沿，中心有一桥形钮，以钮为中心装饰有 "卍" 字纹图案，其外饰双圈细弦纹，镜背整体装饰风格简洁大方，主题突出。

铜松下抚琴图挂镜

金（1115 ~ 1234 年）

直径 7.6 厘米

Bronze hanging mirror with the design of playing the *qin* in the pine shade

Jin dynasty (1115 ~ 1234)

Diameter 7.6cm

圆形挂镜，边缘厚实，镜体小巧。镜边缘正上方有一挂柄，中心纹饰为松下抚琴图，周围近缘处饰以联珠纹一周。

铜权

元（1271 ~ 1368 年）
底部直径 4.3 厘米，高 8.5 厘米
1985 年北京市海淀区四王府地区出土

Bronze weight

Yuan dynasty (1271 ~ 1368)
Diameter of base 4.3cm, height 8.5cm
Unearthed from Siwangfu, Haidian district in 1985

　　覆钵式塔形、钮为方形圆孔、腹部呈圆形、束腰、喇叭式圆底座、底座和肩部均铸有弦纹、铜权通体黄铜铸造。

　　权、俗称秤砣、秤锤、秤权、是悬挂在秤杆上可以移动的器物、也就是称重量之用、名曰衡器。古权材质有铜、铁、陶、瓷、石等、造型多种多样、重量不等、这件铜权为研究元代的计量制度提供了珍贵的实物资料。

金元宝(半个)

明（1368 ~ 1644 年）
长 4.4 厘米，宽 3.3 厘米
1985 年北京市海淀区八里庄出土

Gold ingot (half)

Ming dynasty (1368 ~ 1644)
Length 4.4cm, width 3.3cm
Unearthed from Balizhuang, Haidian district in 1985

　　半个金元宝、重 184.5 克、色泽金黄莹亮。元宝为腰形、中间内凹、边缘弯曲内折、有明显切割的痕迹。

吉语鎏金钱

明（1368 ~ 1644 年）

直径 3.5 厘米

1991 年北京市海淀区北下关出土

Gilt coin with auspicious text

Ming dynasty (1368 ~ 1644)

Diameter 3.5cm

Unearthed from Beixiaguan, Haidian district in 1991

  银质，通体鎏金，钱为圆形方孔，边缘较为宽厚。此钱两面均顺时针满刻"南无消灾延寿药师佛"，雕工精细、边廓深峻、文字遒劲、间架结构舒展，呈浅浮雕效果。

  吉语铸在钱上称之为"吉语钱"，寄托着当时人们的愿望和追求。

（正面）　　　　　　　　　　　　　　　（背面）

"天启通宝" 金币

明·天启（1621 ～ 1627 年）

直径 3.8 厘米

1991 年北京市海淀区北下关出土

Gold coin with the inscriptions "*Tianqi tongbao*"

Tianqi reign, Ming dynasty (1621 ~ 1627)

Diameter 3.8cm

Unearthed from Beixiaguan, Haidian district in 1991

金质。圆形方孔，边廓较平宽，内廓方直。钱面文为十字交叉"天启通宝"，背文有位于穿上部的"金"及右侧的"五钱"，均为正书。钱文笔画肥硕，间架结构舒展。

"万历年造"款铜文字圆挂牌（两块）

明·万历（1573 ～ 1620 年）

直径 8 厘米

1991 年北京市海淀区北下关出土

Round brass hanging tags engraved with "*Wanli nian zao*" (made in the Wanli period) (two)

Wanli reign, Ming dynasty (1573 ~ 1620)

Diameter 8cm

Unearthed from Beixiaguan, Haidian district in 1991

 铜质，挂牌中部刻"万历年造"款、边缘有穿孔五个。

银元宝

清·光绪（1875 ~ 1908 年）

长 8.2 厘米，宽 4.9 厘米，高 7.9 厘米

Silver ingot

Guangxu reign, Qing dynasty (1875 ~ 1908)

Length 8.2cm, width 4.9cm, height 7.9cm

银质，船形元宝。面上有"光绪十七年"、"协成号匠王松"、"江汉关"戳记。

银元宝

清·光绪（1875 ~ 1908 年）

长 8.5 厘米，宽 5.5 厘米，高 8.1 厘米

Silver ingot

Guangxu reign, Qing dynasty (1875 ~ 1908)

Length 8.5cm, width 5.5cm, height 8.1cm

银锭，实重 1756 克，面上铸刻有"光绪十年六月"、"湖北监饷"、"兴记"。

银元宝

清（1644 ～ 1911 年）

长 6.7 厘米，宽 4.1 厘米，高 4.4 厘米

Silver ingot

Qing dynasty (1644 ~ 1911)

Length 6.7cm, width 4.1cm, height 4.4cm

　　银锭，实重 357 克，面上铸刻有"十足色"、"匠德聚"。

银元宝

清·光绪（1875 ～ 1908 年）

长 7.2 厘米、宽 6.8 厘米、高 6 厘米

Silver ingot

Guangxu reign, Qing dynasty (1875 ~ 1908)

Length 7.2cm, width 6.8cm, height 6cm

　　银锭，实重 1885 克，面上铸刻有铭文："光绪十年八月"、"五十两"、"匠朱万"、"万年县"，主要记录了铸造的时间、地点、重量、工匠等信息。

铜烧蓝云龙纹鼻烟壶

清（1644 ～ 1911 年）

口径 1.5 厘米，足径 1.5 厘米，高 7.2 厘米

2002 年北京市海淀区巨山农场出土

Brass snuff bottle with enamel cloud and dragon design

Qing dynasty (1644 ~ 1911)

Diameter of mouth rim 1.5cm, diameter of base 1.5cm, height 7.2cm

Unearthed from Jushan Farm, Haidian district in 2002

铜质、短颈、扁形腹、矮圈足、带盖。颈部饰回纹、蕉叶纹各一周，腹部饰以龙纹。盖、腹部间隙处以烧蓝工艺作辅助装饰。

烧蓝又称点蓝、与点翠工艺相似，是景泰蓝的工序。它不是一个独立工种，而是金属器的辅助工种，用以点缀、装饰金属器的色彩美。

蜜蜡雕刘海戏金蟾鼻烟壶

清 （1644 ～ 1911 年）

高 5.2 厘米

2002 年北京市海淀区巨山农场出土

Mellite snuff bottle carved with *Liu Hai* playing with a golden frog

Qing dynasty (1644 ~ 1911)

Height 5.2cm

Unearthed from Jushan Farm, Haidian district in 2002

蜜蜡质，圆雕，刘海身着宽袍，腰间束带，前额被整齐的短发遮盖，右手舞贴右肩铜钱一串，左手于左肩戏金蟾一只，笑容满面、憨态可掬。金蟾卧处实为鼻烟壶口，金蟾可拆装，并带烟勺一支。整器小巧别致，雕工细腻，设计亦十分精妙。

刘海，是传说中的仙童，也是中国传统文化中的"福神"，更有准财神一说。金蟾则是仙宫灵物，据传可源源不断地带来财宝。刘海戏金蟾，具有财源广进、大富大贵的美好寓意。

黄杨木雕童子献寿像

清（1644 ~ 1911 年）

高 18.8 厘米

Boxwood figure carved with Boy offering a peach (means longevity) to an elder

Qing dynasty (1644 ~ 1911)

Height 18.8cm

　　黄杨木质，圆雕，一老者长须飘飘，额部高隆，右手持杖，左手牵一幼童，幼童左手擎镂雕寿桃，奉于老者，取童子献寿之意。整体雕工精湛，形象生动自然。

竹刻花卉纹烟袋

民国（1912 ～ 1949 年）

通长 70.5 厘米

Bamboo tobacco pouch carved with floral pattern

Republic of China (1912 ~ 1949)

Overall length 70.5cm

复合质地：竹质烟杆，铜质烟锅，青白玉质烟嘴。细长竹质烟杆上刻有兰叶、竹节、花卉纹。

锡錾花温壶

民国（1912 ～ 1949 年）

底部直径 8.8 厘米，高 7.6 厘米

Tin pot for warming carved with floral pattern

Republic of China (1912 ~ 1949)

Diameter of base 8.8cm, height 7.6cm

扁圆形腹，圆形盖，单提梁。盖上中心錾刻团寿纹，外围刻动物花卉纹，腹部中部刻花卉纹，并点缀有杂宝纹，底部有款"浙瓯，潘震丰，真、足点、低、假、不真包换"。

海淀区域内的两汉时期考古发现

岳升阳

海淀地区在汉代位于蓟城西北郊。汉代蓟城是北方重镇和交通枢纽，联系着中原农耕文化与北方游牧文化的交往。《史记》说它是"夫燕亦勃、碣之间一都会也。南通齐、赵、东北边胡。"（《史记》卷一二九《货殖列传》第六九）《盐铁论》赞之为："燕之涿、蓟…富冠海内，为天下名都。"蓟城在汉代是富甲一方的都会，蓟城通往居庸关的大道经过海淀地区，它对区域发展产生巨大影响，造就了历史上海淀地区发展的第一个高峰。

本地区的村庄格局在汉代已现雏形，许多现代村落的历史可以追溯至两汉时期。海淀地区汉代村落分布的主要特征，一是沿古代路道分布，二是沿河湖岸边分布，三是沿西山分布。在通往居庸关的古道沿途，不但分布有众多村落，还建有城池。墓葬则大多分布于村落、城池附近。

一、汉代村落遗址

海淀区出土过许多汉代灰坑、瓦砾层、水井等遗物，它们多是汉代聚落留下的遗迹。

海淀地区最重要的汉代遗址是海淀镇汉代村落遗址。海淀镇起源于战国至西汉时期，最早的起源地位于苏州街旁的乐家花园一带，20 世纪 80 年代初，乐家花园内出土了战国或西汉时期的陶三足器。1985 年在倒座庙旁出土汉代陶罐，1996 年扩建苏州街时，在乐家花园东门出土西汉时期的汲水陶罐，随后又在海淀区龙凤桥北侧出土汉代灰坑。2001 年中关村西区修建环形地下车道时，在原南大街小学旁发现西汉灰坑，出土夹云母红陶片，灰坑经 ^{14}C 同位素测年为距今 2030±90 年，属于西汉时期。

海淀地区有两条通往居庸关的古道，海淀古聚落位于其中的一条古道上。这条大道由蓟城向北，经苏州街、海淀镇、六里屯、东马房、常乐村至双塔村，在大道沿线多次出土汉代遗物。20 世纪 80 年代末，在青年政治学院南面三环路西侧，出土两口

汉代陶井。20 世纪 90 年代，在东马坊发现西汉时期的陶片，常乐村发现汉代陶片和地层，辛力屯砖厂发现先秦、汉代至元代的遗址或墓葬。而双塔村北的土城则是汉军都故城，双塔村旁多有汉代遗物出土。

古河道两岸是汉代聚落分布较多的地方。1983 年在万泉庄小学出土西汉时期的遗址和墓葬，遗址内有面积近百平方米的汉代板瓦堆积层，应是建筑遗址。2001 年又在遗址旁的古万泉河故道中，发现战国末或西汉初年的半圆饕餮纹方瓦以及大量绳纹陶片。1970 年在北京大学俄文楼后出土 1 口汉代陶井，有陶罐、铁剪等遗物。1990 年以来在北京大学电话室一带多次出土汉代灰坑，有夹云母红陶片和绳纹灰陶片。1999 年修建中关村北大街时，在成府村东侧高地边缘出土多座汉代灰坑，有陶豆、陶罐等残片。1988 年在清华大学危险品仓库工地，出土战国晚期至西汉时期的遗址，出土陶罐、陶纺轮和大量绳纹陶片等。

沿山地带也发现汉代遗址。1985 年，北京结核病医院在温泉显龙山下施工时发现汉代遗址，出土陶罐、石斧和一处汉代泉眼遗迹。20 世纪 80 年代初，在北安河村南某工厂内，发现战国至西汉时期的遗迹。

二、汉代城址

清河汉城遗址是海淀区唯一的汉代城址。城址位于清河镇西面的朱房村，万泉河与清河交汇处的清河北岸。蓟城通往居庸关的另一条大道由此经过，古城扼守着清河岸边的要津，曾具有重要的战略地位。城为方形，接近正南北向，边长约 500 米，相当于当时县城的规模。今保存有城垣西南角，为北京市文物保护单位。

20 世纪 50 年代曾对城址进行过 5 次发掘，2011 年为配合京包高速路建设，对城址进行了第 6 次发掘。在历次发掘中出土

了大量陶器、铜器和铁器，以及汉代铜、铁冶炼遗迹。遗址中出土的铁器类型比较丰富，兵器包括刀、剑、戟、钺等，生产用具有锄、铲、耧、镜、轴瓦等。铜器有熏炉、印章、钱币、箭镞等，并有铸钱用的钱范。城址内出土大量汉代筒瓦、板瓦和一些瓦当。瓦当纹饰有卷云、"卍"字、篆书"千秋万岁"等式样。在城址内发现房基和墙基遗迹，以及汉代陶井十多口。城址东西两侧有汉墓分布，20 世纪 50 年代，在遗址西侧出土了一座规模较大的汉代多室砖墓。2011 年的调查表明，城址西南角城垣遗址尚保存有 187.2 米长的城垣遗迹，城垣底宽 10.2~12 米，顶残宽 0.8~3.5 米，残高 1~4.1 米，为夯土筑成。

三、汉代墓葬

海淀地区的汉墓数量较大，分布广泛，大多与汉代村落、城址相伴而生。选址多位于河旁高地的顶面或阳坡，以及古城址附近的高地上。海淀区分布最广的汉墓区位于万寿路至永定路一带，那里是古蓟城西北方的一处高岗，墓葬多在岗的顶部，沿岗分布绵延数千米。多年来在当地的机关大院和道路两旁出土了不少汉墓。如 20 世纪 50 年代以来，在万寿路、炮兵司令部、五棵松、永定路等地出土了许多汉墓，器物包括陶器、铜镜和五铢钱等。2004 年在五棵松体育馆建设时，出土 8 座汉墓，包括 7 座土坑墓和 1 座砖室墓，器物包括陶鼎、陶壶、陶盒等，以及五铢钱、铜带钩和铁刀等。

海淀区的另一处与城址有关的大型汉墓区位于上地村，它处于清河汉城遗址的西北方，选址于古清河故道北侧的一处高地上，墓葬主要分布于高地的阳坡。墓地发现于 1982 年，1991 年正式发掘，历时 10 年，至 2001 年完成，出土战国和汉代墓葬 1000 余座，是海淀区乃至北京市出土汉墓最多的地方。墓葬形式包括土坑墓、砖墓和积石墓。砖墓包括多室墓、双室墓、单室墓和砖椁墓。出土遗物包括陶器、铜镜、铜钱等，陶器类型丰富，包括鼎、盒、壶、罐、仓、灶、耳杯、熏炉、方盒、托盘、豆、文字瓦当等，同时发现的还有多座汉代砖窑。

海淀台地西北边缘是汉墓的又一处集中分布地。这一带是汉代村落分布较为密集的地区，因而墓葬也多，由万泉庄至八家村，沿古清河故道边缘高地分布有多处汉墓。1983 年出土的万泉庄汉墓旁依汉代建筑遗址，出土土坑墓 3 座，器物有鼎、壶、罐等。1998 年在海淀镇八一学校南部出土汉代土坑墓多座，器物以罐为主。1991 年在北京大学燕南园内出土东汉土坑墓 1 座，1988 年在清华大学危险品仓库以北，出土汉墓多座。

在海淀北部地区的河旁高地上也有汉墓分布。1983 年在苏家坨村砖厂出土一座西汉墓群，墓位于苏家坨村北的土坨上，有土坑墓和砖室墓

20 世纪 90 年代上地村出土的汉墓群
Han dynasty tombs excavated in Shangdi Village during 1990s.

多座，出土遗物包括陶壶、陶罐、铜镜、铜器构件以及漆器残迹等。1985 年。在西玉河砖厂发现东汉墓群。墓群位于村东北南沙河南岸高地上，分布范围约有上万平方米，主要为砖室墓，出土银簪、银环、陶猪等遗物。20 世纪 90 年代，在双塔村西北沙河南岸高地上，发现汉代墓葬，出土陶罐等遗物。

海淀区的汉墓多为中小型，有土坑墓、砖椁墓和砖室墓等形制。墓葬方向以南北向为主，也有少量东西向的。万泉庄汉墓是土坑墓的代表，一座墓中出土随葬陶器 20 余件，而一般的土坑墓则仅有一件或数件陶器。砖椁墓在上地出土较多，数十座墓葬整齐排列，场面壮观，但墓内随葬品不多。砖室墓多为单室、2 室和 3 室墓，超过 3 室的墓很少，有的墓装饰有印花纹铺地方砖。

海淀区出土的汉代器物形式多样，陶器中有鼎、壶、仓、罐、盒、豆、灯、楼、熏炉、樽、托盘、杯、猪、纺轮等器形，有的陶器上绘制有精美的彩绘，或涂有红色。陶器以灰陶为主，并有夹云母红陶和夹云母灰陶，以及泥质红陶。金属器物主要有镜、簪、环、剪、铲、钱币、带钩、车马具模型构件等。砖以绳纹砖为主，也有素面砖。瓦有板瓦和筒瓦，瓦装饰有绳纹，也有的装饰由坑点构成的图案。瓦当有卷云、"万岁"或"千秋万岁"等图案。此外，还曾出土过施用白膏泥的墓葬，墓中保存有汉代织品，这在北京地区是少有的。

参考文献：

1. 北京市海淀区文物管理所档案。
2. 胡传耸：《北京考古史汉代卷》，上海古籍出版社，2012。
3. 北京市文物研究所编：《北京考古四十年》北京燕山出版社，1990。
4. 岳升阳、夏正楷、徐海鹏：《海淀古镇环境变迁》，开明出版社，2009。
5. 苏天钧主编：《北京考古集成》，北京出版社，2000。
6. 北京市文物研究所编：《北京考古地图集》，科学出版社，2009。

Han Dynasty Archaeological Findings in Haidian District

Yue Shengyang

Haidian District was the northwest suburb of Ji City in Han dynasty. Ji City was the important northern town and transportation hub which connected farming culture in the Central Plains and nomadic culture in northern China. Records of the Grand Historian said State Yan was a big city; it was the intersection of State Qi and Zhao in the south and minority area in the north and east. (Social Economy Commentary Section P.169, Records of the Grand Historian Vol.129) Discourses on Salt and Iron praised Ji and Zhuo of State Yan were the rich and famous cities at that time. Because Ji was prosperous and built a wide road to Juyong Pass through present Haidian area, Ji left a great influence on the development of the area. It was the first peak of the area in history.

The layout of the village in Haidian was basically formed in Han dynasty. Several present villages can be traced to the time. The villages were located along roads, rivers or Western Hills. There were also small towns lining the road to Juyong Pass besides villages. And the tombs were close to villages and towns.

I. Village Sites of Han Dynasty

Ash pits, rubble layers and wells of Han dynasty were excavated in Haidian, which were all the sites of villages.

The most important heritage of Han dynasty is the village sites of Haidian Town. The Haidian Town was built during the period of Warring States and Western Han. The earliest town was located in the Prince Li Mansion (Qing dynasty) beside Suzhou Street. In the early 1980s, a pottery tripod vessel of the Warring States or Western Han was unearthed from Prince Li Mansion. In 1985, a pot of Han dynasty was found in Daozuo Taoist Temple. In 1996, as the expansion of Suzhou Street, a pot for drawing water of Western Han dynasty was found at the east gate of Prince Li Mansion, and later an ash pit of Han dynasty was found at the north side of Dragon Phoenix Bridge. In 2001, as the construction of the underground driveway of western Zhongguancun, an ash pit of Western Han was found at the original Nandajie Primer School. There are red pottery pieces with micas. The ash pit was about 2,030 years (± 90 years) old by 14C dating, in the period of Western Han dynasty.

There are two old roads to Juyong Pass. Haidian village sites were located in one of the two. This road started from Ji City towards north through present-day Suzhou Street, Haidian Town, Liulitun, Dongmafang, Changle Village, and Shuangta Village. In the end of 1980s, two wells of Han dynasty were found from the west side of Western Third-ring Road, close to Beijing Youth Politics College. In 1990s, the pottery pieces of Western Han were found in Dongmafang; pottery pieces and stratum of Han dynasty were found; sites and tombs of Pre-Qin, Han to Yuan dynasties were found at Xinlitun Brickyard; the north of Shuangta Village is the site of Jundu City of Han dynasty, and there are objects of Han unearthed beside the village.

Many village sites were situated along the both banks of old river channel of Han dynasty. In 1983, the sites and tombs of Western Han were unearthed from Wanquan Zhuang Primer School. Inside the sites, there are nearly a hundred of square meters' layer of tiles from Han dynasty, so they must be building sites. In 2001, in the old channel of Wanquan River close to the former sites, semi-circle tile-ends with taotie pattern and many pottery pieces with rope impressions of late Warring States or Western Han were excavated. In 1970, behind the building of Russian Department of Peking University, a well of Han dynasty with potter pots, iron scissors and other objects were found. In 1990,

several ash pits of Han dynasty were found at the telephone room of Peking University. In the pits there are red pottery fragments with micas and grey pottery fragments with rope impressions. In 1999, in the construction of Northern Zhongguancun Street, several ash pits of Han dynasty with fragments of pottery dou vessels and pots from highland of eastern Dongfu Village. In 1988, in the construction sites of granary of Tsinghua University, pottery pots, spinning wheel and many pottery pieces were found from the sites of Warring States and Western Han.

There are also sites of Han dynasty along the hill. In 1985, during the construction of Beijing Tuberculosis Hospital down the Xianlong Hill of Wenquan, a site of Han dynasty with pottery pot, stone axe and a site of spring mouth. In early 1980s, sites of Warring States to Han dynasty were found in a factory south of Beianhe Village.

II. Town site of Han dynasty

Qinghe town site is the only town site of Han dynasty in Haidian District. It is situated at the Zhufang Village west of Qinghe Town, north bank of Qinghe River close to Wanquan River. Another road towards Juyong Pass got past here. The Qinghe Town forted here on the bank of Qinghe River, So it used to be a stronghold. The town is square almost backing south and facing south with 500 meters on one side. It was close to the scope of a county at that time. Now the southwest corner of the wall is remained, and it is one of the Key Units of Historical and Cultural Heritage in Beijing.

In 1950s the town site was excavated five times. In 2011, the 6th excavation was done as the support to the construction of Jingbao Highway. Many pottery pots, bronze objects, iron objects, and sites of bronze and iron smelters were found. In the sites, objects are various. Weapons include saber, sword, halberd, Chinese hatchet; production tools contain hoe, spade, animal-drawn seed plough, and main bearings; bronze objects include censer, seal, coin, arrow head and mold of coin. Inside the town site plenty of cylinderical tiles, flat tiles and tile-ends were found. The patterns on tile-ends are cirrus cloud, swastika, and characters of "Qianqiu Wansui". There are also foundations, footing of walls, and dozens of pottery wells. Tombs are situated by the east and west sides of the town. The west one is a big brick tomb with several chambers of Han dynasty. According to data of 2011, the southwest corner of town wall, which was rammed, has remained 187.2 meters long, 10.2 – 12 meters wide on base, 0.8 – 3.5 meters wide on top, and 1 – 4.1 meters high.

III. Tombs of Han dynasty

There are a large amount of tombs of Han dynasty distributing widely, which usually are close to village and town sites. Most tombs are located at upland or north bank of rivers or highland close to towns. The biggest Han tomb area is situated from Wanshou Street to Yongding Street, which is the upland northwest of ancient Ji City. Tombs were buried on the top of the land. Since 1950s, there have been many Han tombs found along roads or organizations in Wanshou Road, Wukesong and Yongding Road areas. Objects excavated include pottery pots, bronze mirrors, and coins. In 2004, the excavation in the construction of Wukesong Gymnasium found 8 Han tombs including 7 earthen-pit tombs and 1 brick tomb. There are objects such as pottery ding vessel, pottery hu vessel, pottery box, coin, belt hook and iron sword.

Another Han tomb area close to town site is situated at Shangdi Village. It is in the northwest of Qinghe Town of Han dynasty. It was on an upland north to the ancient Qinghe River. Most tombs were buried on the side facing to south. The tomb complex was found in 1982 but excavated from 1991 and finished in 2001. 1000 tombs of the Warring States and Han dynasty were unearthed, which is the most Han tombs found in Beijing. It includes earthen-pit tomb, brick tomb and stone tomb. The brick tombs divide into several-chamber tomb, double-chamber tomb, single-chamber tomb, and brick outer-coffin tomb. Objects are pottery vessel, bronze mirror, and bronze coin. Pottery vessels are various including ding, box, hu, pot, granary, stove, cup with handles, censer, square box, tray, dou, tile-end with characters. And several brick kilns of Han dynasty were also found.

The northwest edge of the Handian Platform is another collection of Han tombs. It closes to the concentration of village sites of the time. Along the upland edge of ancient Qinghe River, from Wanquanzhuang to Bajiacun, there are many Han tombs. In 1983, Wanquanzhuang Han tomb was unearthed beside the building site of the time. There are 3 earthen-pit tombs with objects of ding, hu and pot. In 1998, several earth tombs of Han dynasty with pots were found in the south of Bayi School. In 1991, an earth tomb was found in the Yannanyuan of Peking University. In 1988, several Han tombs were found in the north of granary of Tsinghua University.

There are also Han tombs distributed on the upland beside rivers in the north of Haidian. In 1983, a Han tomb complex was found at the brickyard of Sujiatuo Village. It was situated at a platform north of the village. There are several earthen-pit tombs and brick tombs with objects of pottery hu and pot, bronze mirror, bronze elements and fragments of lacquer ware. In 1985, a tomb complex of eastern Han was found in Xiyuhe Brickyard, which is located in the northeast of a village, the upland of south bank of Nanshahe River. The tomb complex covers ten thousand sq. m. area and consists of brick tombs mainly with objects of silver hairpin, silver ring, and pottery pig. In 1990s, other Han tombs were found in the northwest of Shuangta Village, the upland of south bank of Shahe River. Pottery pots were unearthed.

The Han tombs found in Haidian District are mostly in medium or small size and have types of earthen-pit tomb, brick outer-coffin tomb, and brick tomb. Most tombs are in south-north direction, and only a few are in east-west direction. Wanquanzhuang Han tomb complex represents the earthen-pit tomb. One tomb has more than 20 pieces of grave goods; others all only have one or several grave goods. Most brick outer-coffin tombs were excavated in Shangdi area. The several decades of tombs were arranged in perfect order, but there are little grave good. Most brick tombs have single chamber, double chambers or three chambers, and few tombs has chambers more than three. Some tombs were decorated with square floor tiles with floral patterns.

Heritage objects of Han dynasty excavated in Haidian are various. Pottery wares include ding, hu, granary, pot, box, dou, lamp, model building, censer, zun, tray, cup, pig, spinning wheel and so on. Some were painted with patterns or painted in red. Most objects are made of grey clay, and some are red or grey pottery with micas even the red pottery with pure clay. Metal wares mainly have mirror, hairpin, ring, scissor, spade, coin, belt hook, and model of chariot and gear element. The floor tiles have rope impressions or no patterns. Roof tiles are flat tile and cylindrical tile with rope or spot impressions. The tile ends are decorated with cirrus cloud and characters of "Wansui" and "Qianqiu Wansui". Moreover, some textiles of Han dynasty were excavated from the tombs sealed by white clay, which are precious in Beijing.

Bibliography:

1. Archives of Cultural Relics Management Institute, Haidian District, Beijing

2. Hu, Ch.S. (2012). *Archaeology History of Beijng: Volume of Han Dynasty*, Shanghai: Shanghai Classics Publishing House.

3. Beijing Cultural Relics Research Institute. (1990). *Fourty Years of Beijing Archaeology*. Beijing: Beijing Yanshan Press.

4. Yue, Sh.Y & Xia, Zh.K & Xu, H.P. (2009). *Environmental Change of Haidian Ancient Town*. Beijing: Kaiming Press.

5. Su, T.J. (2000). *Collection of Beijing Archaeology*. Beijing: Beijing Publishing House.

6. Beijing Cultural Relics Research Institute. (2009). *Beijing Archaeology Atlas*. Beijing: Science Press.

海淀区域内的明清时期墓葬考古工作概况

李伟

1421 年明永乐帝将都城由应天府迁至北京，明亡后，1644 年清顺治帝亦"定鼎燕京"，并在元朝营建的大都城的基础上，由当时的统治者进行了新的规划和营建。在中国封建社会末期的最后两个王朝统治时期，北京城作为王朝的都城，在政治、经济、文化等方方面面都发挥着重要的作用，有着其他城市无法比拟的优势。

海淀区从地理位置上讲，位于明清时期北京城的西北郊，从新中国建立以来六十余年的调查和考古工作情况来看，这一区域内明清时期的地上和地下遗物、遗迹、遗址等类型丰富多样，如园林水系、建筑遗址、墓葬遗迹等，是整个北京地区文物考古工作的重要组成部分，同时具有鲜明的地域特色。本文主要介绍该区域内已经开展的明清时期墓葬考古工作概况。

海淀区域内的明清时期墓葬发现数量众多，覆盖的区域范围广阔，在过去的六十余年间，随着考古工作者对本地区文物考古研究和区域内建设的不断深入，以北京市文物研究所为主的考古工作者主动发掘或配合工程基建发掘了大量的明清时期的墓葬，依照墓主人身份的不同，主要有皇室成员墓葬、贵族墓葬、太监墓葬、平民墓葬等。以下将分别加以说明。

一、皇室成员墓葬

1. 明代皇室成员墓葬：

明代在 270 多年的统治时间内，共营建了六处帝陵，即江苏省盱眙县的明祖陵、安徽凤阳的明皇陵、南京的明孝陵、北京昌平县的明十三陵、北京海淀区的景泰陵以及湖北钟祥的明显陵。其中北京有两处，其一是位于今昌平区天寿山的十三陵，其二是位于今海淀区金山一带的景泰陵。十三陵埋葬的是从明成祖到崇祯帝的十三个皇帝以及他们的皇后，另有少量享受了特殊礼遇的嫔妃亦丛葬于此；景泰陵埋葬的则是在"夺门之变"后被废的景泰皇帝，以及部分早夭的诸王、公主以及不丛葬的

嫔妃等。《长安客话》中曾记载："凡诸王、公主夭殇者，并葬金山口，其地与景皇陵相属。又诸妃多葬于此。"《日下旧闻考》中也曾有明代妃嫔不丛葬者"俱葬金山"的说法，可见位于今海淀区范围内的景泰陵，应为海淀区范围内最高级别的一处明代墓葬区域。

明代遗留在海淀区的这一片皇室成员墓葬，除景泰帝外，依身份而论，包括诸王、公主及后妃等，数量达百余处。从目前的考古发现来看，以嫔妃墓数量较多，且保存相对完好，因墓葬较集中，多有墓志出土，身份明确，很多信息可以同文献记载相印证，因此具有十分重要的学术研究价值。这些不丛葬于十三陵的嫔妃墓，主要包括发现于海淀区董四墓村的嫔妃墓以及海淀区厢红旗营的妃子墓。

董四墓村嫔妃墓的考古工作于 1951 年 8 月至 11 月开展，共发掘出两座明代嫔妃墓，其中一号墓由宝顶、墓门、前室、主室组成。宝顶位于主室之后，呈圆台形，由夯土夯筑而成，异常坚固。墓室平面呈"工"字形，分为前室和主室两部分，中间有石门相通。墓门正脊长 5.3 米，檐长 7.1 米，正脊至檐口宽 3.3 米，两端饰有鸱吻。前室长 4 米，宽 3.3 米，墓底至脊高 6.6 米。正脊饰绿琉璃瓦，与主室相通的石门背后有顶门石，室内未见遗物。主室后部棺床上放置 3 具棺椁，每具棺椁旁各置墓志一合。由墓志可知，三具棺椁中安置的都是天启皇帝的妃子，中间是段纯妃，左右两侧分别是张裕妃和李成妃。此墓因被盗，所剩陪葬品不多，墓室出土了梅瓶 3 件，其中一件青花梅瓶署有"大明万历年制"款，另有金簪、玉器、珍珠以及钱币、梳、篦等器物出土。二号墓位于一号墓的东北约 300 米处，平面也成"工"字形，由宝顶、墓门、前室、后室组成。前室长 19.1 米，高 5.3 米，宽 5.1 米。石门两侧各安置有仪仗用的木架两副，两侧有两合墓志，东侧有三合墓志。后室北部置棺床，其上正中偏东有两合完整的墓志。整个墓室内共有 7 具棺椁，较为凌

乱，其中 3 具棺椁没有被盗。据圹志记录，二号墓安葬的是万历皇帝的 7 个内嫔：张顺嫔、耿悼嫔、邵敬嫔、魏慎嫔、李荣嫔、李德嫔、梁和嫔。这座墓葬出土器物较一号墓多，且更加精美。其中西侧一棺所幸没有被盗，出土的随葬品有手镯、耳环、凤冠等数十件，另有漆盒一件；旁边一棺出土银盆 3 件、银元宝 2 个、凤冠 1 顶。此外，前后两室还发现木俑百余件，从装束判断，含文臣、武将、宦官、皂隶、平民等。另外还出土有十分珍贵的"大明嘉靖年制"款白釉梅瓶和"大明万历年制"款青花梅瓶。

厢红旗营妃子墓发现于 1963 年，共包括 7 座妃子墓。这 7 座墓都呈南北向，横列成一排，形制也基本相同，平面均呈"工"字形，砖石结构。玄宫由墓门、前室、后室等部分组成。前室中央设宝座，其前安置五供和万年灯。后室中央设大理石棺床，上置棺椁。墓门为整块青石或大理石制成，正面雕兽头铺首，背面刻半圆凸起。前室、后室顶部两坡平铺方砖。7 座妃子墓均已被盗毁，棺椁破碎，尸骨失散。其中有 3 座墓各出土 1 合墓志，随葬器物仅剩少量零散的金饰件、宝石、珍珠等。据出土圹志可知她们是宪庙（成化皇帝）庄静顺妃王氏、庄懿德妃张氏、和惠静妃岳氏。

董四墓村和厢红旗营嫔妃墓的发掘，使我们对今海淀区域内的这片明代皇室成员墓葬，尤其是那些不丛葬的嫔妃墓葬有了较多的了解：墓葬多为砖室墓，且规模较大，一般由宝顶、墓门、前室、后室组成；后室作为主室用来放置葬具、棺椁，并多伴随记录墓主人身份的圹志；无论嫔、妃，均有多人共葬一墓的情形，至于墓葬规模的大小以及随葬器物标准的高低，既与后妃的等级有关，也同生前后妃们受宠程度密切关联。

通过这些发现，我们还了解到明代不丛葬的嫔妃"俱葬金山"的文献记载是基本可信的，而《宛署杂记》中提到的"宪庙十三妃共一墓"，按照厢红旗营这 7 座妃子墓的考古资料来看，应是记载共一墓地或茔域的意思，而这一茔域里的每个妃子都有自己的一个单独的坟穴或墓室。海淀区范围内的这批明代嫔妃墓出土的珍贵圹志以及精美文物，已经成为今天研究明代历史十分重要的实物资料，越来越受到专家和学者们的重视。

2. 清代皇室成员墓葬：

清代的皇室成员墓葬在北京较多。在北京有众多以"王爷坟"和"公主坟"命名的地名即是较好证明。遗憾的是，这一方向的正式的考古发掘工作较为有限。今海淀区复兴门外的公主坟是难得的经过正式考古发掘的一处。1965 年，在北京修建一线地铁时，考古工作者对清仁宗嘉庆皇帝第四女庄静固伦公主和

第三女和硕公主园寝进行了发掘。遗憾的是，因为该处园寝在 1939 年曾被日军盗掘，墓室内发现的遗物较少。

二、贵族墓葬

明清时期，京城内外各等级贵族府宅星罗棋布，环绕于紫禁城周围。自清朝康熙年间开始营建"三山五园"始，北京西郊一带（主要在今海淀区范围内）在出现皇家园林等风景游览区的同时，逐步成为了北京城内除原有的紫禁城政治活动区外，一处新的重要的政治活动区域。于是，在"三山五园"的附近也出现了同紫禁城周围相似的情况，贵族府宅众多，官员大量聚集。在海淀区范围内发现的明清时期贵族墓葬也自然很多，如明代武清侯李伟夫妇合葬墓和清代黑舍里氏墓。

1. 明代武清侯李伟夫妇合葬墓

一般情况下，明代的王公贵族和高级品官墓，多为工部按定制营造。依墓葬形制看，主要有竖穴土坑墓、砖室墓、八角（或六角）砖穴墓以及少量的石室墓，其中竖穴土坑墓最为常见。这些墓葬多使用了当时比较先进的三合土封护技术，既增加了墓室建筑的抗压性能，又尽可能地降低了来自地下水的不断侵袭；同时墓葬中绝大多数有墓志出土，出土时的墓志均带字一面相扣，并缚有铁箍两道；在随葬器物方面，这些高等级的贵族墓也有较严格的级别限制，以体现封建制度等级的森严。

武清侯李伟 1997 年发现于海淀区八里庄慈寿寺塔西北约 1 公里处，为南北向的竖穴土坑墓，葬制为一棺一椁，两椁之间有约 10 厘米厚的夯土，男椁在东，女椁在西，椁内置棺。在两椁外侧，各发现墓志一合，以铁箍捆绑。李伟墓志边长 95 厘米，厚 22 厘米，志盖篆额"明故武清侯赠太傅安国公谥恭俭李公墓志"，有志文 50 行。李伟夫人王氏墓志边长 85 厘米，厚 22 厘米，志盖篆额"皇明诰封武清侯赠太傅安国公夫人王氏合葬墓志铭"，志文 43 行，礼部尚书申时行撰。

据《明史》记载："李伟，字世奇，　县人，神宗生母李太后父也。……封武清伯，再进武清侯。"

武清侯李伟墓由于早期被盗，出土器物很少，其妻王氏棺中则出土了大量珍贵的金银器。既有壶、盘、盏、盆、洗等用具，也有头簪、戒指、花钗以及宝石等饰物。尤其特殊的是，这批出土器物大都是宫廷制品，银盆和银洗上刻"慈宁宫"、"万历壬午年御用监造"等字样。刻有"慈宁宫"字样的物品原是李太后的日用器皿，而它们出现在王氏墓中，表明李太后与其生母王氏来往密切。李伟夫妇合葬墓的发掘，为研究明代外戚的

政治和经济生活提供了重要的可靠资料。

2. 索家坟清代墓地

今海淀区范围内发现过较多的清代满族贵族墓，其中大多数为砖室墓，清代早期满族贵族墓常见骨灰葬方式，这是沿袭了满族人原始丧葬习俗，后期则更多见尸骨葬，由此亦可见满汉民族文化融合之一斑。

索家坟清代墓地位于今北京德胜门外小西天西南角（海淀区辖域内），共包括五座墓葬，但因为其一严重破坏未进行考古发掘，另外四座于1962年7月配合基建工程进行考古发掘。四座墓皆为砖室墓，分别编号为M1、M2、M3、M4，其中M1、M2规格较高，除M2为尸骨葬外，M1、M3、M4均为火葬，保留了早期的满族丧葬习俗。

M1墓室平面作正方形，顶为三层拱券，南北向。墓室离地表深4米，以砖为主要建筑材料，局部镶大理石。边长1.82米，高2.95米。东、西、北三壁分设壁龛，南壁正中设甬道，南端有一青石质墓门。墓室北部有棺床，高24厘米，整个棺床占墓室的一半有余。棺床面上铺砖，中央放置边长44厘米、高48厘米的木质骨灰盒一个。棺床前正中设有汉白玉供桌一个，上置镂雕铜方炉、烛台等祭器。甬道中央有汉白玉石碑一通，上刻"清故淑女黑舍里氏圹志铭"。北壁龛为门楼式雕砖仿木建筑，上涂朱漆彩画，壁龛内放置笔、墨、砚、图章等随葬品。东西两壁龛也是雕砖仿木结构，两者形制相同，龛内分别放置瓷器、玉器等随葬品。其中瓷器以斗彩、五彩、青花三类最为珍贵，玉器则有瓶、杯、洗、砚等种类以及多种玉佩饰，共28件，另有铜器6件，包括铜壶、铜方壶、铜炉、铜镜各一件，蜡台2件。据出土墓志可知，墓主人黑舍里氏是索额图之女，清初辅政大臣一等公索尼之孙女。去世时年仅7岁，但墓室修建却如此豪华，随葬器物如此丰厚，可见史书记载的索额图"居官贪黩"概确有其事。

M2为南北向，墓室平面呈长方形。墓室长5.4米，宽2.5米，高1.4米。四壁用青砖平铺垒砌，上顶平铺石板。东西两壁各有壁龛一个，内置青花小瓶和小罐各一个。墓底部平铺青砖，未设棺床，仅在四角用两层砖垫起，示意性地代表棺床。墓室中有长方形金丝楠木棺椁一具，尸体着单、夹、棉衣7层，外裹大衾，头部插满金饰，左右手腕戴金镯。出土遗物大多为金器，有手镯、凤饰、钗簪、耳挖、纽扣等，共计39件。这些金饰用累丝、雕花、镂空等工艺制作，技艺极其精湛，式样也十分古朴。另外，该墓还出土"康熙通宝"铜钱2枚。这座墓葬在尺寸上甚至超过了黑舍里墓，随葬的器物等级也很高，推断墓主人应该是一个十分重要的人物。

M3、M4内葬骨灰，均出土"康熙通宝"铜钱。从出土遗物来看，索家坟4座清代墓应为康熙年间墓葬，很可能是康熙年间索尼、索额图家族的一处墓葬区。

三、太监墓葬

1. 明代太监墓葬

明朝自中后期开始，太监机构变得异常庞大，仅是宫廷内以太监为主体的常设衙门就有十二监、四司、八局，统称为二十四衙门，另外还有为数不少的非常设宦官机构，负责监军、采办、征税、开矿等事务。宫廷以外的宗室和王公贵族也大量使用太监。这些太监大多数是朝廷的忠实奴仆，政治地位低微卑贱，但也有少数太监因为受到皇帝的过度宠信而骄纵跋扈，不仅威震朝堂，更有甚者，将皇帝视若傀儡，操纵大权，此即为明代后期的宦官专权时期。最为大家熟悉的如魏忠贤与刘瑾两大权监。这些太监多数庸庸无为，但也有少数权倾一时，相同的是，多数太监终老于北京。因为太监的身份常为世人不齿，多数太监在出宫后凄惨过世（少部分是主动出宫，当然更多是年老无法继续服役而被动出宫），且无法入葬自己原本家族的坟茔。北京地区的明代太监墓葬数量很多，堪称一种独特的文化现象。

海淀区范围内发现过很多的明代太监墓葬，据不完全统计，经过清理的有40多座，多数墓葬中出土有记录墓主人身份的墓志，以及与其身份相当的随葬器物，对研究当时的政治、经济等具有重要的意义。在这些已经发掘的太监墓葬中，多数都是简单的单室砖石墓，随葬器物种类较少，质量亦不高。这些年来在海淀区域内较重要的几次发现有：香山饭店发现的太监刘忠墓、海淀区地质力学研究所院内发现的杨太监墓、海淀区马神庙的北京工商大学操场上发现的太监墓（3座）、海淀区上园饭店附近发现的御马监太监墓、海淀区八里庄百花印刷厂发现的司礼监秉笔太监杜茂墓以及海淀区白石桥附近国家气象局院内发现的明代太监墓（这里出土过珍贵的成化时期青花携琴访友图罐，现存海淀博物馆）。这里以地质力学研究所院内的杨太监墓为例。

该墓发现于1999年9月，由北京市文物研究所主持发掘。墓呈南北向，内葬石椁、木棺，保存状况较好。椁室呈长方形，带盖，用石板以榫卯连接而成。石椁长1.77米，宽1.68米，通高 2.12 米。石椁盖刻有阳文铭文"乾清宫牌子尚衣监掌印太监杨公之墓石椁",且知墓主人卒于万历四十七年（1619 年）。椁底为须弥座式,椁壁饰有精美的浅浮雕图案,各壁四周为卷草纹,中部饰云鹤纹以及海水江崖、岁寒三友、阴阳八卦等图案,以浅浮雕结合线刻的工艺制成,造型生动。椁内红漆木棺及尸骨、服饰已经腐朽,木棺残片上可见描金云鹤纹图案。随葬品有玉带、釉陶罐、买地券等。

2. 清代太监墓葬

北京地区的清代太监墓葬数量亦相当可观,并且自雍正皇帝开始,太监们终老之后有了较明代更幸福更集中的去处。《日下旧闻考》记载:"雍正十二年,世宗宪皇帝赐内监等茔地一区,名恩济庄,并于其地敕建关帝庙,于乾隆三年二月落成。"清朝末年最著名的太监李莲英的墓就位于此地。此外,据调查,恩济庄有墓碑并留有拓片的太监有近 300 人,其中乾隆朝约占三分之一。碑文上提到的太监官职、品级,与乾隆七年十月"钦定太监凡例"基本相符。碑文所记太监入宫年龄及升迁情况,也基本符合当时的文献记载。

除恩济庄外,海淀区范围内的清代太监墓葬较集中的区域还包括:西直门西北七里的皂君庙、西直门西北的大钟寺、西直门西北二十里的槐树居遗光寺（始名龙泉庵）、西直门外豆腐闸。此外还有部分太监葬于海淀区的东冉村、西冉村、万寿寺、青龙桥四槐居等地。

四、平民墓葬

今海淀区范围发现的明清时期平民墓葬数量较多,大多数是在建设施工过程中发现并进行抢救性发掘,既有零散的发现,也有很多是大量集中发现的平民墓葬。这些墓葬一般形制较小,随葬品也比较贫乏,墓主人多为一般贫民或士绅或低级品官。从墓葬形制上看,绝大多数是竖穴土坑墓,墓葬尺寸较小,葬具简单,基本上只有木棺或骨灰罐,随葬品数量少、质量不高,多以简单的陶器、瓷器、铜器为主,少量稍显富裕的墓葬亦有少量银器及铜钱等物出土。这些平民墓葬的发掘,对研究明代墓葬形制的演变、随葬品组合、丧葬习俗等具有重要意义。

综上,在过去的六十余年间,海淀区域内的明清时期考古工作为今天的我们了解这片土地的过去提供了大量珍贵而难得的第一手资料,对整个明清时期历史的研究具有重要的意义,随着更多考古工作的展开,我们期待着专业的考古工作者带来更多的值得期待的惊喜。

主要参考文献:

1、宋大川主编:《北京考古发现与研究》(1949—2009),科学出版社,2009 年。
2、苏天钧:《北京西郊小西天清代墓葬发掘简报》,《文物》1963 年第 1 期。
3、北京市文物研究所编:《北京考古四十年》,北京燕山出版社,1990 年。

A Survey of Archaeological Excavations of the Ming and Qing Tombs Located in the Haidian Area

Li Wei

In 1421, Emperor Yongle of Ming dynasty moved the capital from Yingtian (Nanjing) to Beijing. In 1644, under the leadership of Emperor Shunzhi, Yanjing (which is now Beijing) was reestablished as the imperial capital of the Qing dynasty after the collapse of Ming. It was again reconstructed as well as re-planned on the basis of the construction of the Khanbaliq of Yuan thereafter by the rulers at the time. The city of Beijing which takes advantages of being the imperial capital of the last two dynasties played a pivotal role in all aspects of politics, economics and cultures throughout the later years of the Chinese feudalistic society that no other cities can be matched with.

Geographically, Haidian District is located in the northwest of the city of Beijing during the Ming and Qing dynasties. This place has been found diversified from the sixty-year archaeological discoveries either in its cultural remains, or in its cultural relics, or in its ruins sites since the establishment of the People's Republic of China. Gardens, rivers, architectural ruins, tombs or burial sites characterized by extensive regional cultural differences are considered to be an important part of the whole archaeological process conducted in the Beijing area. This paper is an overview of the archaeological work that has been carried out in many of the Ming and Qing tombs within the area of Beijing.

A large number of tombs of Ming and Qing dynasties were widely found in the Haidian area. In the last more than six decades, with the further and deeper studies on the cultural relics discovered by archaeologists along with the architectural development in the local region, more Ming and Qing tombs were excavated under the auspices of the Beijing Municipal Institute of Cultural Relics. Basically, tombs constructed during Ming and Qing period could be classified into different types in terms of the tomb owner's identity, for example, the royal family members, or the nobles, or the eunuchs, or the civilians, etc. I am going to explain this as follows respectively.

I. Tombs of the Royal Family Members

1. Tombs of the Ming Royal Family Members

A total of six imperial mausoleums were constructed throughout the 270 years of Ming's rule. Among them, two are located in the Beijing area. One referring to the Ming Thirteen-Tombs is located within the suburban Changping District on the Tianshou Mountain, the other is the Jingtai Tomb hidden at the bottom of Jinshan (literally as the Gold Mountain) in Haidian District. From the Emperor Chengzu onward until the last Emperor Chongzhen, 13 Ming dynasty emperors and their empresses all together with a small number of concubine consorts who had ever enjoyed special privileges were buried in the same area. The Emperor Jingtai was buried in the Jingtai Tomb who was dethroned after a military coup or what we called the Restoration Accident. Some princes and princesses who died at young age and other concubine consorts who were not buried with the emperor were also buried in the Jingtai Tomb. The Dialogue by a Traveler from Chang'an writes that all princes and princesses were buried at the entrance of the Gold Mountain, a place no less than the Jing mausoleum, and the concubine consorts were buried at the same place too. The same accounts could be found in the Serious of Documents about the History of Beijing as well that those concubine consorts who were not buried with the emperor were buried in Jinshan. It is thus clear that the Jingtai Tomb should be the highest honor in burying for the deceased comparing to other Ming tombs within the Haidian District.

Besides the Emperor Jingtai, amounted to more than 100 Ming tombs owned by the imperial family members, including princes, princesses, and concubine consorts, were remained behind their death in Haidian. A numerous tombs owned by the concubines were found relatively well unscathed. These tombs were concentrated in the same place and the owners of the tombs could be identified very clear from the inscription on the memorial tablets, and many of which had got unearthed. Since a lot of information could be corroborated in the existing historical documents, there was no doubt that the value of academic research on Ming tombs became very important for whatsoever. Concubines who were not buried with the emperor in the Thirteen Ming Tombs were found buried near to the Dongsi Tomb Village and the Camp Xianghongqi.

Archaeological excavations of the tombs of concubines were being carried out between August and November in the year of 1951. A total of two tombs of concubines were excavated. Tomb No. 1 was consisted of a dome-shaped roof, a tomb door, an antechamber, and a coffin chamber. The dome-shaped roof was firmly and strongly constructed in rammed earth behind the coffin chamber. The sketch plan of the tomb chambers was H-shaped in two parts---the antechamber and the coffin chamber, which were interlinked with a stone door in between. The main ridge of the door was 5.3 meters long, the eave was 7.1 meters long, the distance between the main ridge and the cornice was 3.3 meters wide. Two ornaments in the shape of a legendary animal were decorated on the two ends of the ridge. The antechamber was 4 meters long, 3.3 meters wide, and the distance between the bottom of the tomb and the top of the ridge was 6.6 meters high. The main ridge was covered with the glazed tiles. A stone bar found behind the door was used to push against the door for security concerns, and here was the entrance to the coffin chamber where no remains existed. Three coffins were found placed on the coffin platform at the rear of the chamber. Each one of the memorial tablets was set next to the coffins. We could figure out from the inscription of the tablet that the concubine consorts of Emperor Tianqi were rested in the three coffins. The one in the middle belonged to the Concubine Consort Duanchun, the one on the left belonged to the Concubine Consort Zhangyu and the one on the right to the Concubine Consort Licheng. The tomb had been robbed and stolen for many times, thus not many objects buried with the deceased were remained. Three bluish white plum porcelain vases were unearthed, and one of the three was a blue-and-white plum porcelain vase inscribed as "made in the year of Emperor Wanli of the Great Ming Empire". In addition, gold hairpins, jade wares, pearls, coins and combs were also unearthed. Tomb No. 2 was located about 300 meters to the northeast of Tomb No. 1. The sketch plan of this tomb was also H-shaped, consisted of a dome-shaped roof, a tomb door, an antechamber, and a rear chamber. The antechamber was 19.1 meters long, 5.3 meters high and 5.1 meters wide. Two wooden stands used for carrying coffins in the royal ceremonial procession were set on two sides of the stone door. We could find that two memorial tablets were on two sides, and the other three were on the east side of the tomb. A coffin platform was built to the north side of the rear chamber, and two well preserved memorial tablets were found in the middle of the platform to the east. A total of seven coffins were found in the coffin chamber but too much in disorder. Only three coffins hadn't been robbed and stolen yet. According to the records from those memorial tablets, there were seven concubine consorts of Emperor Wanli buried in the Tomb No. 2. They were Zhang Shun, Geng Dao, Shao Jing, Wei Shen, Li Rong, Li De, and Liang He. Objects unearthed from the Tomb No. 2 were more than what we found in the Tomb No. 1, and there looked especially more exquisitely beautiful. Luckily, a coffin set to the west side was not robbed, in which dozens of objects buried with the dead were found including bracelets, earrings, one phoenix cornet, and one lacquer box. Besides, three silver basins, two silver ingots and one phoenix cornet were also found in the other coffin next to the former one. In addition, more than 100 figurines made of wood were discovered both in the antechamber and the rear chamber. We could decide from what were dressed in appearance to the figurines that they represented the people of different status and walks including Confucius officials, military generals, eunuchs, yamen runners and civilians, etc. Other unearthed precious were a white glazed plum porcelain vase inscribed as "made in the year of Emperor Jiajing of Great Ming" and a blue-and-white plum porcelain vase inscribed as "made in the year of Emperor Wanli of Great Ming".

A total of seven tombs of the concubines located in Xianghongqiying (literally as compartment red banner camp) were discovered in the year of 1963. The seven tombs were lined up in south-north oriented direction. The sketch plan of the tombs was basically the same as what we had discovered in other tombs mentioned above. They were all H-shaped brick-and-stone constructions. Let's take an example of the tomb; it was consisted of a tomb door, an antechamber and a rear chamber. A throne was set up at the center in the antechamber, in front of which sacrificial offerings to the ancestors and the ever-burning lamps were placed on an altar. In the rear chamber a coffin platform made of marbles was found at the center. Coffins were rested on the coffin platform. The tomb door was made of a mono-block of bluestone or a mono-block of marbles carved with the animal head appliqué holding rings pattern. A semi-spherical convex was carved on the back of the door. The antechamber as well as the rear chamber slopes leading to the top of the chamber room was paved with square bricks. The seven tombs of concubines had been robbed and stolen, coffins in the tombs were broken too with the bones of the dead scattered here and there. Memorial tablets were also found in the three tombs, in each of which one tablet was found buried with the dead. Other objects excavated from the tombs were remained nothing but some gold accessories, gems and pearls, etc. We could know from inscriptions inscribed on the memorial tablets that the owners of the three tombs were concubine consort Zhuangjingshun, concubine consort Zhuangyide, and concubine consort Hehuijing to Emperor Chenghua.

Excavations of the tombs of concubines located either in Dongsi Tomb Village or in Camp Xianghongqi made us understand more details about the tombs owned by the royal family members of Ming dynasty, especially those concubines who were not buried with the dead emperor. Most of the tombs were brick-chambered constructions in large scale, normally consisted of a dome-shaped roof, a door, an antechamber and a rear chamber. The rear chamber usually functioned as the main chamber for keeping coffins and funerary objects, and memorial tablets that could identify the owners of the tombs were very often found in the rear chamber too. No matter what status that the concubine consorts or the imperial concubines held in the imperial court, the fact that they were often buried together in a same tomb after their death. As for the scale of the tomb and the objects that were buried with the dead according to the standardized burial customs, the way of burying the concubines not only should have something to do with their rankings they had ever held in the imperial harem but closely depend on how much they were able to serve to satisfy the emperor before their death.

What we knew from the historical fact through archaeological discoveries was that the concubines of Ming dynasty who were not buried with the dead emperor were buried in Jinshan area. This data should be credible in historical sense. Besides, it was mentioned in the Miscellanea at the Wanping Governmental Office that there were "13 concubines of Emperor Chenghua buried in one tomb". By taking the archaeological data from excavations of the seven tombs of concubines in Camp Xianghongqi, we understand that those concubines were buried in one tomb or in one mausoleum in which every one of them had her own single chamber to be buried. It was worth mentioning that the memorial tablets as well as the cultural relics excavated from the concubines' tombs of the Ming dynasty in Haidian provided us the most important material evidence for the studies of the history of Ming. There should be no doubt that more and more experts and scholars would turn their attention to those archaeological discoveries.

2. Tombs of the Qing Royal Family Members

It seemed that many Qing royal family members were buried in the Beijing area; we could know this from the geographical names like Wangyefen (literally as the Tomb of a Prince) or Gongzhufen (literally as the Tomb of a Princess). But professional archaeological excavations of the tombs of princes and princesses were pretty much limited. One of the tombs of princesses located in what is now the Outer Street of Fuxingmen in Haidian had ever been a typical archaeological site under professional excavation. In 1965, excavations of the tombs of Gurun Princess Zhuangjing and the Hošoi Princess Zhuangjing, the fourth and the third daughters of the Emperor Jiaqing were carried out by archaeologists at the time when the subway Line 1 was being built. But unfortunately, remains found in the tombs were not many most of which were gone because the Tombs Garden here were invaded and robbed by the Japanese troops in 1939.

II. Tombs of the Nobles

Mansions owned by the nobles of Ming and Qing dynasties at all levels were more or less like satellite buildings around the Forbidden City inside and outside of the imperial capital. The grand landscape construction of the famous "Three Mountains and Five Gardens" had started since the period of the Emperor Kangxi in the western suburb of the city of Beijing (mostly in the domain of Haidian District) during the Qing dynasty. Meanwhile, this area had been developed as a new section for political activities outside the Forbidden City. We could see the constructions appeared in the vicinity of the "Three Mountains and Five Gardens" similar to what we saw around the Forbidden City. A favorite place where a mount of mansions of nobles and a lot of court officials used to go. Thus, it was normally recognized that a large number of tombs of Ming and Qing nobles were found in Haidian area. We took the examples of the tomb of Marquise Liwei of Wuqing with his wife of the Ming dynasty, and the tomb of Heseri Hala of the Qing dynasty.

1. The Tomb of Marquise Liwei of Wuqing with His Wife

Commonly, tombs of the nobility in the time of Ming dynasty were constructed by the Ministry of Works and Infrastructure under the imperial rules and regulations. According to the architectural design for the tombs as well as for the tomb structures, we could know that tombs were specified in different types, mostly vertical pit tombs, brick-chambered tombs. They were constructed either in octagonal or in hexagonal shapes, a small number of stone-chambered tombs could be found as well. The vertical pit tomb was the most common type among other types of tombs. All tombs were found sealed by using a kind of rammed earth consisted of clay, sand and gravel. The use of the rammed earth to build tombs could not only assure the compressive strength to be increased, but also could reduce the continuous impact on the tombs caused by the underground water. It was known that the memorial tablets were discovered in most of the tombs. The unearthed stone tablets in the form of paired stones were found tightened up with iron hoops, they were put against each other on the flat surfaces of the stones on which words were inscribed. For the objects that were buried with the deceased in these tombs owned by the nobility demonstrated that there was a strict raking system embedded in the feudalistic society.

The tomb of Marquise Liwei of Wuqing was discovered at the place one kilometer away from the pagoda of Cishou Temple to the northwest in Balizhuang in Haidian in the year of 1997. It was a north-south oriented vertical pit tomb in which a coffin within a coffin was found. The rammed earth that was poured into the space between the two coffins was about 10 cm thick. One of this sort of coffins with the deceased man rested inside was put on the east, and anther one with the woman was put on the west. Two pairs of memorial stone tablets tightened up with iron hoops were found next to the coffins, one of the pairs for each coffin. The memorial tablet to Li Wei was 95 cm long and 22 cm thick. It was a 50 lines of inscription identifying him as the Marquis of Wuqing, the Honored Grand Tutor and the Honored Lord Anguo posthumously named as Your Excellency of Courtesy and Magnanimity. The memorial tablet to Li Wei's wife Wang was 85 cm long and 22 cm thick. It was 43 lines of inscription demonstrating her as the mandated woman, the wife of the Marquis of Wuqing, the Honored Grand Tutor and the Honored Lord Anguo. By looking at the memorial tablets we knew that the texts of the inscriptions were written by the Director of the Board of Rites during the time period from 3 pm to 5 pm.

According to the accounts recorded in the History of Ming Dynasty, we understood that Li Wei was born in the County Guo, his literary name was Shiqi, and he was the father of Empress Dowager Li who was the mother of Emperor Shenzong, and he was ever conferred as the Earl of Wuqing, and was promoted as the Marquise of Wuqing thereafter.

Li Wei's tomb had ever robbed and stolen in its early years, thus, the unearthed objects were relatively not many. A mount of rare gold and silver wares including kettles, plates, cups, basins, washers, hairpins, flower hairpins, rings, and gemstones were unearthed from the tomb in which Li Wei's wife was buried. Particularly, most of the unearthed pieces were made for the royal court. There were silver basins and silver washers on which the Chinese characters like "Palace of Benevolent Peace", "Made and Supervised by the Royal Court in the Year of 1582 during Emperor Wanli's Reign" were engraved. Pieces engraved with the "Palace of Benevolent Peace" were believed to belong to Empress Dowager Li. They were considered as the household wares for every day use. Presumably there might be a close and good relationship kept between the Empress Dowager Li and her mother Wang, and this reckoning could be inferred from those wares that were buried in the Wang's tomb. The excavations of the tombs owned by Li Wei and his wife had provided the reliable and important information on the study of the relatives of the Emperor on the side of his mother and his wife about their political and economic life.

2. The Suojiafen Cemetery of Qing Dynasty

A large number of tombs owned by the Manchu Qing nobility were found in what is now Haidian District. Most of them were the brick-chambered tombs. Burial of the human ashes of the deceased were very often seen in the tombs of Manchu nobles in the early years of Qing dynasty, and this funeral tradition was followed down by the Manchu people. But the burial of the human bones of the dead were found more common in the later years of Qing. This change in the funeral tradition at this point highlighted the integration of Manchu and Han people as well as their cultures.

The Suojiafen cemetery, including five tombs, was located at the southwest corner of what is now Xiaoxitian in Haidian area. In July 1962, the excavation of four tombs here was being carried out at the construction site where an infrastructure project was under way, while the other one was not excavated because of its serious destruction. All of the four were brick chambered tombs which had been numbered as M1, M2, M3 and M4 excavated by an archaeological work team from Beijing. M1 and M2 were built at a higher level of construction standards. M1, M3 and M4 were the tombs in which the ashes of the dead were buried, but the bones of the dead were buried only in M2. Burial of the ashes was a funeral tradition followed by the Manchu people in the early years of Qing.

M1 was a south-north oriented and square shaped tomb with a triple arched roof on top. The tomb was 4 meters below the ground and mainly constructed with brick, while partly with marble. It was 1.82 meters long and 2.95 meters high. Niches were built in the walls on three directions of east, west and north. A tomb passageway was built in the middle of the south wall, and a tomb door made of black slabstones was opened at the southern side of the tomb. A coffin platform, covering more than a half area of the tomb, paved with bricks 24 cm in height was built to the north on which a wooden cinerary casket about 44 cm long and 48 cm thick was placed at the center. An alter made of marbles was set up in front of the platform in the middle, on which an openwork bronze square shaped incense burner, a candlestick and other sacrificial utensils were put. A memorial tablet made of marbles was erected up in the middle of the passageway. An inscription carved on the tablet in memory of the dead was "Qing Dynasty Young Lady Heseri Hala Past Away". The north wall styled in the shape of a classical gatehouse was constructed in a wood imitation structure by using faux bricks and painted with red lacquer. Objects buried with the dead including writing brushes, ink sticks, inkstones and seals were placed in the wall niches. The east and west walls were built similar to the north wall in terms of structure and design. Some objects were put in those walls too. Porcelain wares painted either in contending colors, or in five colors, or in blue-and-white colors were considered to be the most precious ones discovered in the tomb. A total of 28 jade wares, including vases, cups, brush washers, inkstones, and accessories designed in a variety of styles, were found. In addition, 6 copper wares, including a kettle, a square shaped pot, an incense burner, a mirror, and two candlesticks were found as well. We could know from the inscription carved on an unearthed memorial tablet that the owner of the tomb Heseri Hala who died at age 7 was the granddaughter of Sonin, a duke

and a senior regent during the early years of Qing dynasty. Her father was Songgotu, an educator of the crown prince and a grand secretary of the imperial central government. It was probably true according to some historical records that Songgotu was extremely corrupted during the years when he held his official position in the imperial court. And this could be seen from the objects buried with a 7-year-old young lady in the tomb which was extravagantly and splendidly constructed at the time.

M2 was a north-south oriented tomb in the shape of rectangular, 5.4 meters long, 2.5 meters wide and 1.4 meter high. Walls on four sides were constructed by laying black bricks up to the top on which slabstones were paved. Two wall niches, one on each side, were built into the east and the west walls. A little blue-and-white porcelain bottle and a little blue-and-white porcelain pot were put in each one of the niches. There was no coffin platform in the tomb except a schematic one paved with black bricks which was raised by two layers of bricks in the four corners. The floor of the tomb was paved with black bricks, but no coffin platform except a schematic one rectangular shaped coffin made of Acacia wood was placed in the chamber. The corpse rested in the coffin was wrapped up in seven layers of dresses, garments, and cotton-padded coats, and a large quilt was the outermost layer for protection. The corpse head was decorated with gold hair accessories, and two gold bracelets were found on both wrists. Most of the funerary objects unearthed were gold jewelries including bracelets, phoenix pendants, hairpins, earpicks (curette), and buttons, 39 pieces in total. Some superb skills and techniques had been widely used in making these artifacts which were artistically simple in design, for example, the filigreeing technique, carving in a floral design technique, and openwork carving technique, etc. Besides, two "Kang'xi Tongbao" copper coins were found in the tomb as well. Not only was M2 much larger than M1 in scale, but some unusual objects buried with the deceased were discovered too. Thus, we could imagine that the owner of M2 should be a very important person in this family.

Ashes of the dead were buried in M3 and M4 from which the "Kang'xi Tongbao" copper coins were unearthed. It could be deduced from the unearth remains that the four tombs should be buried in Kangxi reign, Qing dynasty. And this cemetery where the four tombs was located in should belong to the family of Sonin and Songgotu.

III. Tombs of the Eunuchs

1. Tombs of the Eunuchs of the Ming Dynasty

The power of the eunuchs in the government reached its zenith during the Ming dynasty, and the units of eunuchs at this time had been massively developed since the late Ming period. The permanent bureaucratic units in which mainly the eunuchs served were commonly called "the 24 Yamens" including 12 superintendents, 4 departments and 8 bureaus. In addition, eunuchs who served in a large number of ad hoc units were put in charge of domestic affairs, such as, military supervising, goods purchasing, taxes collecting and mining, etc. Eunuchs also served either in the royal or in the noble households outside the central court. Most of the eunuchs who held low social and political status were very much loyal to the imperial court, but a mall number of them who were specially favored and unduly trusted by the emperor held the excessive tyrannical power and dominated the court, and even took the control of the emperor who was treated as the puppet. This was the period of late Ming dynasty during which eunuchs gained despotic power over state affairs. Wei Zhongxian and Liu Jin were the most powerful eunuchs well known in history. The majority of the eunuchs were lazy or incapable to interfere with state affairs, but a few of them enabled to enjoy supreme power and privileges over the years. Similar to each other in destiny, most of them died in Beijing. People usually looked down on eunuchs regarding to their social identity, thus many eunuchs were kind of forced to lead a miserable life after they stopped serving at the court and got out of the palace. A minority of the eunuchs volunteered to apply for getting out of the palace, actually because they were too old to be able to continue serving in the Forbidden City, they had to leave with no choice. Unfortunately, they were not qualified to be buried in their own family tombs. Eunuch tombs of the Ming dynasty were large in number in the Beijing area, which was taken as a unique cultural phenomenon in history.

Eunuch tombs of the Ming dynasty were found many in Haidian District. According to incomplete statistics, more than 40 tombs had already been cleared up and sorted out. Memorial tablets that commemorate the life and the identity of the tomb owners were unearthed in most of the above mentioned tombs. Funerary objects that could equivalently indicate the social status of the tomb owners were also discovered. These discoveries could have important significance in the study of politics and economics at the time. Eunuch tombs that had been excavated in most cases were simply single brick (or stone)-chambered construction in which funerary objects were found less in number and poor in quality. A couple of relatively important discoveries in archaeology in Haidian area over the years were listed as follows: the tomb of eunuch Liu Zhong (found at the Xiangshan Hotel), the tomb of eunuch Yang (found in the compound of the Haidian Geological Mechanics Institute), three eunuch tombs (found in the playground of the Beijing Technology and Business University in Mashenmiao), the tomb of a eunuch from the Imperial Stable Department (found near to the Shangyuan Hotel), the tomb of eunuch secretary Du Mao from the Imperial Household Department (discovered at the Baihua Printing Plant in Balizhuang), and finally another eunuch tomb (found in the National Weather Service compound in Baishiqiao in which a precious blue-and-white porcelain jar designed with the "carrying a Chinese zither to visit a friend" pattern made in Chenghua era was unearthed). (This jar was in the Haidian Museum's collection.) Here we took the tomb of eunuch Yang as an example to see what we could know from it.

This tomb was excavated in September 1999 under the auspices of the Beijing Municipal Institute of Cultural Relics. It was a south-north oriented tomb in which a stone outer coffin and a wooden inner coffin were remained in good condition. The outer coffin made by tenon-and-mortise joints in slabstone was in the shape of rectangular and was closed with a lid on which the inscription was carved. We could know from the inscription that the eunuch Yang was in charge of daily affairs inside the Palace of Heavenly Purity and he was also a supervisor from the department of the emperor's crown, robes, slippers, boots and socks. And we could also know that eunuch Yang died in the year 47 (1619) of Emperor Wanli's era. The stone outer coffin was 1.77 meters long, 1.68 meters wide and 2.12 meters high. A Sumerian base was found under the outer coffin. We could find some bas reliefs in fancy patterns being carved on outside of the outer coffin. On each one of the faces of the outer coffin it was thematically decorated with all kinds of patterns like the clouds and cranes, or the rivers and cliffs, or the pine-bamboo-plum blossoms, or the eight diagrams of Yin and Yang. A line-engraving-into-a-shallow-relief carving technique was used to make the thematic pattern on each face of the coffin. And each kind of the pattern was carved in the center of the face surrounded by a floral scroll design on the four sides. The wooden coffin painted with red lacquer could be clearly distinguished, but at the same time we could see that the corpse and the clothes had become putrid. A gold traced design of clouds and cranes could still be identified from the fragments of the coffin. Objects buried with the dead were the jade belt, glazed pottery pots and a certificate of land purchase.

2. Tombs of the Eunuchs of the Qing Dynasty

Eunuch tombs of the Qing dynasty were found considerably many in Beijing area. Eunuchs who served in the imperial court during the period of Qing were able to find better and happier ending places than the eunuchs who served in the imperial court during the period of Ming. Those places were specifically reserved for them to be rested after their death, and this had happened since the time when Emperor Yongzheng came into power. According to the textural records from the Serious of Documents about the History of Beijing, a cemetery property called Enjizhuang was constructed by royal grant in the 12th year of Emperor Yongzheng's reign. Moreover, a Temple of Guanyu (to enshrine Guan as an emperor and an ancient Chinese hero) was being built at Enjizhuang under imperial order as well. The construction of Enjizhuang was completed in February, the 3rd year of Emperor Qianglong's reign. The tomb of the best-known eunuch Li Lianying was just built in this place by the end of Qing dynasty. Besides, according to some relevant survey data that about 300 eunuchs were buried in Enjizhuang, and the tombstones to them as well as the rubbing texts taken from the tombstones survived. Some one third of the 300 eunuchs were buried during the Qianlong period. Ranks that the eunuchs achieved as well as positions that the eunuchs held in the imperial offices mentioned in the inscriptions were carved on the tombstones. Basically, what we had known from the inscriptions could be consistently confirmed with the records in the Bureaucratic Management of the Eunuchs authorized by the Emperor Qianlong in November of the 7th year of his reign. The ages at which the eunuchs entered into service

at the Forbidden City and how the eunuchs got promoted throughout the years were all inscribed on the tombstones. And this could be found in the historical literature sources of the time.

Besides Enjizhuang, other areas where eunuch tombs were concentrated within were Zaojunmiao (7 kilometers northwest of Xizhimen), Dazhongsi (northwest to Xizhimen), Yiguang Temple (originally Longquan Monastery located in Huaishuju 10 kilometers northwest of Xizhimen), and Doufuzha (located in the Xizhimen Outer Street). Again, we could also find the eunuch tombs in other places in Haidian District, including Dongran Village, Xiran Village, Wanshousi, Qinglongqiao and Sihuaiju, etc.

IV. Tombs of Civilians

A great number of civilian tombs of the Ming and Qing dynasties located in the Haidian area were usually found at the construction sites of nowadays. People in all walks of life engaged in this sort of excavations for rescuing history from the cultural relics. Sometimes the civilian tombs were found here and there, but sometimes civilian tombs were largely concentrated in certain area. These tombs were normally constructed in small scale, and the objects buried with the dead civilians were less. This was because the owners of the tombs were poor people or people from the lower gentry or just low ranking officials. The civilian tombs in most cases were vertical coffin pits in structure, small in scale, and simply with the wooden coffin or a jar containing human ashes inside. Besides, funerary objects buried with the dead civilians were few in number and poor in quality. Poorly designed pottery wares, porcelain wares or copper wares were commonly found in the civilian tombs in general. Only a few of objects such as silver wares and copper coins seldom unearthed from a small number of civilian tombs demonstrated that the owners of these tombs presumably might be slightly well-off then. The excavations of the civilian tombs were the most important step in the studies of the Ming dynasty that focused on the development of structure in tomb construction, and the associated funerary objects as well as the funeral customs at the time.

To sum up what we had here in this paper, the archaeological discoveries featured through Ming and Qing dynasties in Haidian area in the past six decades had provided abundance of primary sources to help us understand the history of our land where we lived in. The excavations of the tombs sites offered important materials for the study of a complete history of Ming and Qing dynasties. We expected that more archaeological excavations undertaken by professional archaeologists would continue to surprise us from this day on.

References

1. Archaeological Discoveries and Studies in Beijing 1949-2009 Part Two, edited by Song Dachuan, published by the Science Press, 2009.

2. A Concise Report on the Qing Tombs Discovered in Xiaoxitian in Western Suburbs of Beijing, authored by Su Tianjun, Cultural Heritage, Issue No. 1, 1963.

3. 40 Years Archaeological Discoveries in Beijing, edited by the Beijing Municipal Institute of Cultural Relics, published by the Beijing Yanshan Press, 1990.

后记

李昂

　　海淀博物馆于 2003 年成立，2005 年正式对公众开放。10 年来，通过举办展览、教育活动等方式满足了广大观众对海淀、北京乃至中国历史与传统文化的需求。博物馆先后推出基本陈列"心灵与历史的对话——海淀历史文物展"、"沉香越千年——海淀历史文物展"，并出版多部海淀文物图录，先后向公众展示了近 500 件馆藏的珍贵文物，介绍了海淀发展的历史脉络。

　　海淀博物馆馆藏丰富、珍贵文物众多，其中绝大部分来自于海淀区范围内特别是先后出土的墓葬，对于研究海淀区各个时期的历史提供了宝贵的实物依据。由于展厅条件等诸多因素制约，海淀博物馆尚有大量馆藏文物未能呈现于观众面前。为此，我们自 2013 年开始认真着手这本文物图录的出版工作，此刻终于呈现在大家面前。

　　本图录所汇集的文物集中了更多的馆藏文物精品，更大范围地展示了海淀区文物的精华，它不仅反映了海淀辉煌灿烂的历史痕迹，也记录了海淀区文物工作者几十年来辛勤工作的成果。图录出版的过程中得到了热心海淀区文博事业的专家学者的大力支持和帮助：北京大学考古文博学院秦大树教授为本图录撰写了《红叶黄花自一川》同时审阅了《海淀区域内的明清时期墓葬考古工作概况》一文；北京大学城市与环境学院岳升阳教授为本图录撰写了《海淀区域内的两汉时期考古发现》一文；首都博物馆黄春和研究员为本图录中佛道造像的说明文字进行了细致的审核，在此一并致以诚挚的谢意。

　　由于时间仓促、水平有限，图录中恐多有疏漏，请读者批评指正。

Epilogue

Li Ang

Haidian Museum was established in 2003, it officially opened to the public in 2005. The Museum is dedicated to its pivotal role as a cultural institution and provides opportunities to the general public in approaching and understanding the cultures of the world. The Museum has been trying to offer exhibitions and education programs to satisfy our visitors' hunger for understanding the history and traditional Chinese culture of Haidian, of Beijing as well as of the country as a whole for the last decade. The permanent exhibitions that have been launched at the museum are A Communication between Human Souls and History--the Cultural Relics in Haidian, and Thousands of Years throughout History-Historical Relics in Haidian. At the same time, a number of illustrated catalogs of cultural relics in Haidian are published. Close to 500 pieces of precious objects collected by the museum were put on display, which demonstrate an evolutionary development of Haidian in different periods of history.

Haidian Museum houses a rich collection of cultural relics, most of which unearthed from the ancient tombs are found within the area of Haidian. The discovery of those precious objects makes its contribution to the study of the history of Haidian in various periods of time. Considering the observance of optimal display conditions is not adequately supported and secured, a large number of museum collections failed to meet an audience. We started preparing for the publication of this catalog which we have been working on since 2013 and now the collections presented in this catalog eventually find their way to make its debut in front of you.

More core collection of important selected objects of Haidian is collected in this catalog that attempts to not only broaden the scope of splendid history of Haidian but also reflect the accomplishments and the hard work that the archaeologists have put into over the last several decades. Experts and scholars who are enthusiastic in the development of cultural undertakings of Haidian offered strong support and assistance to the actual publication of the catalog. Professor Qin Dashu from the School of Archaeology and Museology of Peking University wrote a paper titled with Red Leaves and Chrysanthemum are Cultivated from the Same Plains for this catalog; moreover, he has reviewed an article on the Survey of Ming and Qing Tombs Located in Haidian Area. Professor Yue Shengyang from the College of Urban and Environmental Sciences of Peking University also contributed to a paper on The Archaeological Discoveries of Western Han and Eastern Han Dynasties in Haidian Area. A research fellow Mr. Huang Chunhe from Capital Museum did a careful screening check on the description texts regarding the Buddhist statues appeared in this catalog too. We wish to express our sincere gratitude to all those people for their valuable assistance and encouragement in the preparation of this publication.

We will remain solely here responsible for any inaccuracies, errors and omissions that might come out after the publication of the catalog. We would also like to thank people from all walks of life who helped us a lot in finishing this project within the limited time.

责任编辑：贾东营

责任印制：梁秋卉

图书在版编目（CIP）数据

海淀文物精选集 / 海淀博物馆编 .-- 北京 : 文物

出版社 , 2014.10

ISBN 978-7-5010-4023-0

Ⅰ . ①海… Ⅱ . ①海… Ⅲ . ①出土文物－海淀区－图

录 Ⅳ . ① K873.1

中国版本图书馆 CIP 数据核字 (2014) 第 128807 号

《海淀文物精选集》编委会

主　　编：李　昂

副 主 编：李　志

执行主编：李　伟

编　　委：马明杉　鲍晓文　王承浩　姜英鎏

摄　　影：谷中秀　罗　征　刘小放　李　志

设　　计：肖　晓

策　　划：北京博物天成文化发展有限公司 (BWTC)

海淀文物精选集

海淀博物馆　编

出版发行：文物出版社

社　　址：北京东直门内北小街 2 号楼

邮　　编：100007

网　　址：http://www.wenwu.com

邮　　箱：web@wenwu.com

经　　销：全国新华书店

印　　刷：北京雅昌艺术印刷有限公司

开　　本：889×1194 毫米　　1/16

印　　张：19.5

版　　次：2014 年 10 月第 1 版

印　　次：2014 年 10 月第 1 次印刷

书　　号：ISBN 978-7-5010-4023-0

定　　价：380.00 元